Reviewing Singapore

C000037073

GENERAL EDITOR
Shirley Chew

EDITORS
Fiona Becket
Sam Durrant
Lynette Hunter
John McLeod
Stuart Murray
Brendon Nicholls
Jane Plastow

ADVISORY BOARD
Ranjana Ash
Martin Banham
Catherine Batt
Elleke Boehmer
Susan Burns
Isabel Carrera Suárez
Denise deCaires Narain
Romesh Gunesekera
Githa Hariharan
Salima Hashmi
Elaine Ho
Koh Tai Ann
Bénédicte Ledent
Russell McDougall
Niyi Osundare
Nima Poovaya-Smith
David Richards
Neluka Silva
Aritha van Herk
Mark Williams

REVIEWS/BOOKS RECEIVED
Sam Durrant
PRODUCTION
Glenda Pattenden
EDITORIAL ASSISTANT
Lucy Evans

VOLUME 10 NUMBER 1 2010

Moving Worlds is a biannual international magazine. It publishes creative, critical, literary, and visual texts. Contributions of unpublished material are invited. Books for notice are welcome. Manuscripts should be double-spaced with footnotes gathered at the end, and should conform to the MHRA (Modern Humanities Research Association) Style Sheet. Wherever possible the submission should be on disc (soft-ware preferably Word for Windows, Wordperfect or Macwrite saved for PC on PC formatted disc) and should be accompanied by a hard copy. Please include a short biography, address, and email contact if available.

Moving Worlds is an internationally refereed journal based at the University of Leeds. The editors do not necessarily endorse the views expressed by its contributors.

All correspondence – manuscripts, books for review, enquiries – should be sent to: The Editor, *Moving Worlds*, School of English, University of Leeds, Leeds LS2 9JT, UK

email: mworlds@leeds.ac.uk
http://www.movingworlds.net

SUBSCRIPTION RATES FOR 2010
Individuals: 1 year £25.00
Institutions: 1 year £50.00
Students: 1 year £10.00
Cheques should be made payable to: University of Leeds (Moving Worlds)
Payment is accepted by Visa or Mastercard, please contact Moving Worlds for details

Published by
Moving Worlds, at School of English
University of Leeds
Leeds
LS2 9JT UK

ISBN 978-0-9553060-7-5   ISSN 1474-4600

Contents

EDITORIAL

KOH TAI ANN   1

FICTION

SUCHEN CHRISTINE LIM, Big Wall Newspaper   22

OVIDIA YU, Big Dog, Small Lives   47

WAI-CHEW SIM, Great Singapore Sale   107

DRAMA

HARESH SHARMA, Eclipse   135

AUTOBIOGRAPHY

GOH POH SENG, 'A Star-Lovely Art'   162

POETRY

NG YI-SHENG, Madonna Enthroned With Saints, Giuseppe Castiglione   20

LEONG LIEW GEOK, How to Cook a Wolf   71

HENG SIOK TIAN, Stairway (157, Neil Road, Singapore),
   Meeting Crow at Karakorum Highway, Pakistan   146

ARTICLES

TERENCE CHONG, 'At least my Singapore is real': The Politics of
   Authenticity in Identity-Formations   3

C.J.W.-L. WEE, Cultural Diversity in the Modern Urbanscape:
   Public Housing in Singapore Film   32

KENNETH CHAN, Maid to Serve: Representations of Female Domestic
   Workers in Singapore Cinema   56

KWOK KIAN-WOON, The Stakes in Contemporary Art:
   Tang Da Wu's Artistic Practice as Exemplar   72

K.K. SEET, From a Theatre of Politics to the Politics of Theatre:
   Ong Keng Sen and Interculturalism   92

DAVID BIRCH, Artistic Citizenship: The Repoliticization of Theatre
   in the New Creative Economy of Singapore   121

QUAH SY REN, Representing Idealism and Activism: Kuo Pao Kun's
   Theatre in the 1960s and the 1970s   148

NEIL MURPHY, 'A way of happening, a mouth': Public Transactions and
   Interior Spaces in the Poetry of Singapore   182

AVIJIT GUPTA, The Singapore River   194

DIALOGUE

LEE TZU PHENG AND ROBERT YEO, 'The 1960s: Being the Second Generation'
                                                                            171

REVIEWS

by NATHAN SUHR-SYTSMA, LIM LEE CHING   196

NOTES ON CONTRIBUTORS   201

Acknowledgements

Moving Worlds is published with funding assistance from the School of English, University of Leeds.

Centre for Liberal Arts and Social Sciences

We would like to thank all the contributors to this journal

Artwork in 'The Stakes in Contemporary Art: Tang Da Wu's Artistic Practice as Exemplar' pp. 72-91
By kind permission of the artist
Photography by Koh Nguang How, Courtesy of Singapore Art Archive Project@Yishun

Cover illustration:
Singapore River, 2010
Ikonos Satellite Image © CRISP, NUS (2010)
By kind permission

Editorial

KOH TAI ANN

A theme that recurs in this issue is the 'reach of the state', and the effect on citizens, the arts, and cultural development of its 'presence ... in every nook and corner of everyday Singapore life with the ultimate pursuit of economic well-being as its justification' (Terence Chong). This goes back historically to the crucial moment when Singapore unexpectedly and reluctantly separated from its hinterland Malaysia in 1965, and the ruling People's Action Party (PAP) made economic development and nation-building urgent priorities, and required the stability to achieve both. In continuous power since 1959 and virtually unopposed, the PAP government has been able to exert its will against anything inimical to, or anyone allegedly subversive of, its national objectives. It is evident where the inspiration for the school and its principal in the story 'Big Wall Newspaper' came from (Suchen Christine Lim), and why, as the film critic observes, the urban landscape depicted in Singapore film seems metonymic of 'the planned, the monolithic, and the repressive' (C.J.W.-L. Wee).

While the reach of the state is a constant, and economic progress a perennial priority, how the arts are considered and treated has depended on an evolving perception of their role. A poem such as ' "My Country and My People" ' was once banned from being broadcast on the radio because it was thought to counter the national discourse of the 1960s and 1970s in rejecting 'a patriotism of the will' for 'humanity's dark soil' (Lee Tzu Pheng and Robert Yeo). It is now read as a 'national' poem. Kuo Pao Kun − whose plays have been described as offering an 'alternative discourse of identity and belonging' and opposing the State's model of economic development − was detained in 1976 with others for his 'idealism and activism' (Quah Sy Ren). Released in 1980, he became highly regarded for his subsequent contributions towards making drama the most vibrant form in that decade and for engaging in a 'theatre of politics' less confrontational, more allegorical, and nuanced. The role of the arts being now regarded as cultural enrichment than just nation-building, both Lee and Kuo received the Cultural Medallion, an award instituted in 1979 for 'exceptional artistic talent and achievement'. The 1980s culminated in the formation of the National Arts Council in 1991 to provide infrastructural and financial support for the arts.

Theatre matured and moved on in different directions − Ong Keng Sen of TheatreWorks, for example, turned to 'a politics of theatre', freely appropriating and reinventing both Asian and Western artistic and performing traditions and forms to create his intercultural performances and docu-dramas (K.K. Seet). It was left to Singapore film, the emerging art form, to take up its social mission with talented filmmakers exploring such issues as the human costs and cultural effects of globalization, and identity, 'home', and belonging (C.J.W.-L. Wee; Kenneth Chan).

Official support for the arts was not necessarily accompanied by liberalization. When the Minister in charge declared in 2000 that maintenance of 'social peace' was an artistic 'social responsibility', one theatre director was provoked to 'demand' – as artist, citizen, father, son, and 'as a person who sees himself having a future in this country' – 'the right to be irresponsible' since 'an artist cannot work unless that right is given'. But another, aware of the realities still of funding support, responded bleakly that 'It's not so easy to say, "I'm an artist, I just want to do what I want", because you're an artist in Singapore, you know' (David Birch).

Thus, performance artist Tang Da Wu's statement, 'Don't Give Money to the Arts', was central in raising 'questions about the interrelationships between the arts, politics and money and, indeed, about the very idea of art' (Kwok Kian-Woon). Ironically, the latest government initiative, the 'Global City of the Arts Project', would co-opt the arts to contribute to economic growth, constituting 'a key competitive advantage in the globalised economy' as part of Singapore's 'creative industries'.

Yet there is cause for optimism as intellectuals and artists continue to 'speak truth to power' and debate key concerns. Kwok (citing Edward Said) warns, 'the aesthetic and the social need to be kept, and often consciously kept, in a state of irreconcilable tension', while Neil Murphy argues that they can and often need to be kept separate. Indeed, the poetry of Arthur Yap and Boey Kim Cheng suggests a trend of turning away from art or writing that is socially or politically engaged, focusing on the interior life without any irritable desire to 'make things happen'. Likewise this could be said to be true of the creative work represented in this issue. Lively and engaging, the stories, poems, and play are (to adapt Martin Amis' comment on the novel) 'not made to achieve things' but to provide 'a framework for thinking about things'.

'At least my Singapore is real': The Politics of Authenticity in Identity-Formations

TERENCE CHONG

The *ethnie*'s absence and the omnipresence of the People's Action Party

Most modernist accounts of national identity ignore the human need for authenticity by explaining national identity as chiefly a by-product of various modernization processes. They explain the emergence of national identity in a variety of ways, as the result of, for example, industrialization, mass literacy, and print capitalism, or uneven wealth distribution and capitalist development.[1] Where these explanations agree is that national identity fulfils a modern and developmental need rather than a primal yearning. Anthony Smith however argues that, unless we accept the yearning for an authentic identity as natural and actively seek it in the 'myths and memories' of the *ethnie*, we would become 'strangers to ourselves because we [would] have no clear idea of the real, the historic self, and the collective identity formed many generations back, from which each and every individual identity takes its life and meaning'.[2] For Smith, the *ethnie* is a national identity that, based on common ancestry, culture, and ethnicity, is inextricably intertwined with the concept of authenticity. The discourse of *ethnie,* constructed from the nostalgic intellectualizing of a 'golden past' and the eulogizing of a pre-modern ethnic community, is an overarching story that people tell themselves about who they are and what they stand for: in short, it is the collective manufacturing of an 'authentic' national identity. This has resulted in ethnic myths resonating strongly in the national identities of countries, such as France, England, Germany and Austria. The *ethnie* identity is retrospective, continually self-referring and self-contextualizing to frame and give meaning to contemporary everyday life, and is perpetuated when historical texts, canons, and myths are quoted and (re)interpreted in popular culture and public discourse. It is permeable and easy to consume because it is crystallized in clichés, stereotypes, and caricatures while conceived as a linear development, evolving uncritically towards the ethno-nation, which is always presented as an identifiable and unchanging subject of history.

However, the *ethnie* does not exist in Singapore. As mainstream history has it, independence was thrust on the city-state upon its expulsion from Malaysia in 1965. Responding to its own multiethnic complexion and Malay-centric policies in Malaysia, the ruling People's Action Party (PAP) presented and still presents itself as an ethnic-neutral entity, best qualified thereby to mediate between fractious ethnic or religious interests. It also discouraged any overt correlation between the distribution of national resources and ethnicity by introducing the ideologies of meritocracy and multiculturalism. The brief flirtation with Confucian ethics in the late 1980s and early 1990s notwithstanding, the search for an authentic national identity in Singapore has rarely been premised on ethnicity. Historical circumstances having blocked the formation of an 'authentic' national identity, it is equally fruitless to seek it in state-sponsored imaginaries of collective identity or to reconcile the search for an 'authentic life' with the constraints in everyday Singapore life.[3]

For Sartre, the individual who wished to lead an authentic life could not define himself by the roles offered by social institutions; the individual could only be authentic if he transcended these social roles and embraced the freedom to choose who to be. Sartrean authenticity thus comprises two modes: confronting the dreadful truth of one's existence, and actively breaking sociocultural codes to fulfil the desires of the self. However, the success of 'the Singapore story from Third World to First' (to echo the title of Lee Kuan Yew's memoirs) is attributed to necessarily comprehensive state structures and institutions that have ordered and disciplined the everyday lives of Singaporeans. The vast array of ubiquitous state mechanisms from trade unions to the press, the paucity of meaningful opposition, and a highly strategic and competent policy-making process have given the PAP State a wide moral jurisdiction over these lives. According to Minister Mentor Lee Kuan Yew, in what is now a classic piece of PAP political-teleological discourse:

> I say without the slightest remorse that we would not be here, would not have made the economic progress, if we had not intervened on very personal matters – who your neighbour is, how you live, the noise you make, how you spit (or where you spit), or what language you use … It was fundamental social and cultural changes that brought us here.[4]

The PAP State's tight organization of citizens' lives and its monopoly of the power to initiate civic and societal change – with the ultimate pursuit of economic well-being as its justification – has, over the years, disempowered Singaporeans.[5] Coupled with the PAP's mantra that it alone has the mandate to lead and govern in the best interests of Singaporeans, this lack of empowerment means that the sense that one is living the Sartrean authentic life is also missing. Indeed, any thinking person living in Singapore cannot help but be struck by the way the PAP State's presence is found in every nook and corner of everyday Singapore life, making it virtually impossible, short of emigration, to choose to live a life beyond the reach of the state.[6] If the Singaporean life is a PAP-processed life, then there is little leeway to achieve the authentic life, defined by Charles Taylor as a 'self-determining freedom [that] demands that I break the hold of all such external impositions, and decide for myself alone'.[7]

The Singapore heartlander as authentic figure

In the absence of the *ethnie* and given the omnipresence of the PAP State, the working class or the 'heartlanders' have become a source of authenticity in the identity-formation process. The term 'heartlander' in its uniquely Singaporean sense of the word was coined by the then Prime Minister, Goh Chok Tong, in his 1999 National Day Rally Speech to describe Singaporeans who are rooted in the local 'heartland' of the public housing or Housing and Development Board (HDB) estates in contrast to 'cosmopolitans' or globally mobile Singaporeans who possess the capacity to surf away on the waves of globalization. The typical heartlander lives in a flat in one of the many HDB satellite towns, holds a blue collar or low-paying white collar job, and is most comfortable speaking Singlish, the local patois influenced in vocabulary and syntax by Chinese and Malay. Significantly, heartlanders, it is claimed, 'tend to be rooted in their cultures and traditions, respectful of authority and less vocal in their demands. Their concerns centre on their livelihood and children's education rather than abstract notions of artistic and political space'.[8]

There are generally three reasons why Singapore heartlanders have emerged as the embodiment of authenticity in the national imagination. Firstly, stereotyped as unsophisticated, frank, and straightforward, they have become a local signifier of unpretentiousness and genuineness. Without the requisite cultural capital or education to navigate high society circles, they are popularly assumed to be more 'natural' and truer to the self. Indeed, the strong link between authenticity and the working class is universal,[9] and may have roots in the Marxist belief that the proletariat possesses the potential to break free from the shackles of false consciousness and begin the process to self-determination. This inherent potential of the proletariat aligns neatly with the Sartrean notion of the individual's capacity to break free from social institutions and structures to pursue the authentic life. Secondly, living in a city-state that embraces global flows, and under a government highly attuned to the logic of neo-capitalism, Singapore heartlanders have become an acceptable means to address such effects as the widening wage gap and structural unemployment, whenever the state-controlled local media highlights the plight of the poor and the need for social assistance or when the government exhorts workers to upgrade their skills in order to stay competitive. The wisdom of the political elite's policies which have led to such outcomes is thus left unchallenged. The heartlanders thereby become socially constructed as a semi-heroic class who take the hard knocks dished out by a capricious global economy. Occasional social assistance and wealth distribution measures – for example, the New Singapore Shares, Economic Restructuring Shares or the Progress Package – provide opportunities for the PAP State to honour its social compact with Singaporeans while deflecting criticism away from its adamant refusal to practise so-called 'welfarism' or to introduce a minimum wage.[10] Finally, belonging to the 'heartland' of Singapore, heartlanders are thought to have firmer ties and commitment to the local, unlike cosmopolitans who, better educated, English-proficient or highly paid professionals, are less reliant on the state and the nation. As the city-state becomes an increasingly global site, it is inevitable that the local should be celebrated in the interest of national identity and belonging. This celebration goes back to the late 1980s when Singlish was first heard in local theatre. Celebration of the heartlanders using Singlish includes popular television sitcoms, such as *Under One Roof* and *Phua Chu Kang,* which dramatized and rendered comic typical situations in their daily lives.[11] The heartlander in popular culture has become so crystallized in meaning for easy consumption that the 'Ah Beng'[12] – an unsophisticated, usually poorly educated and socially inept working class Chinese male – has become 'cool'.

Heartlander identity, being unlike ethnic identity where access is exclusive, becomes an unguarded resource when run through the mill of pop culture, vulnerable to adoption claims, and counter-claims. It is not uncommon to hear well-educated Singaporeans claiming to be heartlanders and speaking Singlish: claims of authenticity are not necessarily premised on the accurate representation of self or actual adherence to intrinsic cultural heritage and traditions but are (in Bourdieusian terms) 'symbolic capital' which can, in turn, be traded and exchanged for social acceptance, material resources, wealth or other advantages in the social field.[13] To be authentic is to be thus more worthy of the rewards at stake in the field of struggle. And because no one can rightfully claim to be authentic, everyone can.

The exploitation of working class authenticity for financial and other gain is, of course, not new. Grazian, studying the Chicago blues bar circuit, found that the blues bars that best fitted the global stereotype were often more successful in attracting the tourist dollar, regardless of the quality of the music these bars offered.[14] Lionel Trilling's observation that 'Authenticity is implicitly a polemical concept' is also apposite because the politics of authenticity is a zero-sum game where each claim is necessarily a refutation of the other's legitimacy.[15]

Relying on a combination of participant observation, interviews, and discourse analysis, I look next at the manufacture, demonstration, and contestation of authenticity in the world of film and theatre in Singapore. The romanticization of the Singaporean working class in the films of Jack Neo,[16] arguably Singapore's most commercially successful film director, will be examined to excavate its exemplary discourses of heartlander authenticity. The way in which heartlander authenticity is demonstrated will also be examined by looking at how other groups champion Singlish and proclaim to be Ah Bengs in order to win legitimacy for themselves. Lastly, I will look at how certain local theatre companies proclaim themselves to be committed to 'authentic' Singaporean narratives, while others contest the 'authenticity' of their representations. The following sections will explore a specific cultural-political interpretation of the local by various actors and will be sociologically framed to understand the way such 'authenticity' is used to resist, negotiate, and leverage on the logic of globalization processes and the Singapore State's response to the latter.

Manufacturing authenticity: Heartlanders in Jack Neo's films

The romanticization of the working class has been well documented.[17] It begins when specific everyday actions are portrayed as acts of resistance, heroic struggle, or tragedy – actions tending towards self-realization. Such portrayals are used sweepingly to characterize an entire, often diverse group, making the romanticization process a manufacturing of ideal types and thus an erasure of complexity. Jack Neo has emerged since the late 1990s as Singapore's most popular and populist filmmaker whose work has become metonymic of the Singaporean heartland, and who has significantly declared that 'As a director, I like real. Everything in my movies is real.'[18] His stories about the plight of the Chinese Singaporean working class in a fast-paced global city are drenched in sociopolitical critique and cultural moralizing. His protagonists are predominantly Chinese males who are poorly educated and dialect- or Mandarin-speaking, who are often portrayed as victims of global capitalism and/or the PAP State's bilingual education or 'foreign talent' policies.[19] His production values, being considerably lower than those of his contemporaries, such as Eric Khoo or Royston Tan, give his films a patina of no-frills authenticity while box office success in Singapore not only testifies to their commercial viability but also to the affect of his stories about heartland.[20]

Neo's Chinese working class protagonists are essentially well-meaning, even if sometimes morally misguided. Nevertheless, as the examples below bear out, they are always redeemable and achieve absolution or reprieve through self-realization, such that whatever their struggles, hardships, and luckless escapades, they are ensured a happy ending. *The Best Bet* (2004), a cautionary tale about the evils of gambling, features a luckless-working-man-trying-to-make-good. Tan (Mark Lee), a hawker and incorrigible gambler, dreams of striking it rich. After his lack of success at the lottery, He starts a business with his friends, Yong Shun (Christopher Lee) and Richard (Richard Low) which folds up. Debt-ridden, he is arrested for trying illegally to borrow money from moneylenders. Conveniently, he wins the lottery, and then partners his old friends in a *bak kut teh* (Chinese pork rib herbal 'tea') business, and prospers. In *One More Chance* (2005), a story about convicts and second chances, Zhou (Henry Thia) is a factory supervisor and burglar, but also a devoted son to his senile mother. Released from prison, he decides to change, but finds that he is not accepted, and his romantic overtures to a warden officer are rejected. Desperate and desiring to fulfil one of his mother's wishes, Zhou plans a burglary with his ex-prison mates. However, everything works out in the end and the film closes with the usual heavy dose of moralizing.[21]

Typically, the Chinese heartlander protagonists in both these films are male, subject to hardship yet resilient, crude in manners yet basically kind, materialistic yet sentimental. Each surmounts his sociocultural disadvantages through hard work or well-deserved luck. Each undergoes a formulaic cycle of misdemeanour, struggle, self-realization and, finally, a redemption signified by material success. Given that economic status is the most recognizable and respected sign of legitimacy in capitalist Singapore, this is not surprising. Such romanticized 'heartlander heroes', displaying redeeming qualities in their everyday struggle against social structures, and eventually enjoying the fruits of capitalism, are effective, if not ironic, metaphors for self-awakening and self-purification to a nation of consumers devoid of a past 'golden age'. As Smith notes, hero-making and heroes are necessary for the transmission of values, culture, and customs from generation to generation.[22]

Furthermore, it is not unusual for theatre, television, and film to use stereotypes to embody different cultural values and sociopolitical groups, and Neo's heartlanders are imbued with authenticity by being contrasted with another stereotype – Westernized, English-educated and English-speaking, middle class characters who epitomize political or bureaucratic power (the politician or civil servant), or economic success (the well-educated professional and other beneficiaries of global capitalism), or so-called Western values (such as liberal democracy and freedom). Neo accentuates heartlander authenticity by representing Western values or Western orientation as foreign and alienating. For instance, in *I Not Stupid* (2002), a young, precocious female Chinese student stands up in class to declare that 'if I am a Caucasian, I won't have to learn Chinese anymore'. This prompts a lecture from her teacher on how Chinese is the key to personal and ethnic identity; and that, without it, the young anglophile would not understand who she is or where she comes from. The explicit message is that ethnic Chinese who are more comfortable in English and are Western-oriented, like the young student, are likely to become rootless and inauthentic.

Whether as filmmaker or actor, Neo is also fond of illustrating heartlander authenticity by setting up clashes between, on the one hand, Mandarin speaking and/or dialect-speaking protagonists and, on the other, English-speaking middle class characters in order to accentuate the contrasting worlds of the beneficiaries and non-beneficiaries of globalization and PAP State policies. In Tay Teck Lock's *Money No Enough* (1998), Neo plays the part of Keong, a Mandarin Chinese-speaking senior and deserving worker, who is passed over for promotion. In the film's corporate world, his new colleague, Jeremiah Adolpher Lee, with an overseas (that is, Western) education and superior command of English triumphs over Keong's qualities of industry and sincerity, a situation that subliminally echoes the sentiments of the Mandarin-speaking majority who feel that their nation-building sacrifices have been glossed over by the English-speaking elite. The standard Singapore story seems thus to be only about the achievements and successes of the Western-educated, English-proficient Singaporean.

Indeed, the narrative of the economically marginal protagonist, who strives initially in an English-speaking society, but who eventually surmounts his difficulties through sheer grit and adherence to traditional values, is one of the dominant themes of locally produced Mandarin films and television. Turning from their misguided ways to so-called traditional values, such as filial piety, hard work, honesty, personal sacrifice, discipline, prudence, Neo's protagonists all enjoy happy endings. Authenticity is thus manufactured, with Neo suggesting that everything can be solved by a return to good old-fashioned values. This discourse echoes the PAP State's fear, particularly pronounced in the 1980s, that middle class English-educated Chinese Singaporeans were becoming 'Westernized', impelling at the time the emergence of Confucian ethics discourse as a national ideology and privileging the teaching of so-called Chinese culture and values. Neo's films, by showing that heartlanders need only return to ethnic-based cultural values to be successful, leave unproblematized the co-option of romantic notions, such as the redemptive power of hard work, personal sacrifice, and discipline, by the logic of capitalism.

Demonstrating authenticity: Singlish and the English-proficient middle class

Having become established in popular culture and the media as the embodiment of authenticity, the heartlanders' attributed traits, values, and discourses are sources of cultural capital for individuals or groups looking for legitimacy. Thus sections of the English-proficient middle class have begun, firstly, to proclaim they are heartlanders;[23] and secondly, to champion the use and preservation of Singlish. In the mass media and popular culture, heartlander traits are now seen to be authentic, such that local celebrities are given to declare themselves to be a little 'Ah Beng' or 'Ah Lian' at heart.[24] This rehabilitation, through 'cool' portrayals in the media involves the convenient whitewashing of the Ah Beng's anti-social, loutish traits, and even criminal tendencies[25] in the popular imagination, while playing up his non-threatening traits, such as sincerity, street honour, loyalty, sense of brotherhood, and his unquestioned commitment to the local and the locale of the heartland.

That the English-speaking middle class, the most economically secure and politically best represented group, feels that it needs to assume heartlander characteristics in order to acquire legitimacy indicates a dissonance between notions of authenticity and cosmopolitanism. Unlike contemporary connotations of their being sophisticated and cultured, the cosmopolitan were once seen as 'non-citizens' and 'deviant', refusing to define themselves by location, ancestry, citizenship or language and embodying 'all the worst aspects of classical liberalism – atomism, abstraction, alienation from one's roots, vacuity of commitment, indeterminacy of character, and ambivalence towards the good'.[26] In mid-nineteenth century America, the 'cosmopolite' embodied 'a well-travelled character probably lacking in substance'.[27] Moreover, as Steven Vertovec and Robin Cohen have shown, the cosmopolitan's perceived 'lack of substance' was historically measured against 'a readily identifiable provenance, an integrated and predictable pattern of behavioural practice, including loyalty to a single nation-state or cultural identity'.[28] The discourse of the rootless cosmopolitan was consonant with the binary discourse of the Chinese-educated and English-educated Chinese in pre-independent Singapore. The latter were seen to be Westernized and disengaged from the anti-colonial struggle, in contrast to their Chinese-educated counterparts who were connected to mainland China by language, culture, and emergent nationalism. Furthermore, the Chinese-educated community, marginalized by the colonial administration and subsequently by the PAP State where English was the working language, saw itself as self-sufficient and resourceful, while the English-educated Chinese, situated closer to the colonial administration, were either perceived as second-class citizens or cultural hybrids, and thus had weaker claims to authenticity. The nationalistic energy and ideological conviction of the Chinese-educated Chinese – entrenched as the proletariat who expressed themselves through demonstrations, trade union activities, and guerrilla warfare and 'who bravely put themselves behind the wheel of resistance' – are often starkly contrasted with the ideologically *laissez faire* attitudes of the English-educated Chinese.[29] Minister Mentor Lee Kuan Yew has commented unfavourably about the behaviour of the latter during the World War II years:

> Many of us will remember the unhappy spectacle of English-speaking, Western-educated colleagues suddenly changing in their manners of speech, dress and behaviour, making blatant attempts at being good imitation Japs [sic]. Indeed some were sent to Japan as to be better educated, to enlighten their ignorant countrymen in Malaya and doubtless also to become the privileged class, second only to the genuine Japanese themselves.[30]

In the late 1970s when it was observed that economic prosperity had led to increasingly conspicuous consumption of Western cultural products by English-educated Chinese Singaporeans, fears of 'deculturalization' were expressed by PAP ministers, provoking high-level state reports on moral education and national education to counter the apparently attendant undesirable consequences.[31] Given historical associations of shifting loyalties and rootlessness among the English-educated Chinese, it is arguable that the heartlander-cosmopolitan binary also contains traces of the conflict between nationally-bound and free-floating identities. Such historical associations have therefore made it necessary for sections of the English-educated middle class to seek the legitimacy of authenticity through the assumption of a heartlander identity.

Championing of Singlish is part of the attempt to demonstrate their authenticity and their cultural capital.[32] Since the late 1980s when its use in local English language theatre achieved critical acceptance, Singlish has been lauded by both linguists and members of the public as a marker of Singaporean identity and culture, with strong emotive links to notions of community and national belonging. The national debate over Singlish has, on the one hand, its proponents who argue that it is distinctively Singaporean, recognizable wherever one is in the world, and, most importantly, that it is a 'natural' non-state-engineered expression of indigenous Singaporean culture. On the other hand, its critics (including Lee Kuan Yew and PAP ministers) argue that it is 'broken English', prevents Singaporeans from being understood by non-Singaporeans, and thus subverts Singapore's ambitions to develop a global economy and become a global city.[33]

Unlike the Mandarin or dialect-speaking Chinese-educated or the working class heartlander who struggles with English and uses Singlish more by default than choice, the English-educated are diglossic, able to switch between Singlish and Standard English according to social context.[34] Linguists note that such code-switching occurs when a speaker wishes either to communicate more effectively with another person or to express solidarity with a particular individual or social group. This is well illustrated by a scene from Russell Heng's play, *Half Century* (2004).

> *The final week of the year 1999. Evening. Living room of Curly's Housing Board flat. Curly and Ai Meng are listening to a radio programme.*
>
> **Announcer:** Francis, what do you miss about Singapore in all these years abroad?
> **Francis:** Well, *char kway teow lah*, chicken rice *lah* ...
> **Announcer:** Do you speak like that even in London?
> **Francis:** Oh no no no, my dear girl, in England one speaks as the English do. One has to be very *propah*. But now that I am talking to a Singapore audience, I use some Singlish *lor*. That is also what I miss about Singapore, the patois. Of course, I miss my family too.

Rapport is immediately established among Singaporeans by such code-switching, opening pathways to understanding and empathy, enabling the English-educated middle class to cross class divisions in social contexts where different sections of society come into contact, such as during

National Service, when out shopping, and on local university campuses. Code-switching, however, is not available to the heartlander who can only speak Singlish. The English-educated, in using Singlish to cross boundaries between class and identity, display their cultural capital – that is, an embodied form of knowledge and experience – to negotiate the social world to fulfil specific interests.

Another example comes from Stella Kon's now canonical play, *Emily of Emerald Hill* (1985), which is set in the 1950s. Emily, an English-educated Peranakan Chinese matriarch, spontaneously code-switches in the course of her morning trips to the low-end open market and then the high-end supermarket:

> *She goes on to the next stall.*
> Ah Soh! How are you, chiak pah boey? Ya I'm fine, family is fine, chin ho, chin ho. I want to buy sixteen cucumbers today, half a kati of long beans, half a kati of French beans. Yes, you guessed correctly, I'm making achar for the New Year …
>
> *She moves to the next stall.*
> Ai tambi! Give me sesame seed please, dried chilli, peanuts. Thank you, thank you.
>
> Hai Mat, put all the marketing into the car and wait for me, I am just popping in to Cold Storage.
>
> *She enters Cold Storage and assumes a posh accent.*
> Good morning Mr Chai. I would like to order one honey-baked ham for the Chinese New Year. Eleven pounds will be excellent, please deliver it to Emerald Hill.
>
> Oh, good morning Mrs Schneider, how nice to run into you! Yes indeed, I shall send you some orchids for the Church Bazaar as usual. Not at all, with my sons at Anglo-Chinese School I'm very glad to make my little contribution. Do give the Bishop my best wishes won't you?

Both Francis and Emily, like most well-educated English-speaking Singaporeans, move effortlessly, code-switching both to communicate effectively, and to establish, albeit briefly and superficially, a connection or solidarity with other Singaporeans. Francis' ability to drop 'propah' English allows him to assume a Singaporean identity, while Emily, speaking Singlish to Chinese and Indian stall-holders, the Malay driver and other service providers, marks herself as a local, thereby discouraging over-charging and eliciting prompt service.

Contesting authenticity: 'Real' Singaporean stories in theatre

In the struggle for authenticity and legitimacy, it becomes necessary for individuals and groups to contest the claims of others to similar economic and symbolic capital, and this contest is evident in the Singapore theatre scene.[35] Public funds for local theatre companies are distributed according to a hierarchy imposed by the National Arts Council.[36] First in financial terms is the 2-Year Major Grant, then the Annual Grant, and, last, the *ad hoc* General Grant. The struggle is primarily between smaller amateur companies who only qualify for the General Grant and the larger, more established, predominantly English-language professional companies who enjoy the Annual and 2-Year Major Grants.[37]

Discourses of authenticity, and thus 'Singaporeanness', are important to local theatre companies for several reasons. Firstly, audiences generally expect local narratives and stories. Secondly, in light of the government's public commitment to the promotion of local arts and cultural industry, the production of such plays enables theatre companies to compete more effectively for public funds. In short, theatre companies are endowed with symbolic capital in the eyes of theatre-goers and critics for articulating the local. A claim of authenticity begins with a typical assertion of interest in the 'ordinary', that is, an interest in the lives of Singaporeans and in issues important to heartlanders, thereby (un)consciously engaging in the global-local binary. According to an artistic director of a small amateur English-language theatre company,

> My plays are about Singaporean life. I think you have to be Singaporean and be part of the culture in order to understand my stuff. I respect what the other [bigger] theatre companies are doing but I want to tell the story of the 'Ah Sohs' ['sisters-in-law' or a manner of addressing middle aged, married women] who have to deal with her HDB neighbours and their *mahjong* sessions. I think ordinary Singaporeans respond more instinctively to local stories that are happening around them than abstract ones.

Such comments could be interpreted as thinly veiled jibes at the bigger Annual and 2-Year Major Grant theatre companies who are known to engage more with abstract themes and theoretical concepts of the pan-Asian and the intercultural. Another director of a small amateur bilingual theatre company declares,

> [We have] no pretensions of who we are and what we do. We're not some jet-set theatre company or some global cosmopolitan artistic director who talks about interculturalism or transculturalism … At least my Singapore is real … unlike his. My experience as a Singaporean who has lived in Singapore his whole life does not qualify me to be, you know, pan-Asian and all that fashionable jazz. I am more interested in the local. I am more interested in the Ah Bengs, the billiard salons, the seedy karaoke bars, the underbelly of Singapore, so to speak…

The proclaimed commitment to the life-worlds of HDB residents, to the

Ah Bengs or heartlanders, is the appeal to a national culture and all that it stands for – community, security, familiarity, and belonging – in contrast to the foreign, cosmopolitan or global culture allegedly embraced by the Annual and 2-Year Major Grants theatre companies. Commitment to the local is thus a form of capital in the field because it has value in that it can be traded or exchanged for desired outcomes, such as legitimacy and prestige in the eyes of local audiences. After attending a small budget production by an amateur theatre company held at the Substation (a small black box performance space), a twenty-year-old Humanities undergraduate told me, 'I think we need more theatre companies like this. They aren't big but they are pretty independent in their direction. They also tend to be more raw and honest which [is what] I like in theatre.' Positioning themselves as an embedding force against the de-territorializing and de-localizing affects of globalization is particularly powerful because the local-global dichotomy is often played out as the dichotomy between 'home' and the 'transient'.[38] This home-transient binary is used to good effect by those who do not subscribe to cosmopolitan values and who are without global cultural capital: accentuating the de-territorializing and de-localizing effects of globalization not only stirs up the spectre of loss but also highlights the material disparities between those who are 'global' (and mobile) and those who have no choice but to remain 'local' (and stay put). Besides, as people begin to understand the darker consequences of globalization and neo-capitalism, telling Singaporean stories of forgotten, marginal, and dispensable identities also becomes fashionable – indeed some might say important – even among the larger professional companies.

Understandably, among these professional theatre companies, there are some who are sceptical of claims of authenticity from the smaller amateur companies. According to the artistic director of a 2-Year Major Grants English-language theatre company,

> [Amateur and marginal practitioners] say they talk about Singaporean stories. But sometimes you get the feeling that they are more Singaporean than Singaporeans … I mean, it's always easier to go overboard with Singlish [on stage]. Most of us [established practitioners] have passed that phase back in the late eighties, early nineties.

He continues,

> It's sometimes a little condescending when you say you're doing local reality and Singaporean lives. People live Singaporean lives, do they need to hear you say you're staging it for them? What makes you so special? … They all want to be little Prometheuses, bringing fire and light to the masses.

In sum, while different practitioners occupy different positions of power in the local theatre field, all are engaged in the struggle for recognition from audiences and critics, and for financial rewards from the state. Less established amateur theatre companies, unable to compete in terms of ticket sales, media attention, large production budgets or professional technical crew, proclaim their authenticity as an asset to build up reputations as narrators of Singaporean stories and experience. Such contestations of authenticity when unpacked reveal the politics of class, language, and culture.

Conclusion

Historical and political circumstances have rendered impossible the nurturing of an ethnic-based national identity as a source of authenticity in Singapore. The *ethnie* – a population with a myth of common ancestry, shared historical memories, and culture – did not flourish despite the majority status of the Chinese because of their immigrant past. While this absence of the *ethnie* has denied individuals or groups the opportunity to declare their authenticity, it has also stemmed the possibility for ethno-nationalism. At the same time, the overwhelming presence of the PAP State has resulted in heavily regulated spaces, limiting opportunities for individuals to lead the 'authentic life'. It has been argued that the absence of the *ethnie* and the omnipresence of the PAP State, coupled with the universal propensity to romanticize the working class, has resulted in the representation of the heartlander as a source of authenticity. Other contributing factors include the politics of class, language, and power in contemporary Singapore. The manufacturing of authenticity in film, drama, and the media allows the diverse concerns and interests of the Singapore working class to be stereotyped as easily consumable narratives or identities. This enables well-educated English-speaking members of the middle class to assume these identities at will in order to demonstrate their 'authenticity'. As with all claims to authenticity, contestation ensues between individuals and groups situated in different locations of power and privilege in the sociocultural landscape.

From the perspective of globalization, the local-global and heartlander-cosmopolitan binaries not only draw attention to the spectre of loss and transience in the global city, reaffirming the human need for authenticity, but also testify to the vacuum in the Singapore national identity that has yet to be filled.

NOTES

1. See Benedict Anderson, *Imagined Communities: Reflections on the Origins and Spread of Nationalism* (London:Verso, 1991); Ernest Gellner, *Nations and Nationalisms* (NewYork: Cornell UP, 1983); and Tom Nairn, *The Faces of Nationalism: Janus Revisited* (London: Verso, 1998), for a deeper exploration of these ideas.
2. Anthony Smith, *Myths and Memories of the Nation* (Oxford: Oxford UP, 1999), p. 67.
3. See Martin Heidegger, *Being and Time* (San Francisco: Harper, 1962) and Jean-Paul Sartre, *Being and Nothingness* (London: Methuen, 1963). Both Heidegger and Sartre were interested in what constituted the 'authentic' life. But their notions of it differed. For Sartre, the authenticity of the individual comes from acting, choosing, and deciding. For Heidegger, the authentic life comes from understanding and interpreting ontological meaning and truth. The understanding of meaning, or one's self, unveils to the individual his limits, potential, strengths and weaknesses, all of which influence the array of life choices and options at his disposal.
4. As quoted by Hussin Mutalib, 'Illiberal Democracy and the Future of Opposition in Singapore', *Third World Quarterly*, 2:2 (2000) 321.
5. See Terence Chong, 'Embodying Society's Best: Hegel and the Singapore State', *Journal of Contemporary Asia*, 36:3 (2007) 283-304.
6. The omnipresence of the PAP State is seen in its cradle-to-grave policies and institutions which govern every stage of a Singaporean's life, including education in public schools that must conform to a national curriculum and common-streaming examinations (controlled by the Ministry of Education); compulsory military service for all males age 18 and above (National Service); housing (over 80% live in Housing and Development Board flats); compulsory retirement and health care savings (the Central Provident Fund; MediSave).
7. Charles Taylor, *The Ethics of Authenticity* (Cambridge, MA: Harvard UP, 1991), p. 27.
8. Elaine Ho, 'Negotiating Belonging and Perceptions of Citizenship in a Transnational World: Singapore, a Cosmopolis?', *Social & Cultural Geography*, 7:3 (2006) 388-89.
9. See Richard A. Peterson, *Creating Country Music: Fabricating Authenticity* (Chicago: U of Chicago P, 1997); Gary Alan Fine, *Everyday Genius: Self-Taught Art and the Culture of Authenticity* (Chicago: U of Chicago P, 2004); and David Grazian, *Blue Chicago: The Search for Authenticity in Urban Blues Clubs* (Chicago: U of Chicago P, 2003).
10. The New Singapore Shares were introduced in 2001 to help the lower income group cope with the economic downturn. The Economic Restructuring Shares are part of a broader offset package to help Singaporeans adapt to the structural changes in the economy. The Progress Package introduced in 2006 was a budget surplus-sharing exercise which also contained several social and political objectives.
11. *Under One Roof* revolves around a typical Chinese middle class family living in a HDB flat with multiracial neighbours. *Phua Chu Kang* is the name of the main character, a poorly educated renovation contractor with crude manners but a kind heart.
12. The female counterpart of 'Ah Beng' is known as 'Ah Lian' or 'Ah Huay'.
13. See Pierre Bourdieu, 'The Forms of Capital', *Handbook of Theory and Research for the Sociology of Education*, ed. John G. Richardson (NewYork: Greenwood Press, 1986); also *The Field of Cultural Production: Essays on Art and Literature*, trans. Richard Nice (Cambridge: Polity Press, 1993); and *Distinction: A Social Critique of the Judgement of Taste*, trans. Richard Nice ([1979] London: Routledge, 2002).
14. David Grazian, *Blue Chicago*, p. 36.
15. Lionel Trilling, *Sincerity and Authenticity* (Cambridge, MA: Harvard UP, 1972), p. 94.

16. See also Chua Beng Huat and Yeo Wei Wei, 'Singapore Cinema: Eric Khoo and Jack Neo – critique from the margins and the mainstream', *Inter-Asia Cultural Studies* 4:1 (2003) 117-25, for discussions of Neo's work. To date, Neo has written, directed, and acted in 14 films. They include *Money No Enough* (1998); *That One No Enough* (1999); *Liang Po Po: The Movie* (1999); *I Not Stupid* (2002); *Homerun* (2003); *The Best Bet* (2004); *I Do, I Do* (2005); *One More Chance* (2005); *I Not Stupid Too* (2006); *Just Follow Law* (2007); *Money No Enough 2* (2008); *Love Matters* (2009); *Where Got Ghost?* (2009); *Being Human Being* (2010).

17. See Risa Whitson, 'Redundant Masculinities: Employment Change and White Working Class Youth', *International Journal of Urban and Regional Research*, 29:1 (2005) 206-08; and Stacey J. Lee, 'Theorizing Class Through Ethnography', *Educational Researcher*, 36:1 (2007) 33-36.

18. As quoted by Bryan Walsh, 'Neo is the One', *Time Magazine*, 1 April 2002.

19. The term 'foreign talent' is used locally to describe highly skilled foreign professionals working in Singapore.

20. It has been argued that Neo's ability to speak simply and straightforwardly to his audience is traceable to his National Service days when he served in the Singapore Armed Forces' Music and Drama Company (MDC). At the MDC, Neo quickly learnt the craft of efficient storytelling, acquiring ways to get his points across to national servicemen, many of whom were not particularly well-educated or did not have the patience for abstract plays. It is also suggested that the ideologically strict and prohibitive army environment also made Neo sensitive to the boundaries of acceptable critique of the Singapore condition; see Royston Chan, 'Socio-Political Commentary in the films of Jack Neo', <www.sgnewwave.com/sg_jackneo.htm, 2006> accessed 15 April 2007.

21. It is noteworthy that *One More Chance* was supported by the Yellow Ribbon Campaign, a government-inspired effort to assimilate ex-convicts back into society. Interestingly, the film's Mandarin title in English translation is literally 'Three Good Men' and not the version in Singlish, *One More Chance*.

22. Smith, *Myths and Memories*, p. 65.

23. Chua Beng Huat, *Life is not Complete without Shopping: Consumption Culture in Singapore* (Singapore: National U of Singapore P, 2003).

24. John Lui, 'Born to be Beng', *The Straits Times*, 10 September 2008.

25. According to the Singapore Police Force, 3,645 youths were arrested for crime in 2006, accounting for 19 per cent of the total persons arrested, and 5,050 in 2005 or 23 per cent, both percentages higher than the proportion of youths in Singapore. Of 361 cases of rioting in 2006, 137 cases involved young people. <www.spf.gov.sg/stats/stats2006_overview.htm> accessed 3 May, 2007.

26. Jeremy Waldron, 'Minority Cultures and the Cosmopolitan Alternative', *University of Michigan Journal of Law Reform*, 23:3 (1992) 764.

27. David A. Hollinger, *Postethnic America: Beyond Multiculturalism* (New York: Basic Books, 1995), p. 89.

28. Steven Vertovec and Robin Cohen, eds, *Conceiving Cosmopolitanism: Theory, Context, and Practice* (Oxford: Oxford UP, 2002), p. 6.

29. Yao Souchou, *Singapore: The State and the Culture of Excess* (London and New York: Routledge, 2007), p. 34.

30. Han Fook Kwang, Warren Fernandez, and Tan Sumiko, *Lee Kuan Yew: The Man and His Ideas* (Singapore: Times Publishing, 1998), p. 257.

31. Interestingly, only the Chinese were thought to be vulnerable to 'deculturalization', while the Malay and Indian communities were thought to be more deeply anchored to their respective cultures. See Goh Keng Swee, *Report on the Ministry of Education* (Singapore: Ministry of Education, 1978).

32. For a fuller discussion, see Terence Chong, 'The Cultural Politics of English and Singlish in Singapore', in *Border Crossings: Moving Between Languages & Cultural Frameworks*, eds, Lee Su Kin, Thang Siew Ming and Lee King Siong (Malaysia: Pelunduk, 2007).

33. The debate's importance was underscored by the then Prime Minister, Goh Chok Tong, who used his 1999 National Day Rally speech to warn the nation that 'if we carry on using Singlish, the logical final outcome is that we too will develop our own type of pidgin English, spoken only by 3 million Singaporeans, which the rest of the world will find quaint but incomprehensible. We are already half-way there'. Goh, Chok Tong, 1999 National Day Rally Speech (22 August) <www.goodenglish.org.sg/sgemsite/pm22.htm> accessed 6 February 2005. He thereafter initiated the national Speak Good English Movement in 2000.

34. Anthea Fraser Gupta, 'Contact Features of Singapore Colloquial English', in *Sociolinguistics Today: International Perspectives*, eds, K. Bolton and H. Kwok (London and New York: Routledge, 1992).

35. The data and analysis in this section is a result of research between 2007-2008 funded by the National Arts Council under its Arts R &D [Research & Development] grant scheme. The author is grateful to NAC for its support.

36. For further discussion of the stratification of the theatre field and its consequences see Terence Chong, 'From Global to Local: Singapore's Cultural Policy and Its Consequences', *Critical Asian Studies*, 37:4 (2005) 551-65.

37. A typical 2-Year Major Grant English-language professional theatre company would be The Necessary Stage or TheatreWorks. They have full-time staff members of between 8 to 14 people with clearly-defined administrative roles, such as General Manager, Publicity Officer or Arts Administrator, etc., a permanent or regular technical crew, including sound engineers, lighting designers and stage managers, and so on. Furthermore, many of these theatre companies have their own Boards of Directors. In 2005-2006, The Necessary Stage and TheatreWorks received S$370,000 and S$460,000 respectively from the National Arts Council. A typical amateur theatre company would be The Native's Art Society (TNAS). While members of TNAS have assigned designations like 'artistic director', it is common for individuals to juggle different roles. In the same Financial Year 2005-2006, TNAS received S$2,000 from the National Arts Council.

38. John Tomlinson, *Globalisation and Culture* (Cambridge: Polity Press, 1999).

NG YI-SHENG

Madonna Enthroned With Saints

Dammit, he's crying again.
Does he want milk or a wiping?
Is he frightened?
Jerome, chain your lion.
Lucy, stop doing that with your eyes.

Is baby bored?
Catherine, will you let him play with your wheel?
Vitus, dance for him.
Augustine, have you any nice stories in your book?

Still he's screaming.
Magdalena, have you a sedative in your amphora?
No, I've changed him already.
The smell is from John the Baptist.

Thank God, it's dying down. Everybody,
take your places.
Straighten your crosiers and your haloes,
no-one stand too close to Sebastian,
Denis, pick up your head.

Come on baby, smile for the photographer.
See how he's waving the Holy Ghost?
Lord, let's try and look for once like a happy family.

Giuseppe Castiglione

The Emperor had heard of this man,
and was curious, for the Christians
had brought many gifts of enduring interest,
such as their bible, and tobacco.
Those were marvellous days to witness.
Everything flowed into the Kingdom
of the Middle, to the court of one, the funnel
of celestial will. Now into the hall
he minced, due deference paid with the robes
of a mandarin, red pigtail of his tonsure, a gilt key
in his lacquered box. Inside, an inkstone,
a cone of paper. Unrolled, a surface of
heathen crosses, no, lines toward
a corona, centred across the tiles
of our very chamber. We craned to look
and were nearly toppled; the painted garden
became a well, a space through which
a concubine's earrings fell; the palace buckled toward
this hole, a ship pulled where
so went his brush, into that fatal
vanishing point. The emperor bellowed,
the foreigner shut his scroll and paid us obeisance.
'It is my people's late invention,' he said,
shuffling gracefully. 'We call it perspective.'

Big Wall Newspaper

SUCHEN CHRISTINE LIM

In one minute's time, the electric bell will bong. The hungry horde will rush down the stairs and out through the school gates. But I'll be here, waiting for the Sengkang Kid. Thanks to the Auntie brigade, this loo is clean and dry. That's how it is in our elite Saints' schools. We take pride in having a clean loo. And that's why the loo is the best place to have a fight. There's a clear space between the sinks and the urinals; and no teacher comes into the boys' loo. This block is deserted after school. There will be no spectators this evening. No smart-ass loudmouths to cheer him. It will be a clean fight between me and the Sengkang Kid. Not that I want to fight him. I don't like to fight. But that Kid tore up my Big Wall Newspaper.

I had written about the fight that the Kid lost after the soccer game last week. That got him so pissed he sent a fist towards my face. But I ducked. And all that punch and weight fell hard onto the floor. That got him madder. He swore to kick the hell out of my smart-ass face. This morning, he tore down our wall newspaper and showed it to the P.

Mr Harry Koh hit the roof when he saw the headline. Inside my pocket now is the P's note I've got to take home and show to my mom; my mom who pats her son on the shoulder each time he brings home a report card filled with As and Bs. These grades make her feel good. These grades make her feel her life is still worthwhile, and her divorce has not affected her boy. This note will make her cry tonight.

★ ★ ★

'You've got nothing better to do? So many other things happened in school. Why didn't you write about them?'

'This is news.'

That was his father's dictum: Dog bites man. Not news. Man bites dog. News. Of course, she understands why a young female teacher crying in front of her class is news in an all boys' school. But did he have to write about it and publish it in his Big Wall Newspaper, as he calls it?

'What happened in that Secondary Four class was none of your business! You didn't make this up, did you?'

'Mom!'

His eyes have that mix of fear and defiance that you see in a young dog when it's cornered. His tone is accusatory.

'You're the one who taught me to tell the truth.'

His face wears the look of a sullen mule. His voice is hoarse; it's changing fast. Soon he'll speak like a man. She wants to hug him and throttle him at the same time. Pride and annoyance surge through her. He's just fourteen and he's started a school newspaper. She reads his Principal's note again.

You are requested to attend an urgent meeting tomorrow at 8 a.m. sharp. Your son's abuse and violations of ... The note reels off a list of Wai Mun's offences: fighting, vandalism of the school's notice board, putting up notices without the Principal's permission, publishing a school newspaper without the Principal's permission, making a teacher cry. The punishment is a public caning. *Should his parents object, they are advised to take their son out of the school.*

Her hands are trembling a little, just a little. Her son is not a criminal. Her first impulse is to protect her boy. Her second is 'damage control'. But what can she do? Vandals and errant students are caned in Singapore. But a public caning for a school boy? Even the most hardened vandal is caned in private in the prison. Not in front of an audience of a thousand students in the school hall! What will Richard say? For a fleeting second, she thinks of phoning him. But what's the point? He won't speak for his son. He can't even speak up for himself. O God! What should she do?

'When did you start this stupid business?' she turns on the boy.

'Three weeks ago,' he growls.

'Haven't you anything better to do?' she screams at him.

'School's boring.'

'School's boring! So you fight and vandalize the school's notice board?'

'I didn't fight, Mom! That boy didn't turn up. I didn't vandalize the notice board! I pinned up *The Towgay News.*'

'What?' The surprise in her voice makes him smile. 'Rajiv said our Big Wall Newspaper should report bits of news about school. I said, ya, bits of news like bean sprouts. So we called it *The Towgay News.*'

She wants to hug and slap him. The audacity of this boy. The pride in his voice is unmistakeable. He brings out the offending newspaper – an A3-sized broadsheet with a green and yellow computer-printed masthead of bean sprouts, and the date, July 1989. Below the masthead are the names of the two reporters, and their editor, John Wong Wai Mun. She was the one who named him 'Wai Mun', a Cantonese name meaning 'For the

People'. She was young and idealistic then. She thought love could change the world.

Can it? Let's find out, Richard had whispered in her ear, his finger tracing the slight depression beneath her collarbone, sliding down the space between her breasts. She wants to scream at him now.

'Honestly, Mun! I don't know what to do with you. So tomorrow I've got to go and see the Principal about your vandalism.'

'I told you! It's not vandalism.'

'Don't you talk back to me like this! You're in deep shit already!'

'We only pinned up our newspaper on the board for everyone to read. We didn't want to print many copies. So we did one big wall newspaper. Like … like the Chinese students in Tiananmen Square.'

'But you're not in China, Mun! You're in Singapore! In St Paul's! What's the matter with you?'

It's the top elite boys' school after Raffles' Institution. 'We don't accept the rejects of RI. Is St Paul's your first choice?' That's how the Principal interrogates each poor sod who begs for a place for his son. Those whose sons are accepted will hear Harry Koh's sonorous voice booming through the loudspeakers. 'Parents! Give us your boys! We will return them to you as men! St Paul's results are exemplary. There are no failures in my school.'

'I'll have to take you out of that school.'

'No, Mom.'

'It's a public caning for God's sake! In the school hall! It's draconian and barbaric! You're only in Sec Two. You can start all over again in a new school.'

'No.'

She can't believe her ears, can't recognize this stubborn, mulish face in front of her. He looks just like Richard now. Just as stupid. Just as blind. The boy can't see that this is censorship of the worst kind. Not even the government would cane people for reporting a fact, however unpalatable that fact. So. A young female teacher cried. So what? She's an adult and a professional who should be able to hold her own against a bunch of boys. Why should the school protect the adult against the child?

Her brain is ticking. She's marshalling all her arguments, lining them up against the school. Her boy and his friends had started a newspaper by themselves. A bunch of fourteen-year-olds. They should be applauded for their initiative. Not caned! *Forty pairs of male eyes stared in shock and wonder as tears rolled down Miss Tan's* … Agreed! The report is a little sensational. The boys should apologize to the teacher, make amends, wash the school toilets, or pick up litter, or whatever! But not caned! Sensational reporting is not a crime punishable by caning. Starting a school newspaper without the Principal's permission is not a crime punishable by caning. What's the matter with this Principal? His school is not the State of Singapore. Does he think he's the Prime Minister?

She's raving and she knows it.

'I'll put you in a private school for now. Next year, I'll send you overseas.'

Her boy shakes his head.

'Why? Are you scared of leaving school?'

The boy stares resolutely at his feet, and refuses to answer her. His sulky silence infuriates her. She resists the temptation to shake him … and hug him. She wants so much to protect him. But she knows he wants to be treated as a grown-up. Especially now that it's just the two of them in the family. But he's only fourteen. Oh God! How can she let this stupid school destroy him?

'Mun, please,' she pleads.

He looks up, his eyes dark and accusing.

'You're the one who said we must accept the consequences of our action.'

★ ★ ★

My mom says school gives you an education. My mom is biased. She's a teacher. School is where you learn your life is over unless you mug and pass exams. School is where you learn to stand up and sing like a bloody idiot, 'Gooooood morrrrr-ning, teeeee-chur!' You find out at great cost to your dignity that you've got to take all the crap that grown-ups vomit out in front of your desk or else you fail. You learn not to challenge, not to argue with grown-ups. Unless. Unless you've a fatal attraction for insults or humiliation, or detention class, or standing outside the classroom until the grown-up is satisfied with your guard duty. School is where you learn power is in the hands of one man – the P. The P's office is a great place to feel small. You can't enter it unless his female dragons say, 'Mr Koh will see you now.'

We're here in the P's office, my mom and I, and Seng and Rajiv's parents. Six chairs are arranged in a semi-circle in front of the P's table. The parents sit down. Five parents and a vacant chair. That must be for Dad. They don't know that my parents have split. We boys are told to stand behind our parents. I want to take away the empty chair next to Mom. It's making her uncomfortable. Rajiv and Seng Huat's parents have come together. My mom is alone. I step forward. I stand between her and the vacant chair. This way, she can't see the chair. This way, she can see me standing beside her. She's not alone.

'Please wait.' The school clerk closes the door.

No one says a word. The parents sit like they're waiting for the funeral service to start. Mom is wearing her dark blue dress. Rajiv's mom is in a grey sari. Seng's mom wears a black pantsuit; and the two fathers are in dark trousers, long-sleeved white shirt and tie. This is how it is when the principal of your son's elite school tells you to come to his office. Rajiv, poor sod, looks like he's been bonked on his head. His father's face is grim. His back is ramrod straight, and his arms are folded in front of his chest. Not a good sign. Poor Rajiv's mom is staring at the floor. Seng Huat's fat face is the only one with a smile. But I know he's scared shit, like Raj and me.

I watch the hands of the clock above Mr Koh's black leather armchair. Its tick, tick, tick is the only sound in the room. Then the door opens. Mr Koh enters. The parents stand up. They introduce themselves.

'Sit down. Please. Sit down. Sorry to keep you waiting. I had some urgent matters to attend to. Thank you for coming. Boys!'

'Yes, sir!'

'You know why your parents are here, don't you?'

'Yes, sir!'

'Vandalism is a serious offence …'

'Mr Koh, sorry, may I interrupt?'

That's my mom. She's not like other parents. She can't keep her gap shut.

'Yes, Mrs Wong.'

'Exactly what constitutes vandalism at St Paul's?'

'We have very strict rules governing the use of the school's notice boards. No teacher or student is allowed to put up anything without the Principal's prior permission. These boys broke that rule. They pinned up all sorts of papers without my knowledge and my permission. That constitutes vandalism. It's a serious violation. The school rules have been made known to all our boys from the day they joined this school. But these boys have flouted the rules.'

'Mr Koh, I agree that these boys have broken the school's rule regarding the use of the notice boards. But does this merit a public caning?'

'Mrs Wong, I cannot allow any Tom, Dick and Harry to pin up anything they wish without the Principal's expressed knowledge and permission. Such flagrant disregard of rules and regulations undermines the authority of the school and the principal. And I cannot allow it. This is a serious offence. And we cane boys for serious offences. Like smoking. They do harm to their own health. We cane them. These three boys have done harm not to themselves. Worse. They've done harm to a teacher's reputation and authority. They've destroyed my teacher's confidence. She's a young woman. New in the service. A scholar sent by the Ministry of Education. Now she wants to resign. Do you know how hard it is for me to retain teachers nowadays? A good teacher is hard to come by. Now if these boys had followed the rules, had come to me first, I wouldn't have let them publish this story. They should have gone to their teachers. Their teachers would've advised them. They would've vetted the boys' writing, corrected their mistakes, and sent them to see me in the office. But these boys went over their teachers' heads! Went over the principal's head! I'm the principal of this school. I cannot let them go unpunished!'

'Mr Koh …'

'Mrs Wong, I'm the principal of this school. I set the rules. I'm in charge. When things go wrong, I'm responsible.'

He stares at Mom. I'm praying. I pray that Mom will keep her word. I place my hand on her shoulders to remind her of her promise. None of the other parents dare to say anything. Rajiv's father's has unfolded his arms. His back is no longer ramrod straight. We watch in silence as Mr Koh opens the brown folder on his desk.

'If any of you wish to take your son out of my school, I will not stop you.'

Silence.

'Well then,' Mr Koh looks at us. 'If there's no objection to corporal punishment, please sign this document to give the school permission to cane your son. Rest assured. I will do the caning myself. Not the discipline master.'

★ ★ ★

That night, she can't sleep. She has failed her son. Where is her lively seven-year-old? Where's the little boy who had so bravely stood up for his friend in Primary Two? As an eight-year-old, her boy had refused to go for a class outing. *Because Miss Tan was unfair to Aziz, Mommy.* She was proud that he had insisted on staying back in school with his friend. At ten, he had written a note (with her help) to tell his class teacher why he and his friends hated Chinese. *Zhen Lao-shi brings a cane to class.* When did her boy change? How did the courageous little fellow turn into this compliant silent teenager who accepts a public caning? Has she been so absorbed in her own despair that she has failed to notice his change? Has he become like his father?

Last night, she looked through the three issues of Big Wall Newspaper again. Full of typical schoolboy humour, but the reports were well written. There were no grammatical errors. The boy had edited the three issues himself. He's meticulous like his father. And like his father, he's gotten into trouble because of what he wrote. She frets about the caning. How will it affect him? Richard never recovered from that fiasco with the now defunct *Singapore Morning Herald*. His report had caught her attention. In clear, crisp English, he had written about a university students' group, critical of the Prime Minister and his cabinet. And he'd quoted her, and, based on something she had told him in confidence, he'd described her as one of the group's leaders. She stared at the report. There it was, her confidence purveyed and packed into a two-inch column of black print with a half-inch high headline. Below that was his byline: *I'm very sorry. Very very sorry. I had to break the news before* The Straits Times *does.*

A single yellow rose and a box of Scottish nougat were proffered. She should have known better then. To think that her heart and forgiveness were so cheaply bought.

When the *Herald* was abruptly closed down by the government, he'd run like the rest of them to Malaysia, and then to Hong Kong, before making his way back a year later after the fallout and debris had cleared, and he knew he wouldn't be detained again. Like a blind fool, she thought he had courage, and married him.

For god's sake! You're my wife! You can act for me. You're a teacher. You work only half a day. I don't have the time to meet these people.

You don't have the time or you don't have the guts?

He'd stormed out of their bedroom. He would rather pay fines, sometimes heavy fines that they could barely afford, than deal with government authorities. She was the one who blundered through, argued, and fought with the Inland Revenue Authority, the Public Utilities Authority, the Housing Board Authority, the Property Tax Authority, the school authorities, the bank authorities, the hospital authorities – anyone and everyone in a position of authority. For years, she had refused to see it, refused to see that he was cowering behind her. Perhaps *cowering* was too strong a word. But what else could she call it? Government officials unnerved him. But he wouldn't admit it. At home, he raved against the powers that be, the fools and tyrants who run this country. But put him in front of a government official, and he scraped and bowed.

Yes, yes, yes, I understand, sir. No problem, sir. Er... er ... I'll ... I'll wait. So sorry. So sorry to bother you, mister, er, mister. Sir.

She suspected that it was his brush with Internal Security that had so unnerved him. But he refused to talk about it.

You were in there two weeks. What did they do to you? Please, Richard. You've got to talk it out.

Stop it, Joan.

He clammed up. She reckoned he was roughed up. She'd heard such stories whispered among friends. Sometimes, alone at night, she thought of him, imagining how they must've stripped him naked, made him sit on a block of ice or shone two hundred megawatt spotlights on him. Sleep-deprived and stripped, he must have said or done things he was now ashamed of. For years, he'd suffered from insomnia and nightmares.

On the day of his release, his chief editor had told him to run. And so he ran. The next day, the chief editor himself was detained. The newspaper was closed down. Its publishing permit was withdrawn. Richard's parents told everyone they didn't know what their son had done, so they could not vouch for him, they said. His parents' reaction had shocked her. How could his parents wash their hands of their only son? But that was the madness of the sixties in Singapore when the air was choked with rumours of 'Black Ops', CIA agents, and student activists as pawns of the Communist Front. Many fled the country in fear. Richard's father denounced them all, including his own son.

Why run if you've done nothing wrong? You say right or not?

But cowardice is in the Wong genes. It's in their bloody DNA. She fears her son will turn out to be like his father. Rave and rant in the safety of home. Cringe and shrink outside when authority appears. How could her son stay on in the school? He will not go against the school. He's refused to leave. Which mother wouldn't cry? She should stop it. She will call the school. Tell them she has changed her mind. She will rescind her agreement. She will withhold her consent. She will not let him become like his father.

'Mun! Where are you? Mun! Answer me! Open your door! Mun!'

★ ★ ★

1 October 2007. It's Mom's birthday. We're having dinner in a little shop-house restaurant along Upper Bukit Timah Road. Just the two of us, the way she likes it. All mothers are suckers for this mother and son thing. She's fifty-five today. So I indulge her. Call her Momsy the way I used to as a kid and make her smile.

'I felt such a failure then.'

'Don't be so melodramatic, Mom. You didn't fail.'

'What do you mean melodramatic? It was traumatic.'

'For you, Mom. You were always so worried about face.'

'That's not fair!'

'But it's true. You made a big fuss. See, you're still thinking about it after all these years. It wasn't such a big deal. I wasn't the only one caned.'

'It was a big deal for me, son. How could I have known it wasn't a big deal for you? We never spoke about it after that. You were so moody and morose as a teenager. Remember? You stopped talking to me after that.'

The waiter brings us our food. I've ordered a white wine for us as well.

'To your health, Mom.'

A pause. Then she starts again. 'Can I ask …?'

'Must we do this? Is this your guilt or nostalgia? Oh, okay, okay.'

I give up. I relent. I haven't flown all the way back from New York to quarrel with her on her birthday. She lives alone. Poor Mom. She's bound to think of the past. Old people do. I know her. She will ponder and fret. She will recall my silence and the long hours I spent in my room as a teenager. She will say I didn't talk to her for days, for weeks, even months. She exaggerates sometimes. She tells me that I'd locked her out of my life, that her divorce took a toll on her poor boy, and many other such things. Mothers love to talk about their children's childhood. Tonight it's the caning in school. She never forgot the caning. Still, it's her birthday today so I will indulge her.

'So what do you want to know, Mom?'

'Why didn't you talk to me about it?'

'I don't know. It really wasn't a big deal. Anyway we weren't caned in the school hall.'

'You mean Harry Koh didn't carry out his threat?'

'No. I was given two strokes in class. Rajiv and Seng Huat had one stroke each.'

'That's not fair. How come you had two?'

'I was the editor. I was the one who decided what to publish.'

'So he gave you one more stroke.'

'Something like that,' I laugh. 'Mr Koh said he had to show that he supported the teacher. Said he had to protect his staff.'

'What? Protect his staff but not his students?'

'I didn't need his protection, Mom. I could protect myself. I protected my future, didn't I? I stayed. I didn't quit.'

'Because you were afraid to change school.'

'Good grief, Mom. Did you think so little of me then?'

'No. You know I didn't mean that. I was proud of you, son. I wanted you to change school because I couldn't stand that bully of a principal.'

'I wanted to handle it myself. I didn't want to have it on my record that

I had to quit school. Like I was expelled. Besides, I reckoned that bullies die. Eventually. Like all of us. Dad said, "All tyrants have to die some day. All that the young have to do is to stay put and wait".'

'Did he say that?'

'He did. He even wrote about it in one of his articles. Write, he said. Write to keep the flame burning. It is Rajiv's mantra now. That guy's a bum but he's one of the best reporters in *The Straits Times* today.'

Mom is silent, thinking.

'Don't you see, Mom? Dad was right. Rajiv and I are still writing today. Huat's into internet publishing. Where's Mr Koh?'

Mom almost falls off her chair, laughing. 'Who was it who said, lose a battle, win a war?' she giggles. 'Oh, this is absolutely my best birthday dinner ever.'

But I take that with a pinch of salt. Mom's humour has always been a bit off tangent. She taught literature before her retirement, and her favourite Shakespearean character was the Fool in *King Lear*.

'So you did go and see your dad. How come I didn't know?'

'I didn't tell you.'

'Oh.'

'Another thing I didn't tell you. Mr Koh coached me in maths for my O Level.'

'And you didn't tell me that either?'

She wanted to know everything in those days. But she could only guess at what her son must have gone through during those difficult years. An only child torn between his parents. Was it her fault he'd hidden from her his visits and consultations with his father and others? Was she too clingy? Too possessive? A divorced parent clinging to her child, afraid of losing him? I can see these thoughts racing through my mother's brain. To distract her, I tell her about Dad.

'Dad said happy birthday to you. I spoke with him this morning.'

'How's he?'

'He's recovering from his op. He wants to continue his freelance writing. And he's learning to blog, he says.'

'Hmmm. Good for him. Did you tell him about Susannah?'

'Not yet. You're the first to know your son's getting married.'

Mother's eyes light up at this. Although she will never admit it, she wants to come first in her son's life.

'I'm proud of you, son.'

'And I'm proud of you, Mom.'

Cultural Diversity in the Modern Urbanscape: Public Housing in Singapore Film

C.J.W.-L. WEE

The cultural home of the Singapore State's utopian impulse was not painting or literature, which cannot feed mouths, but the art of *building*, particularly buildings that we live in.[1] Since Independence, the ruling People's Action Party (PAP) has increasingly revamped the city-state's colonial downtown into a post-national or 'globalized' space, filled with conceptually empty, decontextualized buildings designed by famous foreign architects. Importantly, for many Singaporeans, the PAP also created vast swathes of safe, reasonably well-ordered public housing. Architecturally both are aesthetic expressions of a state which is self-avowedly 'pragmatic' in its cultural policy and *petit bourgeois* in its larger value system.[2] If the new citizens of the city-state that gained independence in 1965 were to live well materially, then high-rise architecture, rapid urbanization, and urban redevelopment became the social art form that nobody could escape.

Singapore's urban development is similar to what can be called the late modernity of parts of East and Southeast Asia that have experienced sustained economic growth since the 1980s,[3] with their 'uniformly high-rise environments'.[4] However, the city-state's urbanism differs in its utopian belief – which once existed in the advanced West in the twentieth century, but has since been discarded – that rational design will make rational societies without superfluity: 'Singapore's well-manicured urban landscape ... [is linked to] its strong belief in the physical perfectibility of the city'.[5]

Given the above, an important part of contemporary art practices in Singapore since the 1980s[6] has been the exploration of the subjectivities of the suppressed and non-elite who reside in the city-state's public housing, euphemistically referred to by the State as 'heartlanders'. Such practices, especially exemplified in independent film from the 1990s, display a strong dissatisfaction with, and an equally strong desire to break free from, the stifling enclosure of the PAP State's quasi-authoritarian late modernity. Notably, some filmmakers have taken public housing to be a space *separate* from that of the fashionable commercial and business sector. Public housing locales are distinguished from the overtly capitalist downtown to constitute a geography of Singapore that indicates sociocultural difference. In attempting to map an urban space capable of yielding knowledge about the non-elite, the filmmakers also attempt to delineate the interiority of a major part of Singapore's city space, given that more than 80 per cent of the population lives in public housing. The films inscribe city space by depicting the ordinary and the potentially tragic cultural meanings that emit from this space. In effect, they represent an interest in depicting class, but not in class-based politics. Such films also mark the disappearance of the 'tropical' city of Singapore, once part of a colonial geographical imaginary that embraced Singapore Slings, enervating or fecund heat and humidity, and a 'jungle' that revealed human corruption. In its place is figured an urban world that is thoroughly modernized.

Among the films which explore class issues and the urban environment are Eric Khoo's imaginative trailblazer, *Mee Pok Man* (1995), and *12 Storeys* (1997); Tay Teck Lock's *Money No Enough* (1998); Kelvin Tong and Jasmine Ng's *Eating Air: A Motorcycle Kungfu Love Story* (1999); Royston Tan's short film *15* (2002) and *15: The Movie* (2003); and Djinn Ong's *Perth: The Geylang Massacre* (2004). These filmmakers accept the extended public housing cityscape built by the Housing and Development Board (HDB) as an iconic marker of Singaporean identity. However, their films look at public housing as locales where the PAP State's utopian impulses foster instead dystopian places where diverse cultures are suppressed or under erasure, and in which there is no past, only endlessly present space. This essay examines the similar and contrasting means by which representative films, such as Khoo's *Mee Pok Man* (Noodle Seller), Tong and Ng's *Eating Air*,[7] and Tan's short film *15*, present the city-state as a palimpsest of suppressed urban cultures.

Class, cultural identity, and utopia's denizens

The three films referred to above take identity politics and class issues as local or narrowly Singaporean in their focus, and therefore specialized – although I will also contend that these are all not as local as they might seem. The films regard as deeply problematic the PAP State's post-Independence urbanism which amounts to an attempt to organize the life and the circulation of the general population. Thus, public housing blocks in all the films are represented as iconic, but not in the way the State's public-relations version for public housing would suggest.

Khoo's *Mee Pok Man* is his first feature-length film, as *Eating Air* is Tong and Ng's. While Tan's *15* is a short film, he went on to make a feature-length version which incorporated the original film almost in its entirety.[8] I will examine the short version as that which enabled Tan to deliver a more focused critique of the exclusionary nature of a hegemonic culture of success. It is significant that, as filmmakers, all three directors cut their teeth on a similar theme: that Singapore's modernity has created new, non-elite subjectivities with little space to manoeuvre and develop. These films assert that marginalized citizens, too, as much as their English-speaking, English-educated political masters, have self-consciousness. Thus among the marginalized, class is linked with ethno-linguistic identity – and mainly Chinese, the men, youths, and women are represented as speaking the State-proscribed Hokkien dialect along with the more acceptable Mandarin, while English, if used, is often the local *patois*.

The films further assert that what appears to be the void produced by the State's architectural aesthetic is the actual if suppressed centre of Singapore life: the directors register their characters as valuable parts of a diverse Singaporean culture and attempt to give the contemporary subaltern a voice. Khoo's *Mee Pok Man*[9] is the prototype for these films. It deals with an intellectually-challenged noodle vendor who, his father having recently died, lives a lonely life in a small HDB flat. A relationship with a prostitute develops when he takes her home to care for her after she is involved in a hit-and-run accident. But she eventually dies as well, and he is once again alone.

Although Khoo has been criticized for his superficial representation of working class life, his film nevertheless manages to capture imaginatively the oddly contradictory space of Singapore's socialist-style and homogenized public housing, and to re-read it as other than an embodiment of the *telos* of PAP modernity. Khoo uses an old staple of the aesthetic-cultural critique of modernity's ills, and posits its existence in HDB estates. The film, it has been noted, makes only oblique reference to the socioeconomic causes of such ills: 'No mention is made of any repressive administrative policies and thus no direct presence of the state is represented, except in the snowy television set in the *mee pok* man's tiny flat.'[10] A broadcast propagating the government's elitist policies on education makes it known that academic under-achievers do not maximize their economic potential for the nation. Although the device that is used in the film of tying together urban location and class immobility is unexceptional, the extreme depiction, verging on the surreal, of the noodle seller's mental fragmentation and the claustrophobic sociophysical environment carries the film along.

For the noodle seller, the urban environment and the growth opportunities it offers are limited: the film mainly moves between his flat and the *kopitiam* (coffee shop) in the red-light district where he has his food stall and meets the young sex worker Bunny. The opening sequence is a montage of close-up shots of raw meat sold by butchers in a 'wet market', open mouths eating, and exposed body parts, such as a woman's breast, set against a flashed larger view of the famed Newton hawker centre, an open-air food court popular with tourists. The hawker centre is an early gesture towards the larger urban society from which the *mee pok* man is excluded.

The plot moves slowly but inexorably towards tragedy. When Bunny is knocked down, the noodle seller takes her to his home in one of the slab blocks of flats (since demolished) sitting on top of the Outram Park Complex. The camera shows how poorly maintained the stairway is, how spartan his flat, and takes in the closed shops at the bottom of the block lit by harsh fluorescent light tubes: the urban environment becomes a blunt externalization of the hawker's unloved and arid existence. Yet, despite the urban bleakness, there is some emotional liberation for the two characters. The noodle seller, in learning to love Bunny, gains a partial centring of his subjectivity. While in earlier sequences he had stammered incoherently, he is later able to express himself more clearly. As for Bunny, her battered physical state paradoxically brings about some emotional clarity which enables her to appreciate his love. As she has admitted in her diary, she cannot escape prostitution, not only because of her pimp's violent unwillingness to free her, but also because she is used to the money. Seeing that the noodle seller is genuine in his love, she surrenders her body and emotions freely – for the first time – but then, starkly, dies during their love-making.

What follows is an intense confrontational depiction of the noodle seller's inability to accept Bunny's death. This 'necrophilic denouement' has been rightly described as 'astounding although it functions as a perfect reprise to the opening … montage'.[11] The *mee pok* man dresses Bunny and goes through the motions of feeding her, even as her body decomposes. In the film's most notorious scene, he strokes and caresses the corpse in his kitchen, the windows draped with a bedsheet for privacy, for a full seven minutes – an eternity when watching the film in a cinema. It would seem, however, that he still gains some strength from his contact with the dead woman. Subsequently, and for the first time in years, the *mee pok* man is able to stand up to an old cadger at his *kopitiam*. Therefore, despite the deadpan camera eye on the character, directorial sympathy is palpable. But the noodle seller's youth is as lost as the dead Bunny's. For all the sensational episodes following Bunny's death, the film appears static – certainly in terms of narrative development, as nothing really happens. An overwhelming sense of social and psychological claustrophobia is thus represented by the images of urban enclosure. That is part of the film's point.

While, in the film, the protagonists do gain momentary freedom in each other, a larger sense of freedom – with sustained human relationships, with participation in mainstream society, with seeing what living abroad might bring – is, however, denied them. Breaking free of the restrictiveness of red-light district Geylang and residential Outram Park[12] are scenes where Bunny – who, unlike the *mee pok* man, can speak English – spends time with Jon, an exploitative Englishman living in a walk-up flat in a salubrious environment and who, it was hoped, was to have been her means of escaping to England. At the end of the film, we see Orchard Road – the city-state's main shopping area – with the 'Christmas Light-Up' sparkling in the night. We are also shown Raffles Place – a part of the bustling central business district – during office hours. Then, we are brought back to the flat and, in a voice-over, hear Bunny as a young girl saying that she will try harder in primary school maths in preparation for the next examination. These concluding scenes, showing the 'other' parts of the city-state against which the two characters have been critically defined throughout the film, make clear how underprivileged Singaporeans are almost physically isolated from participating in the 'international' strategy that has led to Singapore's economic success.

Sociologist Chua Beng Huat and literary critic Yeo Wei Wei have argued that Khoo's *Mee Pok Man* and his later *12 Storeys* – Singapore's first ever entry at the Cannes Film Festival in 1997 – seem 'more voyeuristic than sympathetic', with individual stories 'not told from the inside but represented in the most superficial ethnography'. Furthermore, they note, 'The absence of entry into … inner lives … is, perhaps, the consequence of Khoo's own financially very upper class background … [The] fascination with the poor stems from a fascination of [*sic*] the Other rather than [from] empathy … making his cinema disturbingly voyeuristic'.[13] This analysis mistakenly takes the film for a social-realist text, when filmic verisimilitude has already been forsaken by the director to represent the states of mind *in extremis* that *Mee Pok Man* specifically investigates. That said, the film does assume that modernity as inherited from the West should possess a larger manifestation of freedom than is the case in the city-state. One unfortunate implication is that the non-elite modern can be seen to be 'not free' because they are not bourgeois. Ultimately *Mee Pok Man* may not have escaped therefore the hegemonic bourgeois assumptions of modern life that it seeks to critique – in other words, it may itself be constrained by the state's version of the modern.

Eating Air and youth culture

Kelvin Tong and Jasmine Ng's *Eating Air: A Motorcycle Kungfu Love Story*, released five years after Khoo's *Mee Pok Man*, is a memorable representation of working class youth, and how their personal and social development could be inhibited by the pressures and limits of the city-state. Compared to *Mee Pok Man*, the narrative in *Eating Air* is more expansive and its quasi-realism – given the fantasy kungfu – more stable than the surreal components in Khoo's film.

At the centre of *Eating Air* (a literal translation of a Hokkien phrase meaning to go for a leisurely ride and enjoy the breeze) is a gang of four friends in their late teens. The protagonist, a school dropout, who occasionally lends a hand at his family's home-based catering business, is known only as 'Boy'. He is particularly close to Ah Gu, a trouble-prone 'motor-mouth' who is caught out by his constant and insecure need to brag. Ah Gu foolishly borrows money from a loan shark to purchase new motorcycles and, when there is no means of repaying the loan, violent consequences follow. The motorcycle in the film's subtitle is a metaphor for machismo, excitement, and escape – it becomes an essential part of the sociocultural geography traversed in the film. Poignantly, in the end, the city's highways and byways – especially its underground road tunnels – provide no way out for the bikes and the youths, only death. Boy's love interest – the 'love story' reference of the subtitle – is a schoolgirl, the daughter of a single parent running a roadside news stand. Like the male characters, Girl also wants to escape from the confines of the urban environment.

The opening sequence shows Boy joyriding through the city-state's financial district. Counterposed to it, and making up the sociocultural geography of the film, are the urban spaces he and his friends inhabit. They comprise the city of the night, a city of public housing estate rooftops and their empty ground-floors (aptly called 'void decks' in Singapore), gaming arcades, and stylistically dated shopping centres.[14] Given that glossy Japan- or US-style department stores and shopping malls had already come into existence when the film was shot, these old-fashioned shopping centres from the 1970s reflect the directors' deliberate focus upon the spaces of working class youths in the city-state. The film posits the argument that so-called 'ill-educated' youths possess multilingual skills – a combination of Mandarin and Hokkien, with some English – and have a distinct sociocultural identity and value to Singapore society. However, these skills will not help them obtain a corporate job in the English-speaking financial district depicted at the beginning of the film. Such youths find meaning in their world grounded in the social bonding within gangs and, not surprisingly, when a gang fight occurs in the film, they come to their comrade's defence.

The motorcycles are the means by which, expressing their desire for a larger world, Boy and company 'go for a ride' to 'eat air'; they are also the means by which Boy is felled. Ah Gu's extravagant transactions with the loan shark to buy two flashy bikes for Boy and himself leads inevitably to his inability to repay the loan or outrun the thugs employed by the loan shark. At a point when Boy's girlfriend was hoping to travel somewhere with him – anywhere – Boy pays the price of youthful idealism. After Ah Gu is beaten up by the thugs, Boy decides to avenge his friend and comrade. In the bowels of the city, in the Central Expressway tunnel, he catches up with the loan shark and vengeance is violently exacted. Unfortunately, at that moment, the latter's reinforcements arrive, and leave behind them Boy's battered body to be discovered by his friends. In the final analysis, Boy's motorbike cannot take him – and the others – away from the city and its all-encompassing oppressiveness.

Even more than in *Mee Pok Man*, the spatial images matter in *Eating Air*. In one scene, Boy and Ah Gu are together on a high-rise rooftop, with the financial district in the background. It is close by and yet has no real social link with them. At another point, with Boy and Girl again on the top of an HDB block of flats, the limits of Boy's world are suggested when, to the question why he does not go to school, he replies, in Mandarin, 'Books don't read me, so I don't read books.' When the conversation turns to what is 'out there', Boy says, to begin with, Johor Bahru (the capital of Johor, the Malaysian State nearest to Singapore), then Malaysia, then Thailand and, finally, China. When Girl presses him again, he humorously remarks that that is where his grandmother's house is: ultimately, asking what is 'out there' becomes pointless and incomprehensible.

It is important to note, however, that Boy's sense of enclosure does not entail cultural isolation. Unlike Khoo's film, an 'outside' cultural reference is already embedded as part of local cultural diversity. Specifically, the subculture of Singapore Chinese working and lower-middle class youths is used incisively both to indicate cultural distinctiveness and to reinforce the critique of state-enforced and planned locality. If the motorbike is the metaphor for escape from the urban modern, the structuring device that directors Tong and Ng use to comment upon Boy and Ah Gu's experiences in their attempts to find their free space is the world of Chinese-language comics that adapt *wuxia* (martial arts) and chivalric fiction dating from the fourteenth century or earlier, and that feature as protagonist a non-conformist swordsman or knight-errant hero.

The specific reference in the film is to the *Water Margin Chronicles* (*Shui hu chuan*), sometimes known as *Outlaws of the Marsh*. In the *Chronicles*, 108 outlaws, some of whom have been ill-treated by corrupt officials, band together to become a 'gallant fraternity', obeying the laws of chivalry, and residing on Mt Liang in the region of Liangshan Marsh. If a man has sufficient and right reason, he can break the laws of the empire – that is the code by which the fraternity live. Black-and-white cartoons that reflect this story, one with a lone swordsman, appear from time to time in the film as a commentary on Boy's attempt to find his Mt Liang in the city. There are moments where, without actually wearing period outfits, Boy's movements mimic the stylized martial-arts kicks and blows of the swordsman shown in the cartoon. Boy's commitment to Ah Gu is a commitment to honour and to gallantry in a Singapore that does not permit them the space to be heroic.

An unpatronizing evocation of working class, Chinese-speaking youth culture by *Eating Air*'s directors inheres in the film's sociocultural orientation, which is thus local but also structured with a keen sense of the city-state's participation in a larger regional culture and range of identities. *Wuxia* comic culture is a form of regional youth culture that links *Eating Air*'s young people to their peers in Hong Kong or Taiwan. It is also evident in the genuine appreciation and unforced use of the culture of *manga*, the Japanese term for comics and print-cartoons, as witnessed in the drawings that appear in the film along with an original soundtrack of ballads, electronic dance music, and industrial rock music in a variety of languages (colloquial Singapore-English or Mandarin or Hokkien). The seemingly sterile and extensive spaces of public housing have diverse subcultures that exceed those shown in Khoo's *Mee Pok Man*. Nonetheless the final result is similar: Boy's subjectivity and his conception of himself as a hero do not yield him full self-consciousness or result in a way out.

Youth subculture and *15*

Royston Tan's *15* strongly shares in *Eating Air*'s desire to show how 'heartlanders' in the public housing estates are not an anonymous mass but people who participate in a youth subculture and have a complex sociocultural existence that is an intrinsic part of Singapore's larger multicultural reality. Tan's film, however, differs in its aesthetic strategies in representing non-elite groups. Despite the brevity of the 25-minute film, his text is more stylized – indeed, stylish – varied, and complex, and more systematically fragmented in its visual pastiche than the two films already discussed. The shadow of the culture industry, crucially, is evident in the film's postmodern aesthetic, and contributes to its visual brio and anarchic dynamism. (I will return to the matter of the culture industry later.) Both *Mee Pok Man* and *Eating Air* participate in a more recognizable, if modified, aesthetic-modernist impulse to show that underneath the uniformity of the modern city are other varieties of life which, though not part of the dominant bourgeois culture or mores, are nevertheless *valid* expressions of contemporary existence. However, the central difference between, say, Charles Baudelaire's mid-nineteenth-century Paris and late-twentieth-century Singapore as depicted in the films of Khoo, and Tong and Ng, is that in the latter there is no escape conceivable. Unlike Baudelaire's poems, the streets in the films do not lead to locales of liberation, however limited and/or hidden from the panoptical gaze. Singapore's late modernity – the result of a Cold-War era modernization – has created a more thoroughly rationalized (and therefore postmodern) cityscape than an earlier urban expression of the modern.

Tan's film, which has no plot as such but an episodic structure, features three 15-year-old, under-performing youths from fractured families – Vynn, Melvin, and Shaun – and their counter-mainstream youth practices, such as body-piercing. The idea that friendship can emotionally sustain the less privileged recurs, and when Shaun at a later point chooses to join another gang, he destabilizes a relationship that once buoyed up the trio. The opening scene shows the young men lying on a floor, their bare-bodied and slim torsos covered with tattoos. The voice-over – director Tan himself – says in Mandarin that he only wanted to make a film about their lives, but 'during the process of filming, I [became] reconcile[d] with a part of myself that was forgotten'[15] – forgotten, one surmises, while he was in the process of becoming an artistic filmmaker.[16] We are offered a narrative that claims to be documentary in its portrayal of the lives of the three friends. But, of course, there is a *script*, even if it is one devised in conjunction with the youths. What we are about to see is therefore both 'real', and fictionalized by Tan. The film's ontological and referential status is thus deliberately confused.

After the introductory episode, there is a rush of black-and-white images accompanied by pulsating electronic music with a percussionist hitting a drum-set's high hat. A tunnel with tubes, roads with painted lane dividers, railway tracks then all rush by, bringing us to a wasteland of bare earth visually filtered to a washed, blue tone. We see the three tattooed, bare-bodied youths again, and we hear heavy breathing in the background. Their breath is made to seem frozen visually, despite the tropical atmosphere. The tough statement that their tattoos make is undercut by the exposure of their young physiques which suggests their vulnerability. Another rush of the same black-and-white images appears, only now moving not forwards but suggestively backwards. It is a tightly orchestrated and frenetically paced beginning.

Vynn and Melvin are next shown playing truant, sitting against the backdrop of public housing blocks probably built in the 1990s. With greater national wealth, housing blocks have become more 'designed' compared to the utilitarian white or grey blocks in the older HDB estates. As alienation in this film is not linked directly to utilitarian modern space, public housing is here less a reflection or exteriorization of the youths' subjective fragmentation. Rather, the problem is the general culture of exclusion that is structured into urban space itself.

We then learn that Vynn and Melvin have been nominated to represent their class in a coming school concert. The scene cuts to the two of them rehearsing, 'rapping' in Hokkien about the joys of brotherhood to be found in a gang. Other possible items that they could present – which are all about the different gangs that they know – are rehearsed and become a repeated motif in the film. We are to understand that they are always performing 'badly' for their social environment, even as the film performs in a self-consciously frenzied 'bad-boy' way for the audience. While we see how the subjectivities of these youths are trammelled, we are also made to recognize that a non-conformist, even individuating energy exists, an energy that might erupt from below and interrogate the state's propensity to class its citizens into 'productive' and 'non-productive' categories.

Tan's film wishes to evoke what he takes to be a youth culture that is popular from the bottom up, and the anarchic energy of the youths which arises from the disjunctures in their lives. Interspersed with the various rehearsals mentioned are significant vignettes: Shaun getting various bits of his body pierced or tattooed; and Melvin swearing fluently in Hokkien, a talking head with HDB flats in the background, and with text suddenly superimposed on his face – 'NEWSFLASH!!! Singaporean boy breaks the World Guiness [sic] Record by scolding all the vulgarities from 4 different languages within 5 seconds.'[17] The technique is a modernist montage updated through a contemporary music-video sensibility. Interspersed in the film are also more sober scenes: the suicide of a teenage girl whose body hits the ground with a dull thud, and discussions by Vynn and Melvin of the particular dysfunctional traits of their respective families.

The geography of the characters' lives is similar to the spaces occupied by the protagonists of *Mee Pok Man* and *Eating Air*. They meander their way through the public housing environs which the short film version never strays from.[18] The closing scene shows the three youths sitting in a Mass Rapid Transit (MRT) train. It is a scene of some pathos: the train, like the motorbike in *Eating Air*, foregrounds the technicist modernity of the city-state and its built environment. As the camera looks straight at the three of them, but also through the window behind them, we see the public housing environment that enwraps them flashing by. A Hokkien ballad without musical accompaniment has the singer intoning, 'Young man, why are you always in pain? Where are parents to find their sons? Brothers risk their lives for each other.' At one point, Melvin puts his head on Vynn's shoulder. The progressive modernity of public transport does not in and of itself mean that Singapore's urbanism organizes or circulates life in a sustaining manner.

The young people's subculture that emerges is a multicultural reality which exceeds the ethnic descriptor 'Chinese-Singaporean'. As in *Eating Air*, *15* suggests, despite the apparently fixed environment, the connectedness of local youth to the youth-oriented mass culture of the region even if at the same time, as with Boy and Ah Gu, there is not much evidence among the protagonists of actual knowledge of the region. The regionally shared subculture of teen rebellion provides a *frisson*. There is a fight sequence between two gangs, choreographed as if it were a video game, but the voice-over during the sequence is in Japanese. One rehearsal of their gangster-themed 'raps' – 'The Dragons are ready to fight' – even becomes camp when the youths suddenly rip off their shirts and break into choreographed steps to a Japanese pop song, with feather boas draped around their shoulders, the fan on, streamers billowing. Then suddenly the song grinds to a halt – as if an old-fashioned turntable has been switched off – and Melvin, questioning the Japanese component, starts to quarrel with Vynn as to why he couldn't simply be himself. Did he think that they were SMAP?[19] The two of them then wave their arms at each other, and, as in Hong Kong *wuxia* films with fantasy elements, illuminated forces appear at their hands and are 'thrown' at each other. The two youths thereby perform their daily lives using such mass-cultural resources to express the 'self'. The film's own high-aesthetic/art-film performativity is itself dependent on the invocation of the culture industry's diversity and widespread consumption in East Asia. *15*'s filmic self-reflexive awareness of multiple cultures is significantly higher here than in *Eating Air*. Indeed, at one level, it is the film's *very own* ultra-contemporary presentation and (at times disturbing) 'hip-ness' that connects the world of Tan's film to the globalized world at large. This is *Time* magazine's description of the varied mass-cultural and aesthetic elements that Tan deploys:

> Like American director Spike Jonze, Tan cut his teeth on music videos, and that pedigree shows in the hip-hop numbers that punctuate the film. He mixes documentary realism with dream sequences, rapid montages, video-game graphics ... Despite his experimental forays, Tan knows when to let the camera linger on the faces of his young actors and wait for the pain to surface. With its white skies and overexposed tropical light, his Singapore is a beautiful void, one that mirrors the emptiness inside his characters.[20]

In short, the flashy MTV moments, the choreography with the 'rap' sequences, and the superimposed graphics show incontrovertibly that, although the film is linked through these elements to a global consumerist world and economy, it is one the youths cannot directly participate in, except as low-end consumers.

An actual politics of urbanism?

What is clear, when we consider the three films together, is that the four filmmakers have similar yet differentiated takes in trying to give the urban subaltern a voice in the city of planned modernist voids. All three films attempt to represent subject autonomy within an elitist, relentlessly modernizing environment. Eric Khoo's *Mee Pok Man* in particular should be recognized as that enabling moment in the city-state's history of aesthetic cultural production when the artistic representation of modernist public housing as a *complex* and sometimes *dark* sociocultural environment becomes possible.[21] The aim of these films seems to be to show and produce the class and cultural difference that truly exists 'out there' in the 'real' world, even while the mixed aesthetics and modes of representation deployed means we must eschew ascribing, even to *Mee Pok Man* and *Eating Air,* a simple social-realist genre tag.

What is also significant is that while there is constructed an opposition between the planned, the monolithic, and the repressive on the one hand and, on the other, the diverse, messy lives, and non-mainstream cultures that exist, this opposition is not brought to a head. The general thrust is that the modes of non-privileged lives – despite spatial-emotional alienation – have value in contributing to cultural diversity in the city-state, and such lives need to be regarded as varieties of citizenry worth looking after. 'Class' is linked with 'culture', and both are the main operative terms in all these films. But none of the directors shows how it might be possible to restore non-alienated experience to the modern city. Furthermore, subaltern or proletarian activity does not really pose a serious threat to the social order. The problem lies in the representation of the subjectivity of the respective protagonists. The films evoke a frustration that cannot find resolution within the selves of the key characters and, ultimately, there is also an inability to reinvent imaginatively the world they live in. Instead, the protagonists' collective consciousness is seen as quashed and their bodies as fully imprinted by the PAP State's notions of Progress and History: the protagonists remain non-mobile in a world of increasing mobility. The films indicate that the social matters – but there is no resurrection of the social; a vision of a certain class substratum is offered, but no class vision. In the end, what we see is closure: no one escapes, and the suppressed modes of (post)modern lives remain suppressed. Closure becomes a form of totality.

The films, taken together, seem to reveal how deeply the city-state and its citizens are still entrenched in a modernist *doxa* trying to convert itself into a postmodernist *doxa* in which pluralism, a supposedly creative 'chaos' and post-Fordist flexibility supplant standardization and an iron bureaucracy. The subjectivities of the protagonists of all three films are represented as new parts of the very shifts and changes in modern consciousness in Singapore that have emerged since Independence in 1965. The films jointly recognize that, in Singapore, the 'modern' is the disguised term for 'capitalism' – that, indeed, it *only* refers to capitalism, even though semantically the term 'modern' is more complex than its references here.[22] The modern becomes a one-dimensional idea or perhaps a pseudo-concept which does not intrinsically contain the possibility of self-reflexive consciousness.

NOTES

This article is a revised version of a paper given at a workshop on 'Cinematic Representation of the Tropical Urban/City', Asian Research Institute, National University of Singapore, 17-18 March 2006 and completed during a Visiting Fellowship at the Humanities Research Centre, Australian National University in 2006. I thank Chua Beng Huat, Chen Kuan-Hsing, Jacqueline Lo, Heman Chong, Kenneth Chan and Koh Tai Ann for their responses to this essay.

1. I argue elsewhere that Singapore represents an exuberant socioeconomic modernization with a deficient aesthetic-cultural modernism and a deficient idea of 'culture', taken broadly. See C.J.W.-L. Wee, *The Asian Modern: Culture, Capitalist Development, Singapore* (Hong Kong: Hong Kong UP, 2007).

2. This was so until about the late 1980s when the government began to understand that contemporary aesthetic high culture had its place in Singapore's becoming a 'global city'. However, the fundamental value system has not changed.

3. These were the countries that managed to pursue postwar modernization seriously and were beneficiaries of the USA's largesse during the Cold War years. Modernization was not, however, a neutral term: 'The word "modernization" … was an active propaganda word during the Cold War, and constituted the principal US contribution to its various Third World allies and clients and even to Europe itself during the period of the Marshall Plan. The Soviets' foreign policy turned essentially on the same stakes … and there was an insistence on technology and the export of heavy industry, on catching up with the alleged modern states, which was not different in spirit and ideology from the American version', Fredric Jameson, *A Singular Modernity: Essay on the Ontology of the Present* (London: Verso, 2002), note 5, p. 229.

4. Peter G. Rowe, *East Asian Modern: Shaping the Contemporary City* (London: Reaktion Books, 2005), p. 33.

5. Rowe, *East Asian Modern*, p. 37.

6. The main artistic developments were in theatre and the visual arts. Multilingual and 'devised' theatre that concerned itself with a range of cultural identity issues occurred from the early 1980s onwards. From the late 1980s, performance art, a renewed interest in figuration and installation sculptural practices, largely displaced abstract modernist visual art practices in the city-state. While these contemporary art formations may be generally described as 'postmodern', there was no resuscitation of aesthetics and the issue of beauty, which are linked to some aspects of postmodern art. There was also a noticeable interdisciplinary approach to art making between theatre, visual arts, and, to a lesser extent, literary practitioners.

7. Chris Berry and Mary Farquhar characterize such films as 'low-budget, modernist films that are artistically avant-garde and socially and politically critical. These films circulate on the international festival circuit and are aimed at an educated elite', *China on Screen: Cinema and Nation* (New York: Columbia UP, 2006), p. 214. This is a fair generalization, although it is important to note that the modernist genre ascription is used imprecisely, mainly to indicate that such films are not in the popular-realist mode of commercial filmmaking. Olivia Khoo describes the 'modernist films' as 'highly localized films' that have developed in the period 1991 to 2004, and 'tend to be dramas, told almost in a documentary style although still highly stylized … [that] represent the darker side of Singapore's economic modernization'; the films participate, she thinks, in a 'regional vernacular' of a dark vision of economic modernity. See Olivia Khoo, 'Slang Images: On the "Foreignness" of Contemporary Singaporean Films', *Inter-Asia Cultural Studies*, 7:1 (2006) 86, 87, 91.

8. The extended version posed some challenges as Tan was not able to find all the amateur youth 'actors' – actually youths drawn from the HDB 'heartland' – with whom he had worked in the original version. Tan thus had to use a couple of new people for the extended film. This, in some respects, diluted the force of the original.

9. *Mee pok* is a flat noodle made with egg and flour.

10. Chua Beng Huat and Wei-Wei Yeo, 'Singapore Cinema: Eric Khoo and Jack Neo –

Critique from the Margins and the Mainstream', *Inter-Asian Cultural Studies*, 4:1 (2004) 117-25.

11. Khoo, 'Slang Images', p. 90.

12. The actual *kopitiam* where the *mee pok* man has his stall and where Bunny and her fellow prostitutes hang out is in Tiong Bahru, a district contiguous to Outram Park.

13. Chua and Yeo, 'Singapore Cinema', pp. 119, 120. Khoo's late father was an internationally known banker and property magnate.

14. Older centres such as Katong Shopping Centre, Queensway Shopping Centre, Roxy Square Shopping Centre and Lucky Plaza are among the key locales in the film.

15. The text within quotation marks is the English translation functioning as subtitles in the film.

16. Tan was 26 years old when the short version of *15* was released in 2002.

17. This refers to the four official languages – English, Chinese, Malay and Tamil – recognized by the city-state as part of its official policy of multiracialism.

18. The feature-length version does stray to various parts of the city, as one youth looks for the 'perfect' building from which to commit suicide. The search for the right building effectively becomes a mordant critique of the 'world-class' aspirations of these buildings, all designed by foreign architects in the globalized city-state.

19. SMAP stands for 'Sports, Music Assemble People', a famous Japanese male band that began in the early 1990s, and has been popular since, with the individual members also appearing in regionally circulated TV dramas.

20. Bryan Walsh, 'Street Survivors: Royston Tan's Intense, Graphic Film *15* Explores Teenage Life on the Dark Side of the Lion City', *Time Asia*, 1 September 2003. <www.time.com/time/asia/magazine/article/0,13673,501030901-477974,00.html>. Walsh actually describes the feature-film version, but the quoted text only refers to what occurs in the original short film.

21. *Money No Enough* (1998), written by Jack Neo and directed by Tay Teck Lock, was an inexpensively made film which became the top grosser of 1998. Genuinely demotic and populist in its socioculturalist idiom, it marks another significant cinematic moment in Singapore's recent cultural history. As director, Neo's films, such as *I No Stupid*, are less aesthetically elitist than Khoo's films, and therefore also work less well for the international art house circuit.

22. For example, see Jürgen Habermas, *The Philosophical Discourse of Modernity: Twelve Lectures* (Cambridge, Mass.: MIT Press, 1987).

Big Dog, Small Lives

OVIDIA YU

Sitting again at her mother's dining table after an absence of almost four years, Kat realizes she is sitting in a strange room with a stranger. At least once a month, thanks to her brother and the internet, Kat has received her mother's updates on relatives and neighbours, and assuaged her worries about cold weather, American food, and America in general. She has prided herself on staying in touch while not spending money on vacation trips home. In the back of the taxi coming from the airport, Kat was surprised to be impressed by the width and expanse of the expressway and the shiny modern business city gleaming across the bay. But now the home she is back in, at last, is much smaller than she remembers; and although the extreme cleanliness here strikes her (have her standards slipped so much without her noticing?) so does the shabbiness. Her mother is also much smaller than she remembers – smaller, older, and painfully frail – as she stubbornly moves non-stop around the flat, cleaning and putting things away, and already starting dinner preparations.

Nobody else is here now; her mother has made her sit down at the very clean dining table (sporting the same plastic sunflower arrangement that Kat won in a spelling competition years ago) and put a plate of *kueh dadar* in front of her as though she is a guest. She is a greedy guest, fingers reaching out for another and yet another cake as her mother works around her, refusing to let her help. Her mother has always been proud of her *kueh*. Now that the Chinese-Peranakan women are flooding the market with a combination of their cooking and business skills, you can buy *kueh* everywhere, but their commercial confections are flavoured with powders and coloured by concentrates. Kat's mother only uses fragrant, fresh green pandan leaves that she chops and simmers herself.

Kat wishes her mother would stop working and sit down. She wants to take in this tiny strange woman who loves and would die or kill for her, but who is now too nervous to sit down and talk to her.

'Ma, sit down and rest.'

'Too much work to do.'

And she won't let Kat help either. 'You don't know how to do.'

There is much behind this. Years of pride in her daughter's academic prowess – as a national top student (not to mention being Malay and coming from a 'neighbourhood' school), Kat has had her photograph in the newspapers, on posters at the community centre, and on a banner along the fence of the school – as well as years of worry that her daughter might learn the wrong things or meet the wrong people or frighten away the right people.

Kat eats and her mother relaxes slightly.

'It is the Bangladeshi workers,' Kat's mother says. 'They hang around the place at night and get drunk. Because of them I don't want you coming home alone at night –'

'Ma, you know I have already been living on my own for the past –'

'Sometimes you come home quite late – because even though nothing has happened yet, why should the first time anything happens be you? Huh? If you must go out late, ask your brother go on his motor and fetch you back.'

'Ma, it's probably more dangerous on Yusuf's bike than on a bus.'

'It is much worse if you live in one of the ground floor units, because the workers when they get drunk, go and urine everywhere – like on the pavement at the back and just outside people's kitchen windows –'

It has been over three, almost four years since Kat last sat in this room. Nothing in here has changed, she realizes, picking out familiar old stains on the curtain and an even older mug from Expo 85. The objects here are the ones she left behind, the gap between them and herself has been created by their lack of change. Kat could have come home every year, but there was always a better use for the airfare. Most other Singapore students, especially those on 'Dad's Scholarship' flew home every year in addition to taking sightseeing and skiing vacations. In one sense, their experience of America was much wider; but working through vacations brought Kat unanticipated contacts and advantages. Now she has submitted her PhD thesis it seems like a strange time to finally take her first home vacation. After all she will soon have to return to defend her paper. But she has really returned to Singapore to announce – or to make – a decision. She has been offered a dream job in Pittsburg. A job that means no more worrying about airfares – or her mother's mortgage or medical bills – but it will also mean twenty-eight hour flights (or more, depending on the stopover) every time she wants a taste of homemade *kueh dadar* flavoured with fresh pandan leaves.

She has not told her mother yet. When they first heard her only daughter was going on scholarship to America, relatives and friends warned that her Katijah would end up marrying some American man and never come back. She should tell the girl to stay in Singapore, go to the National Institute of Education, and become a teacher, Kat's uncles told her, America was full of dangers and temptations a young girl could not face alone.

'If you let her go away on her own and get independent, you think she will ever come home and get married?'

Kat's mother had said, 'A ship is always safe at shore but a ship is not built to stay at shore.'

Kat wonders whether her mother regrets allowing her to go so far away. She is realizing now how much she has changed.

'How is Yusuf?' She has not seen her brother yet. He had left for work before she arrived.

'It is time he settles down,' her mother says.

She is a modern woman who does not believe in forcing anything on her educated children, but the message is clear: she would like to see both her son and his elder sister with homes and families of their own.

They are startled by a sudden commotion of raised voices from the flat next door and then the corridor just outside. Kat can't make out what is being said – a man's angry voice screams hysterical protest above the other voices – can that be their old neighbour, Cheng's father?

Kat is on her feet and is halfway to the front door before she thinks to look to her mother. Have such commotions become a common occurrence? Kat doesn't even know if Cheng still lives next door with her family, and has just assumed that someone would have mentioned such a drastic change. Passing their flat just now on her first walk home from the lift, she noticed their window blinds were pulled shut and had thought that unusual without making anything of it.

'Go – go and see – see are they all right!' Her mother is hurrying, rushing to rinse marinade off her hands. She wants to know what is happening, but propriety runs stronger in her than curiosity.

Cheng is standing in the corridor with her father and two other Chinese men. There is also a large brown dog on a leash. Cheng is holding its leash but, from the way she is holding it, Kat can tell she has just taken it by force from the hands of the taller of the visitors. The dog looks round and offers Kat an uncertain but hopeful half wag as she joins the fringe of their group. It is the only welcome she gets. The first look Cheng throws her is hostile – nothing personal, it comes off her automatic defence system. This is the Cheng, Kat remembers, looking upon the whole world with suspicion.

'Mr Lim, you see – you are disturbing your neighbours already – after they go and complain about you again …' The stockier and more authoritative visitor says. He directs a brief placating smile at Kat.

Cheng's father raises his voice again, 'So? If the neighbours come and complain about me then you will come and take me away also, is it?'

'Mr Lim, please understand – Malay people.' The visitor drops his voice slightly. 'Malay people don't like dogs. We must be sensitive to their feelings.'

'Tell them take their bloody feelings back to the kampong – back to Malaysia!'

Kat reaches over and lets the dog sniff her fingers before touching the top of its head gently. 'Nice dog,' she says.

'You're back?'

She shrugs. 'Just. This morning. What's happening here?'

'These guys –' Cheng jerks her head towards the two uncomfortable looking men. 'Want to fine us five thousand dollars and put my Dad's dog down.'

Sensing it is being discussed, the dog gives another tentative wag. A medium-sized brown mongrel, it points its nose in pleading subservience at each of them in turn but most persistently at Old Uncle Lim; it has found shelter and food here. It will do what it can to please these people, so as to be allowed to stay.

No, the officials say. They are not here to remove the dog. They only want to advise Mr Lim that (1) the fine for possessing an unlicensed dog is five thousand dollars, and (2) he cannot obtain a licence for his dog as it does not belong to an HDB approved breed.

'They want to get rid of the dog,' Cheng says. 'They're just not doing the dirty work themselves.'

People have always found Cheng intimidating but, having grown up next door to her, Kat is used to her.

Kat has heard from her brother and mother how, after the death of his wife, Old Mr Lim refused to talk to anybody and spent his days and nights sitting in the void deck where the wake had been. It would only be a matter of months, people said, before he followed her. Without anyone saying anything, she guesses it was the need and companionship of his illegal dog that has brought him back to life.

Like every Singaporean familiar with HDB regulations, Kat knows that dogs (apart from expensive pedigree toy breeds) are not allowed in HDB flats. But this dog has apparently saved an old man from following his wife to the grave and she can understand none of his neighbours saying anything – until now…

'We have received complaints,' the shorter official said. Kat gets the feeling he is speaking for her benefit. 'We have to take action – otherwise we will be in the wrong.'

'Who made the complaint?'

'That we are not at liberty to disclose, Miss.'

'Oh, right,' Cheng snaps back. 'So if I accuse you of raping me then somebody just comes and takes you away because there has been a complaint, but you have no right to ask who accused you, yes?'

Kat senses that till now the officers have been looking to Cheng as the sensible family member, the one who will keep the old man in check, but not any more.

'We can see you value the dog. If you have any friend or relative staying in private property, why not you ask them to take your dog.'

'Your sister lives in a house, doesn't she?' Kat says quietly turning to Cheng. 'Maybe –'

Hwee Yi, the elder Lim daughter, has married, it is said, well. Her husband is not only a lawyer but comes from a family of lawyers. Kat has never met the man but her mother has kept her informed. Although Kat is not the only one to think Cheng the more beautiful sister, Hwee Yi has always intended to make marriage her career and has cemented her role by producing a son within a year.

Surely, it is possible – although Kat cannot say so with government officials present – to register Cheeky's licence at Hwee Yi's address? Surely, once the fuss has died down, no one will bother with where the dog actually lives? Even her own mother, conservative member of an older generation, does not seem to mind the dog next door.

But Cheng does not pick up on that. She passes Cheeky's leash to Kat to hold as she tries to calm her father.

Old Uncle Lim shouts, rants, almost spits at the officials. Where do they think he is going to get five thousand dollars? He does not have five thousand dollars to give them. Even if he has five thousand dollars, he will not give it to them. In his anger he turns on Kat and Kat's mother who is watching from their doorway,

'If you don't like it here, go back to your kampong! You try to drive us all out! You kill me also I don't go!'

The officials try to make a quick and quiet exit. They'll just take the dog with them and leave, they say.

'We'll bring Cheeky to the SPCA ourselves,' Cheng said. 'I got a taxi driver who doesn't mind dogs.' She automatically incorporates Kat, who is willing, 'I've already called him, but can you go down first? I'll just …'

She indicates her father. It is not necessary to say more. The old man is slumped against the wall of the common corridor moaning, hopeless eyes taking his dog in. Fluid still drools from his nostrils and the sides of his open mouth, but his eyes have given up.

Kat's mother moves to help Cheng with the old man and, although he does not resist, it is a deadweight which they walk into the flat.

'We'll wait with you until the taxi comes,' one of the officials says, as they take the lift down to the ground floor with Kat and the dog. They must have instructions to see the animal off the premises.

'We have nothing against dogs. In fact the new rules were put in place to protect dogs ... so that people cannot keep them under poor conditions or abandon them,' the taller, younger official said. 'I have two dogs at home myself – my wife's, actually – so you see, I have nothing against dogs. Maybe if you go SPCA your friend can get a small dog for her father ...'

Kat fantasizes that soon, in Singapore, officials will be telling parents: *Your daughter is obese – beyond the weight range allowed for HDB flats. You must surrender her to the Ministry of Health but, while there, you can pick up a smaller child if you want one.*

Near the wall of mail boxes, a tall Chinese man in a green shirt idles with a child, very likely his son. The child is eager to play with Cheeky. The man warns his son to stay away from the dog. 'Dirty!' he says. He is jocular and uncomfortably friendly; talking loudly to none of them in particular, he tries to get Kat and the officials to agree that dogs are dirty, right? And it is illegal to keep dogs here!

Not that it makes any difference, but Kat does not want to be mistaken for a dog-culling officer. She pats Cheeky. Cheeky seems confused to have been brought downstairs without Old Mr Lim, just to stand by the side of the road, and she accepts the caress gratefully. She is a very gentle, responsive dog. Kat can understand a bereaved old man finding her a comfort and a blessing.

The child tries again to move towards Cheeky, but the man yanks him away roughly, shaking him into silence when he starts to fuss and protest. Kat realizes this is either a well-disciplined child or one very frightened of his father. Perhaps it is the same thing.

When the taxi arrives, Kat leaves Cheeky with the officers and goes to get Cheng. The lift has always been slow and she decides to walk. Inside the stairwell she sees the same tall Chinese man who is now pulling down the toddler's shorts and pull-up diaper, and is helping him to piss against the wall.

Kat remembers what her mother said, but this is no drunk migrant worker. 'Hey!'

The man looks round, but is hampered by having to steady the child who looks up at him, confused,

'Just a small kid –' the man gestures with a lopsided give-chance grin. Kat glares at him stone-faced. This is her home he is instructing his kid to piss on. She will say more, she has just discovered a desire in her to fight, but she hears Cheng calling for her.

In the taxi and at the SPCA, Kat feels alien. It was only while in Pittsburgh that she had come to think of Singapore as 'home', yet already she is missing not the life but the automatic anonymity she had in Carnegie Mellon. The encounter in the stairwell has left a bad echo and she feels the taxi driver is looking at her suspiciously. He is not rude but speaks to Cheng in Hokkien to clarify directions, '*Near the dead people containers that animal place, is it?*' Kat has picked up enough dialect over the years to understand Hokkien, yet today feels racially slighted.

'Take your dog to put down, ah?' The driver switches back to English to ask conversationally. He does not have a problem with English. Speaking a few words of Hokkien to Cheng was just his way of bonding.

It is Cheng (not Kat) the driver asks about Muslims touching dogs. Isn't it not allowed for Muslims to touch dogs? More calmly than Kat expects, Cheng tells the man Muslims place great emphasis on non-cruelty to all animals (a great deal more than most Chinese), and how, while dog saliva is considered unclean, washing it off takes care of the problem. Kat is surprised Cheng knows so much. So is the driver who stops his attempts at small talk.

'I read,' Cheng says. 'Not as much as you, but I do read stuff. And I talk to your Mum. Your Mum told me that, actually. I was afraid she would be worried about Dad's dog. I don't think your mum or your brother made that complaint. I'm sure my Dad doesn't think so either. He's just upset.'

What about taking Cheeky to stay in Hwee Yi's place for a while? Kat asks again. Uncle Lim can visit his dog there. From what she remembers of Hwee Yi, Kat can believe she won't want this dog in her house but surely she will provide temporary shelter, seeing how much it means to her father.

'Hwee has moved back with us,' Cheng says. 'She and her kid.'

It is not necessary to say more.

Kat and Cheng had been close friends once, a long time ago. Together in a housing estate so new that even the streetlamps did not extend beyond the car park at the foot of their block, the two girls explored the scrub wilderness and construction sites around them. There had still been guppies in storm drains and spiders, squirrels, giant lizards and even monkeys in the receding semi-jungle. It was only the stray cats and dogs that preferred to lurk around the expanding human habitations.

Somehow Kat had grown up past that stage into the serious teenager who got so caught up reading religious texts during the fasting month she would forget to break fast.

Coming back from the SPCA they do not talk. But their bond is back. There is the same sense of something valuable being cast away unrecognized for the sake of conformity and clean housing. The taxi driver refuses to take payment for the return trip – he has to come back the same way anyway – he says.

At the foot of their block, at the open door of a dark green Subaru WRX, Kat sees the same tall Chinese man again. She recognizes the small boy first, now being carried by a woman who Kat takes a moment to identify as Hwee Yi. At first she thinks the man is trying to avoid her, trying to hurry the other two into the car, then she sees it is Cheng he wants to get away from.

'It was you!' Cheng goes right up to the car and rests a hand on the windscreen.

'What?'

'You're the one that complained about Dad's dog, aren't you!'

'I don't know what you are talking about. You've got Malays living in this block, they are the ones that cannot *tahan* dogs, why come and accuse me!'

'You did, didn't you?'

The child starts to whine. The man snaps at him. Kat remembers the desperation in Cheeky's eyes as the dog was dragged whining from them at the pound. Docilely compliant up till then, she had struggled and fought. Driving away, they could hear her howling.

'You are a wicked man,' Kat says. She still has Cheeky on her hands and now she rests them on his car, like Cheng is doing.

'He didn't complain about Dad's dog,' Hwee Yi gets out of the car. 'I did, okay!'

'You –'

The man turns to Hwee Li, 'No way I'm letting you bring up my kid around her!'

'Better than around you!' Cheng says.

'You! You don't come and accuse me – your kind is worse than the Mat Sallehs – don't think you are fooling anybody.'

The crash is loud when the old man's body lands. They are all dumbfounded, incredulous, staring. Hwee Yi starts giggling. There is more blood than you'd expect from such a frail, old body, now oozing slowly, pooling like thin gravy, more red than you would think, already gritty from the gravel.

'Yeh-Yeh?' says the child.

Kat goes upstairs to be with her mother. Her brother is back and she tells them what has happened to the family next door.

'We all thought he would die after his wife died,' Kat's mother says. She is less upset than Kat expected.

'I used to tell your Pa, the most important thing is for everybody to be happy, don't fight. But now if you don't fight ...'

Kat cannot tell whether this is an incitement to fight or if she has just run out of breath. Her mother has been breathless of late.

'I am also getting old,' her mother goes on. 'These days you cannot trust your husband, your neighbours ... not even your children.'

'I got offered a job,' Kat suddenly announces. 'A good job. In Pittsburg.'

'Good,' says her mother.

Maid to Serve: Representations of Female Domestic Workers in Singapore Cinema

KENNETH CHAN

Introduction: The 'Foreign Maids' issue

Singapore's rise as an Asian economic powerhouse has attracted an influx of migrant workers from developing countries in the region. Female domestic workers – or 'foreign maids' – constitute a major segment of the migrant worker population owing to the increasing demand for domestic help because of Singapore's shifting gender demographics in the professional workplace.[1] The first work permits were issued in 1978 'to allow a limited recruitment of domestic servants from Thailand, Sri Lanka and the Philippines'.[2] By 2005, the population of foreign domestic help had grown to a staggering 150,000. Most of the migrants are from Indonesia and the Philippines, with the remainder coming from Thailand, Sri Lanka, India, and Myanmar.[3] According to the 2005 Human Rights Watch report on the issue, one finds a foreign maid in one out of seven homes in Singapore today.[4]

This same report, drawing on official statistical information and testimony from numerous interviews, also pieced together an alarming picture of human rights abuses frequently endured by domestic workers. Already suffering the trauma of leaving home and struggling with cultural differences,[5] many are furthermore subjected to verbal, physical, and even sexual abuse. Reports of maid abuse appear frequently in *The Straits Times*, Singapore's national newspaper.[6] Low pay, lack of rest and days off, food deprivation, and restrictions on social activities and family contact are commonplace. Recent cases, where maids have fallen to their death when forced by their employers to clean the windows of apartments in high-rise buildings without safety precautions, have led to public debates on how Singaporeans should or should not treat their maids. Currently, Singaporean employers are required by law to give their maids at least one day off a month, but far too many do not heed this ruling.[7] While the Human Rights Watch acknowledges that the Singapore government 'has taken important steps to provide protections for migrant domestic workers', it warns that the State should not assume its 'current measures are adequate and does nothing more' as 'it will be condemning more domestic workers in Singapore to discrimination, exploitation, and abuse'.[8]

Because the figure of the female domestic worker has come to occupy such a significant place in the Singapore family, and within contemporary Singapore society, her presence is increasingly registered in popular culture, particularly in local television soap operas and comedies as well as films and plays depicting life in the Singapore 'heartland'. At the same time, her presence is often relegated to the narrative background of these works. A less politically conservative approach than state-sponsored television representation, however, has been adopted by Singapore's rising film industry. Led by Raintree Pictures, the more independent filmmaking arm of the state-sponsored MediaCorp, and followed by competitors and collaborators, such as Zhao Wei Films and Boku Films, there is now a critically acclaimed and commercially viable body of work by Singaporean filmmakers, among them Eric Khoo, Jack Neo, Royston Tan, and Kelvin Tong. Through cinematic images that contradict official public and political representations of the nation, this emerging cinema offers its audiences slices of Singapore life through unflattering depictions of heartland denizens or marginalized figures who occupy the fringes of this successful city-state. As the figure of the 'foreign maid' becomes metonymic of an emerging racialized (and even racist) class system produced by Singapore's embrace of global capitalism and its often exploitative strategies, Singapore cinema is beginning to register this social phenomenon in a significant and critical fashion. Eric Khoo's *No Day Off*, premiered during the 2006 'Third Singapore Short Cuts',[9] captures the experiences of an ill-treated Indonesian maid in Singapore. There is also Kelvin Tong's box-office success, *The Maid* (2005), which rode upon the fashionable Asian horror film wave sweeping through Hollywood. Together these filmic representations of foreign domestic workers produce a strong indictment of the often dismissive and, hence, irresponsible attitude of Singaporeans towards those whom they employ. Such a critique participates in the public discussions on internet forums, and in the local and international media, over maid abuse and the State's resistance to passing legislation that protects domestic workers' rights.[10] In examining Kelvin Tong's *The Maid* and Eric Khoo's *No Day Off*, this essay not only foregrounds the narrative and discursive strategies the filmmakers deploy to produce their critique, but also interrogates the political efficacy of these strategies by complicating in each case the modality of the film's gaze and the risk of unwitting complicity that each takes.

At this juncture, some theoretical and critical reflections may help to contextualize the analyses of these films on maid abuse in Singapore. While it is necessary to condemn the flagrant deprivation of the maids' basic human rights, what is cause for disquiet is the emergence of an insidious and deep-rooted cultural essentialism serving as the foundation for a race, class, and gender inflected attitude towards the figure of the maid as an embodiment of alterity. In other words, the everyday discourse of Singaporeans frequently conceptualizes the maid as a cultural and national other. This notion of otherness then serves to justify the unfair treatment and abuse of maids as in frequently heard statements, such as 'Oh they are all like that. If you do not keep them on a tight leash, they will take advantage of you. It is in their nature.' The attempt to naturalize individual flaws as representative of a cultural whole is consequent upon a number of factors.

Firstly, Singapore's culture of economic pragmatism and efficiency demands value for money. The maid, instead of being viewed as a person and as an employee with human rights, is thought of as commodity. Commodification here introduces a process of dehumanization: being from the developing 'Third World', she is while human not as civilized as we are. Desiring to be a cosmopolitan urban node within the network of transnational capitalist flows, Singapore works hard to attract 'foreign talent' to its shores, but the foreign labour pool unfortunately forms a hierarchy where domestic workers, alongside unskilled manual labourers, occupy the lowest rungs. This is symptomatic of what some critics of globalization have termed 'crises of care'.[11] Brenda Yeoh is thus right to foreground the contributions of these domestic workers, which are often taken for granted and rendered invisible by the dehumanizing process of commodification.[12] Another reason for this disparity in status lies in gender inequality arising from the relationship between gender and the perception of domestic care as a vocation of low importance to the nation's interest.[13] The state's response to calls for legislation to protect the rights of domestic workers is often to reject them by invoking the necessity of maintaining labour flexibility in order to meet the shifting needs of Singapore, thereby privileging again economic exigencies over human rights.[14]

Secondly, a culture based on capitalist economics produces a transformation of the employer-employee relationship, where the distinction between the private space of home life and the public space of work life is blurred. The foreign maid becomes an embodiment of cultural difference that needs to be culturally cannibalized and assimilated (as I will show in my discussion of Kelvin Tong's film, *The Maid*). But the project of assimilation is bound to fail, as the maid is an 'abject' figure. With reference to Mary Douglas's contention in her seminal work, *Purity and Danger*, that 'dirt is essentially disorder' and 'There is no such thing as absolute dirt: it exists in the eye of the beholder',[15] Julia Kristeva in *Powers of Horror* theorizes that the 'abject' is 'dirty' or 'impure' because it is 'irreducible to the subject/object and inside/outside oppositions'.[16] The abject necessarily 'partakes of both polarized terms but cannot be clearly identified with either'.[17] The maid is abject in the sense that she transgresses the spatial and temporal boundaries of a conventional employer-employee relationship. She both is and is not a family member and employee. She is a member of the community and yet, by being culturally different, is viewed as being apart. The idea that 'they are all alike' is an attempt to shift her into a category of cultural otherness, thereby restoring the neat us-versus-them binary opposition.

It is arguable that to demonize Singaporean employers in general is unfair when such reported cases of abuse constitute the exception rather than the rule – Singaporeans often do treat their domestic helpers with kindness and human decency.[18] Furthermore, not all maid abuse stems from personal cruelty and could be a by-product of the complex social tensions arising from the fast-paced and stressful lifestyle in Singapore.[19] While these observations are *theoretically* valid, the humane treatment of one's employee is, and should always be considered, a moral and ethical given, undeserving of any fanfare or self-congratulation; and Singapore's stressful lifestyle should never be the pragmatic justification for even incidental ill treatment. In any case, maid abuse as a social phenomenon is now quickly losing its 'exceptional' status in Singapore, particularly when abuse can take on various violent and non-violent forms; and racialized attitudes towards domestic workers as a *minority group acquire more insidiously racist dimensions.*

The Maid: Ghostly abjection and alterity

My earlier discussion of the maid in terms of alterity and abjection enables me to introduce a discursive relationship to the horror film genre. In his pioneering work on the American horror film, Robin Wood argues that 'the repressed/the Other' is represented by 'the figure of the Monster'. He suggests that 'the true subject of the horror genre is the struggle for recognition of all that our civilisation *re*presses or *op*presses'.[20] Wood's politicized reading of horror does not simplistically imbue the genre with an inherent political character. Horror can be politically radical or reactionary, depending on one's reading strategy.[21] Moreover, the spectacle of violence, gore, and the supernatural in horror films tends to eclipse and obscure any intimations of a political, social, or cultural critique.[22] It has been pointed out that the horror elements in Kelvin Tong's *The Maid* are similar to films made in the region such as Malay-language films which depict the *pontianak*.[23] Although such formalist and historical comparisons are valid, this essay will offer a reading where the narrative and structural aspects of the film serve to convey its social and political critique of the treatment of maids in Singapore.

The Maid is a mainstream hit that rides the successful global wave of the Asian horror film phenomenon following in the wake of Hollywood remakes of contemporary Japanese cinematic classics such as *The Ring* (2002), *The Grudge* (2004), and *Dark Water* (2005). Not surprisingly, executive producer Daniel Yun of Raintree Pictures was delighted that '*The Maid* has all the makings of a horror film from Asia that will travel to the West.'[24] It was such a box office success both nationally and regionally that a sequel is being planned.[25] But arguably Tong's real success is that he brings to what could have become another mediocre horror film both an art-house sensibility and a heightened social consciousness, reflecting a deep sensitivity to the plight of maids.[26]

In the film, eighteen-year-old Rosa arrives from the Philippines to work for the Teo family, who are members of a Teochew[27] opera troupe and proud bearers of this age-old Chinese artistic tradition. Chinese opera in Singapore today is mostly performed during the Hungry Ghost Festival in the seventh month of the Chinese lunar calendar, when it is believed the gates of hell are opened and hungry ghosts roam the world of the living in search of food and other offerings. Rosa's arrival coincides with this period when certain rituals were practised that would appear bizarre to the newcomer. She is warned, for instance, not to step on or touch the ashes of the paper money burnt as offerings. Nonetheless, Rosa sweeps up the remaining ashes on the sidewalk outside the Teo's house and, as a result of her transgression, she is able to see the dead (an obvious parallel is M. Night Shyamalan's *The Sixth Sense*, 1999). The terror mounts as she endures a series of hauntings, leading her to confide in the couple and their mentally-challenged son, Ah Soon. Visited by the spectre of the family's previous Filipino maid, Esther, Rosa discovers that Esther had been burnt to death and hidden away in a drum used as a musical instrument by the Chinese opera troupe. It turns out that because Esther had been raped by Ah Soon, Mr Teo torched her to death in order to cover up the crime. Ah Soon eventually died of grief for the maid he loved. The now too familiar surprise ending is that the Ah Soon, whom

Rosa has been dealing with, is really his ghost who, because he had died unmarried, has returned during the seventh month to claim a bride. The Teos' evil plan was to lure Rosa into agreeing to marry their dead son before killing her as a sacrifice. The parents eventually die horrible deaths, thus freeing Rosa to return to the Philippines with the ashes of Esther.

Part of the appeal of *The Maid* as an Asian horror film is the exoticism of the Hungry Ghosts Festival. The prologue of the film narrates the logic of this cultural belief:

> Every year for thirty days during the lunar seventh month, the Chinese believe that the gates of hell are thrown open. Vengeful spirits and hungry ghosts wander among the living, seeking revenge and justice before the gates of hell are closed again for another year.[28]

The horror works on two levels: for Chinese audiences brought up with this belief, the film concretely visualizes terrifying taboos of the seventh month, such as not to stay out or go swimming after dark, not to turn around when someone calls out to you, not to talk about the burning of paper money or tread on the ashes. Urban myths abound of the dire consequences of transgression. Hence, belief in these myths and taboos constitutes a form of cultural belonging and connection, but it also has the disciplinary effect of inculcating conformity to a cultural ideology, its values, and practices. For audiences unfamiliar with these myths, the film can be equally terrifying, though on a slightly different level: the horror experienced is of an exotic cultural unknown, a mystery deepened by its alienness.

My intention is not to essentialize cultural modes of experiencing horror but rather to display the structures of horror in the film that accentuate the notion of difference (cultural difference, in this case) which the maid has to negotiate. The Month of Hungry Ghosts provides a fantastical scenario which brings into relief the struggles of the foreign maid against social oppression and cultural assimilation. The cultural traditionalism represented by the Festival becomes the rhetorical device with which the Teos demarcate the boundaries and limits of Rosa's mobility and freedom. For instance, when Rosa goes out to mail a letter for the very first time and asks the postman where the mailbox is, Mrs Teo chastises her:

> 'You cannot anyhow talk to outside people. Next time you want to post letter, I post for you. You first time come to Singapore, you don't know what kind of people outside. They cheat you, you also don't know. You understand? ... And now it's hungry ghost month. You must be careful.'[29]

Mrs Teo constructs Rosa's cultural ignorance in order to create a relationship of dependency. The deep mysteries of the Hungry Ghosts Festival authenticate Mrs Teo's cultural wisdom. Of course, her cultural wisdom disguises her ulterior motive which is to prevent any kind of communication between Rosa and her family and friends.

The move to contain Rosa within the family sphere is to prepare her for her ultimate role in their evil plan: to offer her to and placate their dead son. In other words, Rosa is to be consumed and assimilated into the familial structure, negating her abject status. This violent process of consumption/assimilation is based on the Chinese cultural logic of the primacy of marriage, family, and children. When Ah Soon suddenly appears, Mrs Teo explains his mental deficiencies to evoke Rosa's sympathy:

> 'Me and sir unlucky. Have baby too late. When Ah Soon born, they say his head got problem. Other people children grow up, go to school, married, have baby. But my Ah Soon, so big already, still like a small boy.'

Mrs Teo uses the cultural imperative that Ah Soon should have a normal family life to convince Rosa that she can be the solution to their sad predicament. Mr and Mrs Teo use kindness to blackmail Rosa emotionally by paying her in advance so that she could remit the money needed for her brother's kidney operation.

When Rosa confronts Mrs Teo about their former maid, Esther, Mrs Teo's explanation is unintentionally revealing:

> 'Two years ago, Esther work here. Like you. She is a very good girl. Very hard working. Me and sir like her very much. Ah Soon also like her very much. We like one big family. Then one day she missing. Nobody know where she go. Sir call the police. The police also don't know where she go. The police say many maid from Philippines like her. They find a boyfriend here and then they run away. We never tell you this because we don't want you to become like Esther. We want you to stay home, work hard, be one family. Do you understand, Rosa?'

Most of us are not unfamiliar with the 'good maid/bad maid' rhetoric. Its strategy is to force Rosa into agreeing to be a good maid, hence denying her other possibilities of being human outside of this binary option. At the heart of the Teos' intention to have Rosa as Ah Soon's wife in the afterlife is the 'be one family' cultural imperative.

In the chilling final sequence when Rosa is dressed up in the traditional Chinese bridal costume, tortured with burning joss sticks, and then bound with a rope around the neck and tied to the ceiling, Mrs Teo reveals the perverse twist to the cultural logic of marriage and family: 'Chinese people believe in many things. Dead people also can marry … All my life me and Sir waiting for Ah Soon to marry.' Inherent in their insertion of Rosa into their formulations of familial obligation and marital fulfilment is their treatment of maids as objects of utility. Her humanity is never a consideration. It only matters that she, as commodity and tool, serves the family's purposes. While their actions may be a monstrous and horrifying caricature of maid abuse, the dehumanizing conception of the maid's purpose is not intrinsically different from the much articulated notion that foreign maids in Singapore must serve Singaporeans in a way that does not disrupt the efficient running of the social machinery.

The film's denouement, in which Rosa takes Esther's ashes home to the Philippines, becomes therefore a sharp critique of this emerging social problem in Singapore. Scenes of her flight are accompanied by a calm voice-over, where Rosa's voice is gradually merged with Esther's:

'A month ago, I came to Singapore. I came to see the world. But I ended up looking into the darkest and saddest part of a human heart. Here, my journey ends. I am finally going back ... and so is another girl who has been away from home for a long, long time.'

The film ends with Rosa walking through the glass doors of Changi Airport's Terminal One building. As the doors close after her, horrific apparitions of the Teo parents and their son appear, looking on.

Kelvin Tong's political intentions obviously motivated a film where the trope of ghostliness is effectively deployed to foreground the plight of domestic workers in Singapore as they struggle with not just culture-shock but also mistreatment and abuse. The spectral return of Esther, the first maid, signifies cinematically the continued haunting of the public and cultural imaginary of Singapore, even as the state disavows and elides *social* and *political* complicity and responsibility for the human rights abuses suffered by maids. It is arguable that this pop cultural invention of a spectacular or 'extreme' instance of maid abuse on screen – with the theatrical elements of the Hungry Ghosts Festival, the atypical Chinese opera family, and the horror elements in the story providing further distraction – does not represent social reality. Singapore audiences could find this filmic representation both alien and exceptional and, therefore, might not see themselves reflected in it. This argument dovetails in a way with my earlier critique of the genre's ability, through spectacular visuality and form, to eclipse any social message that a horror film might have. The figure of the maid thereby once more returns to its role of utility, this time by presenting a pair of 'foreign' eyes to experience the cultural spectacle that is the Hungry Ghosts Festival. As one of the actors involved in the film puts it, 'It is through the eyes of a Filipino maid we explore the customs and traditions of Singaporeans during the seventh month, as well as the strange practices during this month.'[30] In other words, there is a narcissistic cultural turn inwards with the maid being the means to that end, a filmic parallel to the way she functions socially and invisibly (as some hope) to shore up the Singaporean bourgeois lifestyle.

No Day Off: Vicarious chronicling

Director Eric Khoo shares with Kelvin Tong a similar social sensibility when it comes to the question of maid abuse. Confronted with the observation that his film, *No Day Off*, 'portrays Singaporeans too harshly',[31] Khoo retorted ironically that he 'could actually have made them more evil', but that he and his co-writer Wong Kim Hoh did not want the film to 'have ended up more like a horror film',[32] an obvious allusion to Tong's *The Maid*, which had been released the year before. While he may have been playfully signalling a political affinity with Tong, Khoo's statement suggests a rhetorical shift by his adopting a different genre to engage with the same issue. His attempts to capture the lives of the marginalized in Singapore society show he is no stranger to *cinéma vérité*. His gritty portrayals of prostitutes in *Mee Pok Man* (1995), dysfunctional and alienated 'heartlanders' in *12 Storeys* (1997), and lesbian lovers and 'China brides' in *Be with Me* (2005) have impressed film festival audiences the world over; but his work also has the potential of 'deflating the triumphalism [of the state's official discourse] by pointing to the underbelly of the nation where the failures are too well hidden under the new affluence'.[33] *No Day Off*, Khoo's contribution to a trilogy of short films entitled *Talk to Her* (the other two films being Thai filmmaker Pen-ek Ratanaruang's *Twelve Twenty* and Kazakhstan director Darezhan Omirbayev's *About Love*),[34] continues his cinema of political aesthetic by offering viewers a 39-minute fictional chronicle of 1,519 days in the life of Siti Rhama (Syamsiah) from the time she leaves her home village in Sulawesi, Indonesia, to work as maid for three very different Singaporean households to her final return home to her infant son.

Home-video visuality in both technique and effect is strategic in Khoo's simulation of a documentary. To accomplish this, the camera captures and situates Siti front and centre, while following her (mis)adventures. The feel of a video-camera documentary is further emphasized by the placement of numbers on the top left-hand corner of the screen to indicate the passing number of days and by the use of intertitles on a black screen, techniques which one finds in news documentaries or silent films.

The creative use of numbers and the switching on and off of the camera allow Khoo to telescope the diegetic 1,519 days into the short film's 39 minutes; but, more importantly, it sutures the fragmented moments in Siti's life to give viewers a holistic and cumulative sense of the varied trials and tribulations that the domestic worker has to suffer throughout her stay in Singapore. The deployment of intertitles interspersed throughout the film deepens the connection between the viewers' vicarious experience and a social reality by providing a contextual framework:

Title One: There are 150,000 maids working in Singapore. Of these, 60,000 are Indonesians, mostly from families of small farmers or labourers. The majority are married, with children.
Title Two: One in every seven Singapore households has a 'live in' maid.
Title Three: Between 1997 and 2005, an estimated 600 cases of maid abuse were reported in Singapore.
Title Four: Between 1999 and 2005, 147 domestic workers died in Singapore either through accidents or by suicide. Of these, about 80% were Indonesians.
Title Five: As of January 2006, there is no legislation to ensure that domestic workers in Singapore get a rest day each week. Many Indonesian domestic workers work 7 days a week. [35]

The intertitles, providing numbers and data factually, also follow a sociological narrative, which delinks Siti's story from its fictional character and reconnects it to contemporary Singapore, thus rhetorically producing a powerful message that combines the very real factual immediacy of socially dysfunctional maid abuse and the emotional narrative sweep of the fictional story.

The fact that the film's documentary aesthetic relies on images of the everyday also suggests another strategic distancing from the spectacularity of Tong's *The Maid*. By focusing not just on abusive moments of her experience in Singapore but also on the day-to-day life of Siti, involving both good and bad, happy and sad times, Khoo succeeds in constructing a believable account of the life of a maid. Such an account does double duty by imbuing the character with a certain generality that allows viewers to visualize her as the stock version of the Singapore 'foreign maid', while at the same time retaining a cultural specificity and individuality that distinctively belongs to her, Siti. Enabling viewers to perceive Siti as a believable character also means they can empathize with her woes and suffering as a maid. In not accentuating the extreme and 'evil' instances of maid abuse, Khoo circumvents the exceptionalism that the spectacle of cinema is wont to produce.

Another important effect achieved through the compression of Siti's

1,519 days into 39 minutes of film is that it rapidly exposes moments of disconnection and contradiction between the partial truths told by the recruiter in his attempt to lure poverty-stricken women into servitude and the reality as experienced by Siti. The viewer and Siti are simultaneously exposed to the idyllic picture of easy work and financial rewards painted by the recruiter:

> 'What are you hoping to find here in Sulawesi? The land is harsh, life is difficult. You should try for a better life for you and your family. Follow us to Batam, we will train you to be a maid. After that you can go and work as a maid in Singapore. The work is easy, you get a salary every month and a good salary too. You can buy land in your village, look after your family, and educate your kid, and even save. The work is easy. You just need to clean, tidy and you will get a good salary every month ... So think about it. Come to Batam.'

What the recruiter avoids mentioning is the debt that Siti will incur when she arrives in Singapore, a fact that is soon made plain to her by the local maid agency:

> 'Your salary is $230 (US$143) a month. But you have a lot of debts. You have to pay the recruiter, your travel expenses and us – the agent's commission. Do you understand? We will deduct $220 (US$138) from your salary for 9 months. So, you will only get $10 (US$6) each month. You will only get your full salary from the 10th month onwards.'

This voice-over reality-check is coupled with images of the Work Permit Service Centre of the Ministry of Manpower in Singapore and close-up shots of pages from the entry test that Siti has to undergo, thereby registering institutional complicity in her financial exploitation by the recruiting and facilitating agencies.

By showing Siti at work for three very different families, the film effectively illustrates the emotional and psychological toll on the maid as she negotiates racial differences within Singapore, different social classes, and various language barriers. The first family is an extremely wealthy, jet-setting, English-speaking couple with a spoilt daughter. Not only is she not permitted any day off, Siti is subjected to insults from her male employer, who complains that 'she has half a brain ... I talk to her, and she looks at me like a cow'. Her failure to understand basic instructions is simply a matter of the language barrier, which her rich employers do not have the patience to comprehend or the decency to amend. Worst of all, she is subjected to the whims of the spoilt daughter, who is given full authority by her mother to control Siti.[36] This disempowerment of Siti in relation to the child declassifies her as an adult and is altogether demeaning to her person.

Before she can accustom herself to the English-speaking household and their upper class expectations, Siti finds herself transferred to a working class Chinese-speaking family in an HDB flat. Siti is now suddenly expected to acquire a new set of language and lifestyle skills. The accidental breaking of a bowl provokes a torrent of verbal abuse from the foul-mouthed matriarch, who then proceeds to complain to her married daughter:

'When I went into the room to read the papers, I saw her crying. People would think we were mistreating her. I can't stand it! Her face is so black, it will bring bad luck. And I've noticed the lustful looks she casts on your husband. You'd better keep an eye on her, these people are capable of anything.'

The racist rant with its clear prejudices and ironic inconsistencies can be said to come across with convincing verisimilitude.

The last household which Siti works for suggests optimistically that perhaps there are families who take better care of their employees. With this Malay-speaking Indian family, the language barrier no longer exists and the relief on Siti's face is evident as we see her break into a smile in her new work environment. But she finds that she has to quickly adapt from being a babysitter (as with the first family) to becoming a live-in nurse who must care for an infirm old man. The penultimate sequence presents one of the most poignant scenes in the film: Siti witnesses the painful decline and death of the old man, a scene which has his daughter crying in Siti's arms.

Except for the scene where the two women weep in commiseration with one another, viewers do not get to see the other characters but only hear their voices. Siti becomes the central visual focus which is Khoo's method of cinematically evoking 'her isolation'. Because you don't 'see' the other characters, Khoo explains, 'you can ask yourself, is that me?'[37] The continued visual gaze which Siti is subjected to produces in the viewer both the discomfort of a voyeuristic complicity and an identification that begs that question. Another implication of this voyeuristic gaze which I would like to note is the filmmaker's role in rendering this visuality. In their analysis of Khoo's positioning as filmmaker in *12 Storeys,* Chua and Yeo have remarked: 'Khoo's own financially very upper class background' would suggest that 'this absence of entry into the inner lives of the marginal people in a national success story … stems from a fascination with the Other rather than empathy for the Other, making his cinema disturbingly voyeuristic.'[38] A similar point could equally be made in relation to *No Day Off.* Without doubt it is easy, and maybe *too* easy, to speculate on Khoo's motivations, particularly when we see how films depicting human rights abuses in the non-West find willing audiences in film festivals in Europe and North America – prompting the suspicion that Khoo is producing a cinema of auto-ethnography[39] that feeds the West's assumptions about allegedly recalcitrant nations like Singapore. But such conjectures about a filmmaker's motivations are critically and politically less productive than reflections on the possible social and political effect of such films. Both *No Day Off* and *The Maid*, despite their shortcomings, present critically significant cinematic interventions that are both necessary and urgent in a national climate where the rights of the marginalized and disenfranchised are in need of protection.

NOTES

1. 'Singapore's industrialisation programme engendered a relatively rapid influx of women into the labour force, in turn creating an escalated demand for paid substitutes to fulfill responsibilities in the reproductive sphere.' Shirlena Huang and Brenda S.A. Yeoh, 'Ties That Bind: State Policy and Migrant Female Domestic Helpers in Singapore', *Geoforum*, 27 (1996) 479-93, p. 482.
2. Huang and Yeoh, 'Ties That Bind', p. 484.
3. Maruja Milagros B. Asis, Shirlena Huang and Brenda S. A. Yeoh, 'When the Light of the Home is Abroad: Unskilled Female Migration and the Filipino Family', *Singapore Journal of Tropical Geography*, 25 (2004) 198-215, p. 203.
4. Human Rights Watch, *Maid to Order: Ending Abuses against Migrant Domestic Workers in Singapore*, 17:10(C) (2005) pp. 2-3. This report is available for download at <http://hrw.org/reports/2005/singapore1205/> accessed on 10 May 2008.
5. Brenda S. A. Yeoh and Shirlena Huang, '"Home" and "Away": Foreign Domestic Workers and Negotiations of Diasporic Identity in Singapore', *Women's Studies International Forum*, 23 (2000) 413-29.
6. The following is a random sampling of reports appearing during preparation of this article: Elena Chong, 'Doctor's Wife Jailed for Repeatedly Abusing Maid', *The Straits Times*, 25 October 2007, p. H6; Braema Mathi, 'More Now Likely to Tell on Maid Abusers', *The Straits Times*, 17 November 2007, p. H7; Elena Chong, 'Girl, 18, Accused of Pulling Out Maid's Front Teeth', *The Straits Times*, 11 March 2008, p. 3; Diana Othman, 'She Fled to Avoid Beatings', *The Straits Times*, 1 April 2009 <www.straitstimes.com/Breaking+News/Singapore/Story/STIStory_357210.html> accessed on 2 May 2009.
7. There is growing activism by NGOs on behalf of domestic workers. For instance, The Day Off Campaign is 'a joint initiative by the National Committee of UNIFEM Singapore, Humanitarian Organisation for Migration Economics, and Transient Workers Count Too' that seeks to educate the public on the necessity of granting maids at least a day off a week. <www.dayoff.sg/> accessed on 10 May 2008. See also Keith Lin, 'Civic Groups Campaign for Maids' Day-Off', *The Straits Times*, 30 April 2008, p. H2.
8. Human Rights Watch, *Maid to Order*, p. 108.

9. Stephanie Yap, 'Maid's Second Connection', *The Straits Times*, 12 October 2006, Life section, p. 6. 'Singapore Short Cuts' is an annual showcase of outstanding short films organized by the National Museum of Singapore and the Substation, an Arts centre.

10. Apart from Khoo's and Tong's films, Colin Goh and Woo Yen Yen's 'heartlander' film *Singapore Dreaming* (2006) – which won awards at the 54th San Sebastian International Film Festival, the 20th Tokyo International Film Festival, and the 30th Asian American International Film Festival (see <www.sinema.sg/2007/10/> accessed 2 May 2009) – also includes a telling subplot featuring a Filipino maid having to serve two families and being unjustly accused of stealing by her employer.

11. Mary K. Zimmerman, Jacquelyn S. Litt and Christine E. Bose, 'Globalization and Multiple Crises of Care', in *Global Dimensions of Gender and Carework*, eds, Mary K. Zimmerman, Jacquelyn S. Litt and Christine E. Bose (Stanford: Stanford UP, 2006), pp. 9-29 (p. 10).

12. 'It is often "forgotten" that a global city owes its success not only to the presence of multinational corporate headquarters, transnational élites of the professional and managerial class (referred to in Singapore as "foreign talent") and hi-tech, cultural and tourism industries, but also has to be sustained by an underbelly of low-skilled, low-status "foreign workers" who minister to the needs of the privileged in both residential, commercial and industrial settings.' Brenda S. A. Yeoh, 'Cosmopolitanism and its Exclusions in Singapore', *Urban Studies*, 41 (2004) 2431-445, p. 2438.

13. 'Not only is the nature of their work trivialised because it is considered to be no more than what women traditionally undertook in the home as a labour of love and therefore "free", but the conditions of their work, even though it is paid work, are perceived to be governed by the rhythms of the private sphere and therefore beyond the purview of normal state legislation to protect relations in the sphere of work.' Huang and Yeoh, 'Ties That Bind', p. 488.

14. 'Singapore Rejects Maids' Day Off', *BBC News*, 9 March 2006 <http://news.bbc.co.uk/1/hi/world/asia-pacific/4790104.stm> accessed on 24 September 2006. See also 'S'pore's Maid Policy Boosts Economy, Says Harvard Study', *The Straits Times*, 12 October 2006, p. 32. The celebratory publication of this Reuters article is typical of the way the Singapore press reifies governmental policies through the imprimatur of academic authority.

15. Mary Douglas, *Purity and Danger: An Analysis of Concept of Pollution and Taboo* (London: Routledge, 1966), p. 2.

16. Julia Kristeva, *Powers of Horror: An Essay on Abjection*, trans. Leon Roudiez (New York: Columbia UP, 1982), pp.1-2. For Kristeva's discussion of Mary Douglas's ideas, see pp. 65-70.

17. Elizabeth Grosz, *Volatile Bodies: Toward a Corporeal Feminism* (Bloomington: Indiana UP, 1994), p. 192.

18. View, for instance, *Get Real*. Series 1, episode 2, 'Maid Home Leave'. Prod. Raju Jayakumar and Sharon Hun. 23 min. MediaCorp News, Singapore. 2005.

19. The maid subplot in *Singapore Dreaming* (see fn 10) precisely illustrates such an overdetermined moment of incidental mistreatment of the domestic help, who is otherwise usually trusted and not ill-treated. I would like to thank Philip Holden for pointing this out to me at the '(Ir)responsibility' Conference, organized by the Division of English, Nanyang Technological University, Singapore, 2006, where I had presented an early version of this essay.

20. Robin Wood, 'An Introduction to the American Horror Film', in *Movies and Methods:*

Volume II, ed., Bill Nichols (Berkeley: U of California P, 1985), pp. 195-220 (p. 201).

21. Wood excellently demonstrates this point on pp. 215-20.

22. For instance, the flesh-eating violence in George A. Romero's revival of the zombie movie in *Land of the Dead* (2005) consumes much of the film's screen time and narrative, thus overshadowing its intended political allegory.

23. Pieter Aquilia and Chua Ling-Yen, '*The Maid*: The Asian Ghost Story Meets the Hollywood Horror Genre', Conference Presentation, The Film Scene: Cinema, the Arts, and Social Change, U of Hong Kong, Hong Kong, 21-22 April 2006. The *pontianak* is the Malay version of the female vampire.

24. 'The Making of *The Maid*'. Prod. Ler. MediaCorp Raintree Pictures. 2005. In *The Maid*. Dir. Kelvin Tong. MediaCorp Raintree Pictures. 2005. DVD.

25. '"The Maid" Sequel Wins Award from HK-Asia Film Financing Forum', *Yahoo! Asia News*, 24 March 2006 <http://asia.news.yahoo.com/060324/5/singapore199496.html> accessed on 15 September 2007.

26. 'I've always found the idea of Filipino maids very interesting because they are more than just migrant workers. They are often migrant workers without voices, without opinions. They are supposed to come and work in a strange place. They are not supposed to have an opinion. They are not supposed to speak unless spoken to'. 'The Making of *The Maid*'.

27. Teochew is one of the Chinese dialects in Singapore.

28. *The Maid*. Dir. Kelvin Tong. MediaCorp Raintree Pictures. 2005. DVD. All subsequent references to this film are taken from this Singapore DVD version.

29. I have chosen to retain the original Singlish when quoting dialogue. Singlish (described by linguists as Singapore Colloquial English) is a local dialect of English.

30. 'The Making of *The Maid*'. The actor who made this comment is Hong Hui Fang, who plays the character of Mrs Teo.

31. Yap, 'Maid's Second Connection'.

32. As quoted in Yap, 'Maid's Second Connection'.

33. Chua Beng Huat and Wei-Wei Yeo, 'Singapore Cinema: Eric Khoo and Jack Neo – Critique from the Margins and the Mainstream', *Inter-Asia Cultural Studies*, 4 (2003), 117-25, p. 119.

34. Yap, 'Maid's Second Connection'.

35. *No Day Off*. Dir. Eric Khoo. 39 min. 2005. For more discussion of the plight of Indonesian maids in Singapore, see Noorashikin Abdul Rahman, 'Shaping the Migrant Institution: The Agency of Indonesian Domestic Workers in Singapore', in *The Agency of Women in Asia*, ed., Lyn Parker (Singapore: Marshall Cavendish, 2005), pp. 182-216.

36. As her female employer instructs Siti, 'If Dawn wants to do anything, please make sure you do it with her. You look after her, and follow her everywhere. If she comes to me and complains, cries, or is angry that you don't let her have her way or that you are horrible to her, you go back to Sulawesi'.

37. As quoted in Yap, 'Maid's Second Connection'.

38. Chua and Yeo, 'Singapore Cinema', p.120.

39. I am thinking of Rey Chow's critical manoeuvre here in her analysis of the works of Chinese Fifth Generation filmmakers. Rey Chow, *Primitive Passions: Visuality, Sexuality, Ethnography, and Contemporary Chinese Cinema* (New York: Columbia UP, 1995).

LEONG LIEW GEOK

How to Cook a Wolf

Season its mouth with wine,
Then bind the jaws with meat;
Not only will its teeth tear into flesh,
Its bite is far worse than its bark.
Think, when it's eaten you whole,
It'll be too late to slice its belly open
To emerge, a Venus cloaked in blood.

Trap it before it snares you.
What's the best part of a wolf?
Not its tongue, but the tail
Between retreating legs.
When skinned, its nakedness
Will show one wolf is like any other,
An Adam to your Eve, your dinner or his.

What would you have: steaks or ribs,
Prime cuts of loin and leg, or offal
Disguised by pepper, vinegar and ginger?
There's Merlot to go with the meal:
A lesson for pawing your body parts.

Be prepared: for he may come, a sheep with eyes closed,
Ears laid back, or some herbivorous horny goat.

The Stakes in Contemporary Art: Tang Da Wu's Artistic Practice as Exemplar

KWOK KIAN-WOON

Tang Da Wu has a lot to answer for. But who is Tang Da Wu?[1] And what has he to answer for? A clue lies in a note that he handed to the President of Singapore during the opening of the 'Singapore Art 1995' exhibition. Dressed for the occasion, Da Wu walked among the crowd in a black jacket with the words 'Don't Give Money to the Arts' emblazoned on the back. He reportedly 'weaved his way past the bodyguards', but was denied permission to speak to President Ong Teng Cheong, who nevertheless accepted the note. It read: 'I am an artist. I am important.'[2]

By all accounts in the art world, Tang Da Wu *is* an important artist. Born in 1943, he was by the mid-1990s already well-known in Singapore and the Asian region for an impressive corpus of work. It included not only drawing, painting, sculpture but also that broad category known as 'contemporary art' – installation, conceptual, environmental and performance art.[3] However, in his 1995 intervention – which could be considered performance art – he was neither identifying himself as an individual artist nor asserting his own importance. Rather, Da Wu's declaration to the public and the State (as represented by the President) prompted such questions as: 'What do artists do? Why are artists and the arts important?'

'Don't Give Money to the Arts', symbolically embroidered in gold thread, was not telling the Singapore State literally to stop funding the arts – when it had already adopted the development of the arts as part of the national agenda, as indicated, for example, by the establishment of a National Arts Council (NAC) in 1991. Indeed, the President's speech in 1995 repeated the current mantra: 'With greater affluence, we can now afford to pay more attention to improving the spiritual and cultural quality of life.'[4] But, in the previous year, the NAC had discontinued its funding for performance art in particular. This followed the charge made against a performance artist, Josef Ng, for having committed an 'obscene' act in public.[5] As dramatist Kuo Pao Kun (1939-2002), one of Singapore's leading intellectuals noted, this instance of discontinued funding amounted to a 'de facto ban' on an entire art form.[6] Da Wu's intervention raised questions about the interrelationships between the arts, politics, and money and, indeed, about the very idea of art – questions that have not been adequately addressed in Singapore and elsewhere.

Tang Da Wu has to answer particularly for having played a key role in the emergence of contemporary art in Singapore, not just as an individual artist but also as the founder of The Artists Village (TAV) in June 1988. Returning after nearly two decades of art studies and practice at Birmingham Polytechnic of Fine Art and, later, Goldsmiths College, London University,[7] he invited younger artists to share makeshift studio space at a farm in Lorong Gambas, Ulu Sembawang, which was then among the last remaining rural parts of Singapore.[8] Less than two years later, the land was requisitioned by the Government for urban redevelopment. The idyllic setting vanished overnight, but not the intense artistic energies that it unleashed, engendering new developments in the visual arts in Singapore over the next two decades.

TAV held its 'First Open Studio Show' in early 1989. This was followed by many public art activities held under its aegis – even after the artist-collective had long ceased to have its own physical space. In a brochure for the 'Second Open Studio Show' in mid-1989, the art historian, T.K. Sabapathy, wrote of the artists coming together 'in a cluster of zinc-roofed huts, with real farmers and chickens and pigs'.[9] The adjective 'real' pinned on to the farmers and animals ironically indicated that their existence might well have been unreal to the denizens of an almost totally urbanized city-state that had undergone 'perpetual territorial transformation' as part of a state-led modernization since Independence in 1965.[10] But the gestation of contemporary art in such surroundings, involving as many as 35 artists on site and 50 others in exhibitions, was palpably real, as Sabapathy guardedly observed: 'They wish to draw the viewer into an active dynamic relationship with the artwork, the artist and the process of creation. They have made positive beginnings. We wait to see their development.'[11]

For one thing, performance art – relatively new in Singapore – became a regular feature of the collective's agenda, with Da Wu as a leading practitioner. Lorong Gambas provided a unique setting for experimentation among artists and exposure of the art form to new audiences. At the 'Second Open Studio Show', for example, Da Wu's performances engaged viewers in reflecting on the issues of the day. *Gooseman* was one of his many performances relating to the relationship between human beings, animals, and the natural environment. With his

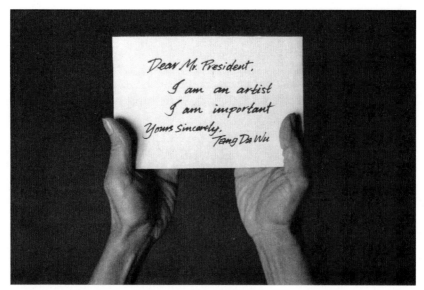

Tang Da Wu, Don't Give Money to the Arts, 1995
Photograph by Koh Nguang How, Courtesy of Singapore Art Archive, Project@Yishun

body painted white, Da Wu adopted the persona of a goose and, using gestures and sounds, communicated with the geese that he had brought up on the farm. The performance ended with him telling the audience: 'I speak English, I speak Chinese, I speak Goose Language.' At the same show, Da Wu, together with a few TAV members, also responded to the Tiananmen Square Massacre which had happened only days before. *Open the Gate* was an allegorical re-enactment of the clampdown on student protesters at Tiananmen (Gate of Heavenly Peace) by state power, drawing a parallel between the arduous journey taken by the students in campaigning for democracy and that of human souls in making their way to Heaven. The performance began in the cramped confines of a chicken coop with Da Wu under a wheelbarrow, which simulated the army tanks. Crawling out of a hole in the coop towards the fishpond – all the while pleading with Heaven to 'Open the Gate! Please Open the Gate!' – Da Wu, here an Everyman figure, found a brief resting place, perched precariously on a plank lying athwart the pond. He then fell into the water, struggling to keep afloat, and dragged himself towards a mound of earth where three towering incense sticks stood. Only then, with the symbol of the Gate of Heaven within reach did Da Wu, still in the water, make the final effort – he lit the incense sticks with a long torch, marking what could be said to be the end of his journey.[12]

Tang Da Wu, Gooseman, *1989*
Photograph by Koh Nguang How, Courtesy of Singapore Art Archive Project@Yishun

In his overview of 'Contemporary Art in Singapore', published since TAV's 'Second Open Studio Show', Sabapathy's wait-and-see tone gave way to a more decisive assessment of Da Wu's contribution to the shaping of a new milieu and an alternative to the mainstream practice. Established art was dominated by painting (and, to a lesser extent, sculpture), that is, by 'objects which are artifactually [*sic*] well-wrought, in which aestheticism is paramount, which exemplify formalistic properties and which are perceived as discrete entities'. Not only were artists who produced such works in the majority, 'the belief in essences, the conviction that a work of art encloses an inviolable universe, and the insistence that the work of art sustains an objective selfhood is deeply entrenched in the public here, and in the minds of very many artists and is fervently defended'. Against this, Da Wu's twofold contribution figured prominently in Sabapathy's discussion on the development of contemporary art in Singapore. On the one hand, the artists' colony that he founded was 'a vital centre for learning and practicing art, an alternative to the academies of art':

> it was an oasis, physically and spiritually. Da Wu provided working space for artistic activity and development, a facility sorely needed and difficult to gain access to in Singapore. He also generated conditions in which creativity was entered into and explored in an open, critical and self-questioning manner; creative practice entailed

Tang Da Wu, Open the Gate, *1989*
Photograph by Koh Nguang How, Courtesy of Singapore Art Archive Project@Yishun

not only making art but also developing critical and discussive dimensions, thereby enabling intentions and processes to be accountable and explicable. The Village was a beacon, and Da Wu both a catalyst and mentor.[13]

On the other hand, Da Wu's own artistic practice took him beyond the oasis that he and fellow artists created. His performance works in the late 1980s and early 1990s – notably *They Poach the Rhino, Chop Off His Horn and Make this Drink* (1989) and *Tiger's Whip* (1991), both of which questioned the Chinese practice of using animal parts as medicines and aphrodisiacs – led Sabapathy to conclude that 'Tang Da Wu, more than anyone else, has taken art into the public realm, testing the limits of practice and tolerance of that practice.' Departing and differing radically from established art practices, the multidisciplinary approaches of Da Wu and younger emerging artists involved 'earnestly re-examining the basis for art activity, and renegotiating and expanding connections between artists, art and the public'. Sabapathy captured a sense of how the public responded to these artists and their art: 'Their works, actions and gestures are met with a variety of responses, ranging from bewilderment to anxiety, and occasionally resistance and hostility.'[14]

I have quoted Sabapathy's carefully chosen words at some length because they serve as a springboard for my reflections on the significance of art and, in particular, *contemporary* art both in and beyond Singapore. It is not Tang Da Wu who has to answer for taking art into the public sphere and provoking a gamut of complex responses on the part of the public, an apparently amorphous and passive entity either taken for granted or conspicuously absent in discussions about art. To begin with, he won't. What we know about Da Wu, as an artist and as a person, suggests that he won't provide direct answers, and certainly not in so many words.[15] Although he has been described as 'charismatic' and 'enigmatic', it is his work which we engage with as 'art' and to which we must look for answers – and not his personality which he struggles to efface in his artistic practice.

Here I pause to clarify just who might be implied, if not implicated, by the collective pronoun 'we'. It refers broadly to all the persons and institutions that play a part in the making of the 'art world' in Singapore and the wider Asian region, which is now also part of a 'global art system' shaped by the activities and discourses associated with museums, biennales, and the international art market. The concept of an 'art world' suggests that 'art' is not just solely created – or defined as such – by individual artists or artist-collectives. As the philosopher, Arthur Danto, observed in 1964 when responding to Andy Warhol's *Brillo Box*, 'To see something as art requires something the eye cannot descry – an atmosphere of artistic theory, a knowledge of the history of art: an art world.'[16] An artwork, constituted as such, depends on the interpretation of its symbolic meanings and the 'mode of their embodiment' within a context of art history, theory, and criticism. This requires a 'discourse of reasons' rather than, as later suggested by George Dickie in his 'institutional theory of art', the mere conferment upon the artwork 'the status of candidate for appreciation' by persons and institutions in the art world (which begs questions of who qualifies for membership and what roles they play in institutionalizing art).[17] All this leads us to an expanded and more open-ended or porous notion of artworks as, in Howard Becker's formulation, 'joint products of all the people who cooperate via an art world's characteristic conventions to bring works like that into existence'.[18] Thus, in the case of contemporary art, the key participants in the art world, other than artists, include the following: critics and other art scholars or writers, art teachers, curators, museum professionals, arts administrators, collectors, gallery owners, dealers, and auction-house professionals.

Given the boom in the market for contemporary art – especially for Asian artworks – from the late 1990s until the global financial crisis of 2008, it might appear that the players in the art market, including speculators, are the most significant in determining the status of artworks.

The art market, however, is itself dependent on the larger art world, a 'symbolic economy' in which a multitude of persons and institutions contribute to the interpretive or cultural evaluation of any work as a work of art, and this in turn influences its commercial valuation.[19] Membership in the art world has its privileges, including that of playing a role in maintaining and shaping the social context within which works of art are understood and evaluated. But, precisely so, what is needed is a reflexive stance on the part of members of the art world, especially in placing oneself and one's role critically alongside other implicated persons and institutions, that is, with a self-questioning attitude and a sense of public accountability. Hence I am concerned here with clarifying the stakes in contemporary art.

To say that artworks are jointly produced by members of an art world is not to downplay or demean the creative efforts of individual artists. Without these efforts, and the sustained practice and experimentation on the part of artists and artist–collectives, the art world would be dominated by established conventions and maintained by mainstream gatekeepers. Da Wu and TAV, as Sabapathy suggests, broke through existing conventions and barriers – and at a time when contemporary art in Singapore was ill-understood and even resisted in the art world, including older-generation artists and state arts administrators, not to mention the wider public. The Village could not have come into existence either as a benign evolution of styles within a longstanding artistic community or as a top-down arts initiative launched by an arts council. Theoretically, if TAV had not come into existence, it would have been a matter of time before the Singapore art world faced the winds of newer artistic movements from elsewhere, whether or not it might have led to a productive tension between mainstream 'modern' art and alternative 'contemporary' art.

Indeed, artists such as Da Wu and his contemporary Cheo Chai-Hiang (b. 1946) – who studied at both Birmingham Polytechnic and Brighton Polytechnic – were personally well-placed to confront new paradigms of artistic practice in a self-critical and productive way. Both artists were educated in traditional Chinese schools and exposed to established painting techniques in Singapore; they were young members of the Modern Art Society in Singapore.[20] In particular, Da Wu has never abandoned drawing and painting, especially the use of Chinese ink, a medium which he continues to explore and reinvent, although retaining representational elements. His untitled self-portrait in oil (1986) – in which he is represented as imbibing *xin gaoyao* (the Chinese term meaning 'new medicine') from a gourd (traditionally used in China to contain herbal remedies and wine) – depicts a turning-point in his artistic life. Nearly two decades later, his self-portrait in ink, *The Village* (2005), recalls the atmosphere of the Lorong Gambas days, symbolized by the goose which, together with the durian, has been adopted by the post-Ulu artists as TAV emblems. In spite of his strengths in drawing, however, Da Wu considers installation and, especially, performance as his main art forms, although he has often incorporated drawings as part of his multimedia works.[21]

Tang and Cheo returned from England with a sense of creative mission that made a significant impact on the Singapore art world. Chai-Hiang's rejection of formalism, articulated in the early 1970s, was accompanied by other elements of contemporary art, especially a sense of personal and emotional engagement, a process-oriented approach, the use of everyday materials, and audience involvement in the process of art-making. His own 'total break from picture-making as the final destination' shifted his focus away from producing 'beautiful pictures' to the idea of 'art as a thought process', which involved 'a slow and rather painful process of changing myself'.[22] *Singapore River* (1972) constitutes an early defining moment in the emergence of contemporary art in Singapore. This was a submission for the annual Modern Art Society exhibition in Singapore. Mailed from England after Chai-Hiang's year of study there, it contained a spare set of instructions, requesting for the outlines of a square, five feet in dimension, to be drawn on a wall and floor, bearing the title 'Singapore River' – which was by the early 1970s a stereotypically iconic and lyrical subject matter among artists in Singapore. Not surprisingly, this act of calling into question the prevailing art conventions elicited a rejection from the Society, which reaffirmed the dominant paradigm in a letter in Chinese from Ho Ho Ying, an established older artist, stating his reasons in a passage that has often been quoted, including by Chai-Hiang himself when he magnified Ho's letter in a floor-to-ceiling installation, *Dear Cai Xiong* (2005).

> Art, besides being new, has to possess a special intrinsic quality in order to strike a sympathetic chord in the hearts of viewers. Imagine if an artist who erects a dead, dry tree in the middle of a large square and claims that it is art. The viewer can likewise point to a dead tree in the park and say it is art too. It is very confusing when an artist mixes art and non-art. I am a formalist, but I will not accept an art which can be casually picked up from anywhere; an art which does not involve an artist's additional effort and fine tuning in terms of improving its composition.[23]

In noting the invidious, even adversarial, way in which the distinction

Tang Da Wu, The Village, *(67x100mm), 2005*
Photograph by Koh Nguang How, Courtesy of Singapore Art Archive Project@Yishun

between art and non-art was defended by Ho, Sabapathy has argued that 'the artists who emerged in the latter half of the 1980s (including those affiliated with TAV) and who consolidated their ideals and practices in the 1990s can be appraised as breaking boundaries separating art from non-art spheres [or] … rendering these boundaries permeable.'[24] These emerging artists included S. Chandrasekaran, Goh Ee Choo, and Salleh Japar whose *Trimurti* show in March 1988, premised on the Hindu conception of Creation, Preservation, and Destruction (as represented by Brahma, Vishnu, and Shiva), sought to transform 'an art space into an energy space, an arena where a total happening takes place involving paintings, sculptures, installations and performances'; this event was regarded as 'one of the most encompassing, considered and intensively collaborative events mounted by artists in Singapore'.[25]

Chai-Hiang's critical interventions as an individual artist, the *Trimurti* artists' multidisciplinary and collaborative works as a trio, and TAV's programmatic efforts in engaging the public as an artist-collective were quite independent of each other, but they received recognition from critics and curators, and opened up the institutional spaces for contemporary art in Singapore. As an artist-collective, TAV strove to rejuvenate itself over time. In February 1992, the collective became an officially registered art society under Singapore's Societies Act, which made its members eligible for state funding from the then newly-established National Arts Council. However, they failed to secure a space under the Council's arts housing scheme and, given the official nervousness about performance and experimental art in the mid-1990s, many of the Village artists went on to follow their individual directions, often outside of Singapore. In 1999, a younger generation of 'Post-Ulu' (that is, post-Village) artists, who were not part of the original nucleus in Ulu Sembawang, reorganized the collective, reinvigorating it with a series of art projects which, in turn, continued to expand the scope of contemporary art in Singapore.

When the Singapore Art Museum (SAM) was established in 1996, it took a keen interest in collecting and exhibiting Singapore art, including the works of many of the Village artists, such as Chng Seok Tin, M. Faizal Fadil, Amanda Heng, Koh Nguang How, Lee Wen, Vincent Leow, Lim Poh Teck, Tang Da Wu, Jose Tence Ruiz, Wong Shih Yeow, and Zai Kuning. In August 2008, SAM and the 'Post-Ulu' artists jointly curated and presented the exhibition 'The Artists Village: 20 Years On'.[26] This modest exhibition elicited at least two kinds of responses. First, it was seen as marking two decades of eventful contemporary art development, focusing on the contributions of a single artist-collective that was founded on alternative artistic ideals and sustained by creative effort. Kuo Pao Kun's view is pertinent here which is that, for an independent arts group, keeping true to its artistic vision while lacking support, mere survival in the longer term is itself a remarkable achievement, not least because this enables it to make breakthroughs when conditions change for the better.[27] Bereft of a physical home after a couple of years, TAV's members took art into public spaces and worked with multiple partners, developing what Russell Storer has described as 'a responsive, collaborative approach that has been highly influential locally, as well as connecting to international tendencies in contemporary art and curatorial practice'.[28]

In Singapore today, the kinds of energies manifested in TAV's earliest shows, and in Da Wu's performances, are few and far between. Since the early 1990s, the relationship between artists and the public realm has been progressively mediated by state institutions, such as the National Arts Council and the National Heritage Board (established in 1993, it also oversees the development of public museums). This leads me to consider the second kind of response to the 2008 exhibition at SAM. At the risk of appearing cynical, one may ask what it means for the short but significant history of an independent artist-collective to be commemorated in a state-sponsored museum. The title – 'The Artists Village: 20 Years On' – is interestingly ambivalent. It suggests a retrospective which, by definition, historicizes a particular period of art-making, and, given a museum museumizes, makes the past *past* or 'safe' in the gaze of the present. At the same time, the title sounds a forward-looking note, symbolically ushering a new phase into existence and, to be sure, the curators in the exhibition brochure enjoined audiences to 'understand [TAV's] artistic activities, objectives and practices, as well as the tensions, disjuncture and collision of the individual and collective memories' of the Village.

The larger institutional context within which the Village as a collective has been given some kind of recognition is significant: 'alternative art' as a movement – and 'alterity' as an ideal – have been inscribed and legitimized as a part of national art history. The official magazine of the National Heritage Board, announcing the opening of a new wing of SAM at Queen Street dedicated to showcasing contemporary art, introduces Marcel Duchamp's *Fountain* (1917) with reference to Vincent Leow's *The Artist's Urine,* performed at Body Fields in 1993, a performance which is described as the artist's 'daring act of urine consumption'; and concludes that 'The Artists Village's members are today acknowledged trailblazers who engaged a public more used to traditional painted canvases and bronze casts'.[29] A bottle of urine on display at the SAM retrospective was accompanied by a curatorial text which explained that the gesture was a statement about 'how sacrifices are needed' in light of the 'difficulties faced by artists in Singapore'. There was perhaps a heroic subtext embedded in the commemoration of TAV's twentieth anniversary and this tracing of the lineage of Leow's *The Artist's Urine* to Duchamp's use of a manufactured urinal: Singapore, it would seem, had come a long way in embracing contemporary art not only through the efforts of trailblazers among artists and other participants in the art world, such as art critics, scholars, and curators, but also the efforts of enlightened state institutions.

Contemporary art, although embodying critical and pluralistic voices, is also now pressed into service in the functioning of an ambitious global city that has, as the state rhetoric goes, to keep 'reinventing' itself in order to 'stay relevant'. Borrowing from Sabapathy's earlier analyses, Wee Wan-Ling argues that the state-led modernization of the post-Independence era brought about homogenizing but also disruptive and alienating conditions, which paradoxically facilitated the emergence of new art movements. This resulted in 'newer forms of cultural pluralism that challenged the existing, constrictive, petit-bourgeois and therefore "philistine" socio-cultural forms the state valorized'; however, in the 'ongoing reinvention', as reflected in the Singapore Biennale 2006, 'the creative and critical sociocultural energies that Tang Da Wu and the Artists Village helped release in the 1980s are already in the process of being contained and instrumentalized'.[30]

The mention of the inaugural Singapore Biennale is not accidental. The fact that it was organized in conjunction with the annual meetings of the International Monetary Fund and World Bank Board of Governors, congregating the captains of finance and business, made it an easy target for the criticism that Singapore had staged the first Biennale as part of the projection of its image as a vibrant and creative global city. While one of its co-curators, Eugene Tan, notes that this was 'very much symptomatic of the role that art festivals and biennales have come to play in the age of globalization … where everything, even art, has been subsumed by the interests of global capitalism', he also argues that 'it was successful as a platform for furthering the conditions of the production and reception of contemporary art in Singapore'.[31] But, given the confluence of interests among state agencies, corporations, and art worlds, how should the 'success' of a biennale be evaluated? Ranger Mills, a New York artist based in Singapore, commented trenchantly that the second Singapore Biennale (2008) was shaped by the 'perceived need to have a creative basis within the society to serve economic development' and 'to provide the illusion of sophisticated cosmopolitan graciousness'. He adds that

> everyone sort of knows this, yet all cleave to the scenario of accepting it and then accommodate to the rigours and limitations of this system. There is no 'equal and opposite' reaction in the form of breakaway systems of independent, creative, cultural production. The effect is internalised and everyone ... is complicit in accepting the protocol. ... so what you do get is a pressure that is exerted through the different functionary groups within this system. ... Because everyone shares guilt, everyone is aware of the other's immoral position. [32]

This scenario reminds me of analyses of totalitarian or fascist systems which are said to be propped up not so much by efficient and rational administrative control by the upper echelons of leadership as by the pervasive and perverse moral corruption of ordinary people practising bad faith in everyday life. If there is any grain of truth in such analyses as applied to the situation of contemporary art, it must be said that the phenomenon is not unique to Singapore. It is symptomatic of the overarching ideological framework of the globalized art system incisively critiqued by Julian Stallabrass: 'That the very concerns of art – creativity, enlightenment, criticality, self-criticism – are as instrumentally grounded as what they serve to conceal – business, state triage, and war – is the consideration that must be concealed.' In particular, 'art's weightless sign-swapping' is analogous to the commodification of everything under the conditions of capitalism, and it is rare to find artistic work that 'does not seek to mystify itself or flatter viewers by assuring them of their own depthless profundity'. [33]

In addition to the usefulness of contemporary art to the state and corporations, two other related phenomena may be highlighted. On the one hand, although contemporary art is often positioned *vis-à-vis* 'popular culture', the radical shift away from the so-called elitism of traditional fine art has also entailed drawing from, and feeding into, the wider 'visual culture' such that, as Thomas Crow says, 'a postmodern outlook can afford no exclusion of the Hollywood films, television productions, glossy advertisements, computer graphics, and all the other enticing visual products of the age.' [34] This also raises issues about the relationship between contemporary art and profit-driven cultural industries whose effects, as David Hesmondhalgh has argued, are 'complex, ambivalent and contested'. [35] On the other hand, the relationship between art and money has taken on mind-boggling dimensions in a spiralling international art market awash with speculative capital. The recent global crisis has exposed the lack of regulation and responsible conduct among banks and financial institutions – and what's more in the art market, which Robert Hughes referred to in 1978 as 'the last refuge of nineteenth-century laissez-faire capitalism', and arguably remains unchanged today.[36] Valuation or pricing in contemporary art, as Don Thompson blithely explains with reference to Damien Hirst's *The Physical Impossibility of Death in the Mind of Someone Living*, also known as 'the $12 million stuffed shark', is in part determined by branding, which 'in the world of contemporary art, can substitute for critical judgement' and, in this case, 'lots of branding was involved here', not least on the part of the artist himself.[37] The very idea that branding can be substituted for critical judgement is itself problematic, especially in the art world where criticality and self-criticism are putatively its core values. The public imagination, influenced by media, is also captured by aggressive branding or sensationalist reporting of developments in the art world.

In this respect, in spite of the national rhetoric on the importance of the arts and creativity, the situation in Singapore, if we are to judge by only the English-language media, may have deteriorated in recent decades. Arts reporting, when it is not submerged under the plethora of news on popular entertainment, often covers everything else – auction prices, collectors' profiles, high society events, ministers' speeches, and state censorship – rather than art, artists, and artworks. The public reception of contemporary art, especially TAV and the art-making of its members, was once mediated by art critics. Sabapathy and T. Sasitharan wrote informed newspaper reviews of exhibitions and artworks, even as the emerging artists were dismissed by some established artists as 'self-indulgent amateurs' or by others as being 'radical for the sake of being radical'.[38] As mentioned earlier, public responses to their works ranged from bafflement to resentment. Any of these responses may be genuinely warranted and no artist or artwork should be above critical judgement, especially when there are proclivities towards gratuitous use of shock tactics and self-mystification in contemporary art, eliciting responses analogous to 'the emperor has no clothes'. By not nurturing a succeeding generation of art critics and arts reviewers (as opposed to arts reporters) who advance the public understanding of art, the media today routinely feature facile and facetious remarks on contemporary art, supposedly in sympathy with readers perplexed by the shifting distinctions between art and non-art.[39]

Critical judgement is all the more required for contemporary art, with its aspirations to being an 'art of ideas' engaging audiences in ways not available through other mediums, and not the kind of 'political art' whose effectiveness in changing public opinion pales in significance when compared with 'events, arguments, press photographs, and TV'.[40] This returns us to the question of the stakes in contemporary art, especially at a time when, on the one hand, it has proven useful in serving political and business interests and, on the other, it has tendencies towards 'weight-lessness' and 'depthlessness', eliciting mixed responses from the public. This again is not unique to Singapore. Consider the titles of two recent reflections by experienced practitioners in the English-speaking art world: Julian Spalding's *The Eclipse of Art* and Peter Timms' *What's Wrong with Contemporary Art?* In discussing 'the crisis in art today', Spalding concludes that 'the concept of the modern avant-garde – the licensed uselessness of art – has been just as restrictive and destructive, in its way, as prescriptions about the social usefulness of art.'[41] Arguing for 'art that is more respectful towards, yet at the same time more demanding of, its audience, art that is neither facile nor wilfully abstruse, rewarding patience, knowledge and dedication', Timms adds:

> we need to shut down the so-called arts industry, drive off the money changers, hucksters and spruikers and acknowledge that art is not merely a business, an entertainment, an expression of national pride, or a substitute for political action, but a means of asking serious and profound questions about who we are, where we have come from, and where we might be going. [42]

It is tempting to adopt Timms' ringing words as a conclusion. However, critical participants in the art world today, including artists, will find it impossible to eliminate cultural industries, monetary interests, and political influences – all of which have become interpenetrated in the globalized art system, giving short shrift to art's capacity for 'asking serious and profound questions'. The art world cannot be hermetically sealed off from worldly interests, and even if some consider art as a sacred realm, artists have to confront what it means to be *in* but not *of* the world. I am reminded here of Edward Said on the public role of writers and intellectuals, which seems to me is as compellingly applicable to artists. Agreeing with Theodore Adorno, Said argues that ultimately 'one of the hallmarks of modernity is how at a very deep level, the aesthetic and the social need to be kept, and often consciously kept, in a state of irreconcilable tension.'[43] Culture as industry, business, and entertainment constitutes 'mass deception' or the breaking of the promise of art in providing us 'with valuable new and authentic experiences that will further the development of our sensibilities and that will permit us to maintain our awareness of alternative possibilities'.[44]

The potential of contemporary art lies in its 'disciplined exploration of ideas and processes' in which 'we develop ideas, make associations … we speculate about the nature of things; we cogitate; we explore other possibilities and we try to make the world more open [and] also respond to change'; in this way, art should be 'read' rather than 'looked at' since to simply look at something does not constitute a critical appraisal'.[45] For Da Wu, art 'makes statements' and, as he says in a 1991 interview on sculpture in Singapore, an artwork should not be thought of 'in terms of a polished object, which people can possess and keep in glass cases or whatever'.

> Here, in Singapore the insistence is on art as commodity. But there are other interests. What of concepts, and showing concepts? These concepts are unpolished … yet they are still very important as artworks or as statements … which can be collected. In this way the artist is questioning: What is art? What is craft? What is it to look at things and understand things? … the concept, thinking as art, is all within that process. But you can't look at things just as objects. … I think that whoever collects art here should pay more attention to the kind of art I am talking about.[46]

Although Da Wu suggests that conceptual artworks are collectable, he is critical of the commodification of art and his work has not been oriented to the art market. In particular, time-based performance art cannot be collected as such, even though recording and documentation extends its reach to a wider public. When asked by a reporter from *Xinming Ribao*, a local Chinese newspaper, whether a performance artist could earn a livelihood without presenting 'concrete' artworks for sale, Da Wu expressed disappointment at her question; for him, a performance event, although ephemeral, has its own value in 'provoking thought' (*jifa guanzhong de siwei*).[47] In so doing, Da Wu's artistic practice eschews crude sloganeering or wilful obfuscation; his installations and performances are based on detailed research and executed with craftsmanship, paying attention to specific sites and audiences. Throughout the 1990s, he also conducted many workshops with students in Singapore and overseas, including them in projects such as *Tapioca Friendship Workshop* (1995 and 1996), *Life in a Tin* (1999), and *Jantung Pisang: The Heart of the Banana* (1999). These projects engaged themes related to the material life, political economy, social history, and natural environment of Southeast Asia, and has been characterized by Lucy Davis as 'serious play with psycho-geography and public memory'.[48]

Intellectuals in Singapore have postulated that as a nation-state Singapore represents a case of 'modernization without modernity' – that is, it has all the superficial trappings and concrete benefits brought about by relentless state-driven modernization, which however does not engender critical reflexivity and personal autonomy.[49] If this is true, then art and intellectual life in Singapore is either woefully impoverished or totally instrumentalized, having no critical presence in the public sphere. John Carey argues that literature is 'the only art ... that can criticize anything, because it is the only art capable of reasoning', in keeping with his thesis that 'a vital element in all literature is indistinctness' which 'generates multiple individual readings'.[50] The same argument could be made for contemporary art, which also involves multiple readings in the intellectual engagement with ideas and concepts. Equally, where Said speaks of the role of invention in intellectual work, I would suggest, too, its applicability to contemporary art:

> [One] invents goals abductively – in the literal use of the Latin word '*inventio*' employed by rhetoricians to stress finding again, or reassembling from past performances, as opposed to the romantic use of invention as something you can create from scratch. That is, one hypothesizes a better situation from the known historical and social facts. So, in effect, this enables intellectual performances on many fronts, in many places, many styles that keep in play both the sense of opposition and the sense of engaged participation. [51]

Indeed, among other things, contemporary art *is* about invention rather than creating something out of little or nothing, as suggested in the hackneyed and hollow notion of creativity that is peddled as the necessary ingredient of capitalist entrepreneurialism. Tang Da Wu's artistic practice has rested on finding sources and resources from past exemplars, drawing materials and ideas from history, tradition, and the environment – re-assembling and re-enacting them in multiple sites and ways that oppose the fixity of the historically and socially given, and engage our sense of alternative possibilities. That his art could have developed on Singapore soil belies any totalizing depiction of the nation-state as the epitome of 'modernization without modernity': it thus keeps alive the ideal of artistic autonomy in a world that tends to incorporate every iota of creativity for its own purposes.

NOTES

1. Tang Da Wu requested not to be formally interviewed for this essay, deflecting attention away from himself and recommending that younger emerging artists be featured. I rely primarily on published sources and, where appropriate (and publicly verifiable), I draw observations from my association – and many discussions – with him and my involvement in the arts in Singapore since the early 1990s. I also refer to Da Wu by the name he has used since the 1970s, in keeping with how he is informally known to artists and art students in Singapore.

2. See 'Pay More Attention to the Arts – President', *The Straits Times*, 12 August 1995, and Sian E. Jay, 'Ironic Twist', *The Straits Times*, 1 November 2000. The latter refers to the apparent irony of Da Wu's donation of the jacket to be auctioned to raise funds for The Substation, a multidisciplinary arts centre. By that time, as Jay notes, the jacket had become 'a piece of Singapore art history'.

3. See, for example, the citation for Da Wu being considered 'a truly worthy recipient for the Arts and Culture Prize of the Fukuoka Asian Culture Prizes' in 1999, especially with reference to his art and his pioneering contributions to the development of contemporary art in Southeast Asia throughout the 1980s and 1990s <www.asianmonth.com/prize/english/winner/10_04.html> accessed 11 April 2008.

4. 'Pay More Attention to the Arts – President', *The Straits Times*, 12 August 1995.

5. Ng's performance, which alluded to the biased media reporting on homosexuality in Singapore, involved a segment where he snipped his pubic hair with his back to the audience. He pleaded guilty to the charge.

6. Kuo Pao Kun, 'Repositioning the Arts', *The Arts Magazine*, Nov/Dec 1999. The ban was rescinded only in 2003.

7. See a summary of his background in <www.nac.gov.sg/eve/eve12.asp> accessed 11 April 2008.

8. Kwok Kian Chow, *Channels & Confluences: A History of Singapore Art* (Singapore: National Heritage Board/Singapore Art Museum, 1996), p. 142.

9. As quoted in Kwok, *Channels & Confluences*, p. 144.

10. See Rodolphe de Koninck, Julie Drolet, and Marc Girard, *Singapore: An Atlas of Perpetual Territorial Transformation* (Singapore: NUS Publishing, 2008). An oft-quoted joke in Singapore: when asked by art teachers to draw chickens, schoolchildren invariably draw chickens without feathers, resembling what is served at fast food restaurants.

11. As quoted in Kwok, *Channels & Confluences*, p. 144. To be sure, earlier beginnings were marked by Tan Teng Kee's *Picnic* (1979) and Tang Da Wu's *Gullies* (1979).

12. The details regarding these two performances were provided by Tang Da Wu and Koh Nguang How, also an early TAV artist, who had single-handedly documented Da Wu's performance art through photography from 1988 to 2000.

13. T.K. Sabapathy, 'Contemporary Art in Singapore: An Introduction', in *Tradition and Change: Contemporary Art in Singapore and the Asia Pacific*, ed., Caroline Turner (Queensland: U of Queensland P, 1993), p. 88.

14. Sabapathy, 'Contemporary Art', p. 85.

15. Sian E. Jay asked the 'notoriously shy' artist about his 'Don't Give Money to the Arts' intervention and found that, characteristically, 'Tang rarely makes straightforward statements. Answers to direct questions are couched in metaphor and allusion. He forces you to think and interpret for yourself, so that even his conversation becomes part of his art.' 'Ironic Twist to Substation Fund-raiser', *The Straits Times*, 15 November 2000.

16. Arthur C. Danto, *Beyond the Brillo Box: The Visual Arts in Post-Historical Perspective* (Berkeley: U of California P, 1992), p. 41.

17. George Dickie, *Art and the Aesthetic* (Ithaca: Cornell UP, 1974), p. 204.

18. Howard S. Becker, *Art Worlds* (Berkeley: U of CP, 1984), pp. 34–35.

19. See, for example, Olav Velthius, *Talking Prices: Symbolic Meanings of Prices on the Market for Contemporary Art* (Princeton: Princeton UP, 2005); Sarah Thornton, *Seven Days in The Art World* (New York: W.W. Norton, 2008).

20. Da Wu grew up in an immigrant Teochew household whose visitors included the Nanyang artist, Fan Chang Tien (1907–1987), a friend of his father, Tang Xue Zhi

(known as Tang Shi Qing in his newspaper columns). He attended the primary school where his father taught Chinese. Da Wu then studied at the Thomson Government Chinese Middle School, where he first met Cheo Chai-Hiang, marking the beginning of a lifelong friendship between two.

21. See, for example, his installation and performance *They Poach the Rhino, Chop off His Horn and Make this Drink* (1991), documented in *Asia Collection 70: From the Collection of the Fukuoka Asian Art Museum* (Japan: Fukuoka City Foundation for Arts and Cultural Production, 2007), pp. 54-55.

22. Cheo Chai-Hiang, 'New Art, New Concepts' (1972) and 'Essay' (1975), in T.K. Sabapathy and Cecily Briggs, *Cheo Chai-Hiang: Thoughts and Processes* (Singapore: Nanyang Academy of Fine Arts and Singapore Art Museum, 2000), pp. 115 and 122.

23. Quoted in Sabapathy and Briggs, *Cheo Chai-Hiang: Thoughts and Processes*, p. 12. See also Ahmad Mashad, 'Southeast Asian Art during the 1970s', in the exhibition publication *Telah Terbit (Out Now): Southeast Asian Contemporary Art Practices* (Singapore: Singapore Art Museum, 2007), pp. 53-54. The *Dear Cai Xiong* installation is featured on p. 55, 'Cai Xiong' being Cheo's personal name in *hanyu pinyin*.

24. T.K. Sabapathy, 'Paradigm Shifts and Histories of Art', in *Selves: The State of the Arts in Singapore*, eds, Kwok Kian-Woon, Arun Mahizhnan and T. Sasitharan (Singapore: National Arts Council, 2002), p. 83.

25. T.K. Sabapathy, 'Trimurti: Thoughts on Contexts', in *Trimurti and Ten Years After* (Singapore: Singapore Art Museum, 1998), p. 23; the artists' statement is quoted on p. 25.

26. See articles and documentation on the exhibition in Kwok Kian-Woon and Lee Wen, eds, *The Artists Village: 20 Years On* (Singapore: Singapore Art Museum, 2009).

27. As well as his artistic and intellectual achievements, Kuo was also the founder of the Practice Performing Arts School in 1965 and The Substation in 1990.

28. Russell Storer, 'The Artists Village: Collaboration as Transformation', in *The Artists Village: 20 Years On*, eds, Kwok and Lee, p. 5.

29. Marcus Ng, 'Contemporary Art, With Class', *BeMUSE*, 5:1 (2008) 28-37.

30. Wee Wan-Ling, 'Tang Da Wu and Contemporary Art in Singapore', in *The Artists Village: 20 Years On*, eds, Kwok and Lee, p. 19.

31. Eugene Tan, 'Believing in Art: The Singapore Biennale', *New Asian Imagination*, eds, Samuel Lee and Chan Hsiao-Yun (Singapore: Nanyang Academy of Fine Arts, 2008), p. 39.

32. See 'The Biennale: Proposing Alternative – Part II, A Talk With Ranger Mills', *Singapore Art Gallery Guide* 4:10 (2008) 10-14.

33. Julian Stallabrass, *Contemporary Art: A Very Short Introduction* (New York: Oxford UP, 2004), pp. 124 and 134.

34. Thomas Crow, *Modern Art in the Common Culture* (New Haven and London: Yale UP, 1996), p. vii.

35. David Hesmondhalgh, *The Cultural Industries* (London: SAGE Publications, 2002), p. 3.

36. Robert Hughes, *Nothing if not Critical: Selected Essays on Art and Artists* (USA: Penguin Books, 1990) p. 236.

37. Don Thompson, *The $12 Million Stuffed Shark* (London: Aurum Press, 2008), p. 1.

38. Seng Yu Jin, 'Re-visiting the Emergence of The Artists Village', in *The Artists Village: 20 Years On*, eds, Kwok and Lee, p. 13.

39. See, for example, the following articles in *The Straits Times*: Jeremy Au Yong, 'More Arty Than Farty', 23 August 2008; 'Art? We Don't Get It' (Editorial), 31 August 2008; Ong Sor Fern, 'Why I Prefer David Over Spacemen', 18 September 2008.

40. Robert Hughes, *Culture of Complaint: A Passionate Look into the Ailing Heart of America*

(New York: Warner Books, 1993), p. 186.

41. Julian Spalding, *The Eclipse of Art: Tackling the Crisis in Art Today* (Munich: Prestel, 2003), p. 115.
42. Peter Timms, 'Introduction' in *What's Wrong with Contemporary Art?* (Sydney: U of New South Wales P, 2004), p. 13.
43. Edward Said, *Humanism and Democratic Criticism* (New York: Columbia UP, 2004), p. 129.
44. Heinz Steinert, *Culture Industry* (Cambridge: Polity Press, 2003), p. 27.
45. Cheo Chai-Hiang, 'Written for the Occasion of 8th Modern Art Exhibition' and 'Artist Statement' in Sabapathy and Briggs, *Cheo Chai-Hiang: Thoughts and Processes*, pp. 119, 126.
46. Interview with Tang Da Wu, in T.K. Sabapathy, *Sculpture in Singapore* (Singapore: National Museum Art Gallery, 1991), p. 55.
47. 'Biao Yan Yi Shu' ('Performance Art'), *Xinming Ribao,* 1 August 1987.
48. Lucy Davis, 'Of Commodities and Kings: Tang Da Wu's Serious Play with Psycho-Geography and Public Memory', *Art Asia Pacific*, 25 (2000) 63.
49. The phrase 'modernization without modernity' is attributed to Tay Kheng Soon, an architect and public intellectual in Singapore.
50. John Carey, *What Good are the Arts?* (Oxford: Oxford UP, 2006), pp. 177, 214.
51. Edward Said, *Humanism and Democratic Criticism*, p. 140.

From a Theatre of Politics to the Politics of Theatre: Ong Keng Sen and Interculturalism

K.K. SEET

Internationally Ong Keng Sen is probably Singapore's best known and recognized theatre practitioner, and is much sought after as collaborator and initiator of cutting-edge artistic projects worldwide.[1] In Singapore, however, his aesthetic and craft, the *raison d'être* behind his approach to theatre and performance, are much misunderstood, even maligned by theatre, academic, and media critics.[2] The criticisms include: increasingly deserting the directorial for the curatorial function; capitulating to Western global cosmopolitanism while supposedly articulating the new Asia in his productions; a facile interculturalism that pays scant attention to the economic implications of late capitalism; hot-housing traditional Asian performative genres under the guise of revivifying and reinventing them; and over-indulgence in an anti-linear, anti-narrative postmodern aesthetic that blatantly ignores audience competence and receptivity. His attempts to ban from his productions critics and reviewers whom he considers unequal to the appreciation of his praxis have only served to reinforce hostile perceptions.[3]

Ong's intercultural productions – *Lear, Desdemona,* and *Search: Hamlet* – are among his most widely discussed works; they have also come in for more than their fair share of criticism, the result of what Robin Loon has identified as the Ideologist Approach to intercultural theatre.[4] Loon attributes this approach to Rustom Bharucha who, in his critique of *Lear,* for example, uses an *a priori* political and theoretical apparatus which has more to do with cultural studies than performance analysis.[5] On his part, Loon prefers the text-imminent Analytic Approach, which explores 'intercultural theatre as a specialized performance practice by studying how it operates, the resources it mobilizes to make itself communicable and how it presents the audience with a set of hybridized coordinates to be decoded'.[6]

The Analytic Approach is also the one I will adopt to examine Ong's most recent intercultural productions – *Sandakan Threnody, Global Soul,* and *Geisha.* This trio, in putting to rest the texts from the Shakespeare canon, transcends what Bharucha calls 'two monolithic entities – Asia and Shakespeare', not to mention their 'potentially conflictual relationships: Asia in Shakespeare, Shakespeare in Asia; Asia without Shakespeare, and Shakespeare without Shakespeare'.[7] This paper argues that in these three works, Ong has moved beyond his earlier experimentation phase. Perhaps, after the vexations of, and controversies over, his Shakespeare trilogy, Ong, as one reviewer succinctly puts it, is finally 'a free man: free of the burden of giving an Asian take on a dead white male text', and also someone 'made lighter by the spirit of travels and regenerated by new collaborations with some of the best artistes in the world'.[8]

Nonetheless, it is worth noting that the three recent intercultural productions continue to bear some of Ong's signature traits. Throughout his oeuvre Ong has sought to give voice to the voiceless, and to correct the misperceptions arising from cultural myopia. These preoccupations have endured in an artistic career which can be divided into two broad phases. First, his stint at the New York University Tisch School of the Arts pursuing an MFA in Directing (1993-94) may be seen as the transitional point. In the late 1980s and early 1990s, he was responsible for what might be termed a theatre of politics in Singapore which touched on taboo subjects in defiance of the State's draconian order. In 1988, his *Safe Sex* double bill demolished myths and misconceptions concerning AIDS, thereby drawing attention to the disenfranchised homosexual community and marginalized HIV victims in Singapore. In the early 1990s, Ong spearheaded the production of the first two parts of Eleanor Wong's ground-breaking trilogy, *Invitation to Treat*,[9] thereby giving the lesbian figure a human face as well as challenging orthodox views of gender roles and sexual orientation. Another major socially engaged production of this period was Tan Tarn How's *Six of the Best* (1996). Based on the caning of the American teenager, Michael Fay, it dissected racial relations, and addressed such issues as the import of so-called 'foreign talent' and postcolonial tensions.

After his New York years, and into the second phase of his career, Ong contemplated a larger canvas. The matrix was no longer Singapore as such, but Singapore within Asia and Asia within the world. The need to shatter what Ong often characterizes as a 'conspiracy of silence', which has obscured stories of trauma and histories of human dignity, galvanized him to bring to the surface true life stories, such as that of the seventy-year-old classical dancer, E.M. Theay of Cambodia, who survived the horrors and mass killings of Pol Pot and the Khmer Rouge. Apart from their topicality, these productions, such as the 2001 docu-drama, *The Continuum:*

Beyond the Killing Fields, serve to explore today's Asia through confrontation with both self and history.

Destinies of Flowers in the Mirror (1997), gathering some 300 people at the monumental fountain in downtown Singapore's Suntec City, reflects this trend by examining oppression and genocide; *Descendants of the Eunuch Admiral* (1995) looks figuratively at varied forms of castration through the historical personage of the Ching imperial era, Admiral Zheng He; *Broken Birds* (1995) delineates the plight of the *karayukisan*, the 'comfort women' of the Japanese Occupation; and *Workhorse Afloat* (1997) makes visible the plight and treatment of foreign workers in Singapore. In this second phase, Ong also initiated *The Flying Circus Project*, an ambitious performance laboratory held biennially, consisting of classes, workshops, improvisation sessions, and seminars with the twin goals in view of cultural negotiation between diverse Asian performative genres and the reinvention of Asian traditions and practices. These were to spawn various intercultural productions in the late 1990s and at the turn of the century.

Under Ong's Artistic Directorship, the attempts of TheatreWorks to position Asian perspectives on the world stage, and 'forge a different relationship to intercultural performance than what has developed in the United States, for instance',[10] can be said to mark its transition from a theatre of politics to a politics of theatre, from dissection of the nation-state's body politic to negotiating the interface of theatre-making in the global arena. This, to Ong, is about re-educating the ordinary spectator. It is also 'about Asians having the choice not only to reinvent ourselves but also reinvent others'.[11] This explains the insistence on 'appropriating Shakespeare to say something else'[12] in his earlier trilogy, since reinvention, and crucially reinvention as political action, calls for reference to an established standard.

It is important to note that Ong's involvement in *Sandakan Threnody* was not the result of deliberate positioning or calculated solicitation. He was in fact approached by the composer Jonathan Mills to expand an original 30-minute orchestral piece into a 90-minute theatrical production.[13] The two had met socially in Sydney in July 2001 and discovered they were both working on some aspect of the World War II. The idea of the *Sandakan Threnody* was also timely in view of contemporaneous events, such as the US Army's abuse of power in Iraq. After a two-year hunt for funding, a collaboration ensued when Singapore Arts Festival programming director, Goh Ching Lee, and her Australian Arts Festival counterpart, Robyn Archer, expressed an interest.

Owing to its subject and presentational mode, *Sandakan Threnody* is not an easy work to digest. It is based on an event which occurred at the end of the Japanese Occupation of Southeast Asia, when 2,345 Allied POWs – the majority of whom were Australians apart from some local Malays – were forced marched the distance of 420 kilometres from Sandakan to Ranau in North Borneo by Japanese soldiers. Only six survived to tell the tale. With its graphic accounts of bayonetings, crucifixions, disembowelments, even cannibalism, conjoined with music, dance, historical narrative, theatre and documentary film, *Sandakan Threnody* is a multilayered, multidimensional piece that spills over with an excess of moments and meanings. What the composer describes as 'musical archeology'[14] is the manner in which the original symphonic piece has been deconstructed and remoulded by Ong to complement or counterpoint the dramaturgy from moment to moment, such that beauty and brutality are always kept in precarious tension and delicately balanced. Like most of Ong's later works, *Sandakan Threnody* demands vigilant decoding of the subtleties of its semiology. The long and arduous process of its evolution from idea to stage production informs not just the piece in its totality but also each strand of the *gesampkunstwerk,* from its musicology and soundscapes to the assembly of talents in its production. A reconnaissance of that trajectory will also cast light on the amount of thought that went into its making.

Sandakan Threnody had its origins in Jonathan Mills' memories of his father's accounts of the war. Frank Mills was a surgeon with the Australian Field Ambulance in Singapore in 1942 when he was captured and sent to Changi Prison and, later, to Sandakan. Mills who escaped the death march when he was summarily dispatched to Kuching was stunned eighteen months later by the news that only six from the Sandakan camp had survived. However, he could recall, too, acts of great honour and dignity by the Japanese forces.[15] These stories handed on by his father inspired Jonathan Mills to compose the original orchestral piece commemorating the victims of the Sandakan death march. Like his father, Mills was disinclined to apportion blame and saw the war as an occasion which revealed the fragility of humanity. Mills found Ong's non-linear style appropriate to his intent to avoid either a straight narrative or historical document. In delineating multiple perspectives, political as well as personal, Mills wanted to assert the importance of collective restraint.

In expanding his composition into a full-length score, Mills conceived its musical development in terms of three movements to enable Ong to devise the appropriate dramaturgical strategies with a multicultural cast. Performed by the Sydney Symphony Orchestra, each movement was intended to allude to a musical archetype. The first movement is an instrumental overture with references to the subtle timbre of traditional Japanese music, like the *gagaku*, interspersed among the aggressive notes of orchestra percussion. As the shortest of the three movements, its brevity also serves as a comment on the abrupt incursion of the brutality of war. The second movement, for obvious reasons, features a march reflecting the deteriorating state of the POWs and sporadic flashes of outrage. This was scored for solo tenor and chorus, and drew its afflatus from two texts. One was the Penitential Psalm 130 used in liturgical prayers for the faithful departed. In this context, the core rhythmic motif was based on a Morse code transcription of the Latin words: *De profundis clamavi ad te Domine* ('Out of the depths do I cry unto thee, O Lord'). Mills' intention was to effect a connection between a dead language, Latin, and a dead technological language, the Morse code, in order to express the tragic dimensions of the death march. The other text was a fragment of a 1930s poem by the Russian poet, Anna Akhmatova, who displayed a quiet optimism in her work, although censored and incarcerated for much of her life. The combination of the two sources, and their transmutation into a musical text, was designed to evoke the complex feelings of guilt, grief, and hope among the POWs.

The third movement is a lyrical poem by Randolph Stow set once again for solo tenor and orchestra. 'Sleep', about a man who can fight a bushfire only if he got some sleep, conjures quintessential Australian landscapes that offer repose as well as hope of renewal. The score thus endeavours to capture both the hopelessness and brutality of war and a sense of redemption and salvation. Mills was prompted by the Greek word *threnos* which emphasizes a public act of grieving as collective catharsis or at least private, individual mourning, because he found in his fellow Australians an inability to grapple with grief and loss. Making it a threnody also breaks the long official silence surrounding the Sandakan tragedy. Finally, a threnody involving a multicultural cast positions it at the crossroads of Australia, Japan, Borneo and Singapore. Singapore might initially appear tangential to the narrative but, since its capitulation to the Japanese army in February 1942 could be said to trigger the events leading to the Sandakan march, it is an important factor in the equation.

Mills also collaborated with sound designer and electro-acoustic composer, Steve Adam, to orchestrate a series of soundscapes to accompany Ong's *mise en scène*. As if to echo the tripartite nature of Mills' score, Ong's drama also unfolds in three movements or acts: the first portrays the postwar trauma of one of the survivors, Bill Moxham, questions the lack of counselling and psychotherapy for such victims, and probes the equivocations of heroism; the second act features Allied tribunals interrogating war criminals and condemning the perpetrators of military atrocities; and the third involves a sequence of contemporary and classical *kabuki* dance, as kinesthetic odes to memories of joy and sadness, before breaking forth into a gestural and symbolic projection of hope. An epilogue envisages a future where legacies of the past, while awaiting resolution, still haunt and linger.

The choice of participating talents reflects an approach that lays stress upon plural and varied perspectives. Veteran Singapore actress, Lok Meng Chue, as the Narrator who reads letters, reports of military tribunals, diaries and interviews throughout the production, embodies Singapore's role as implicit witness to the events of the war. That she serves as the conduit for the mass of factual data and personal reminiscences also exemplifies the archival function of Ong, whose role is to offer an unbiased, comprehensive picture of the events. The main actor is, appropriately, veteran Australian actor, Matthew Crosby, who has been trained both in a Western theatre academy and in Japanese Suzuki technique. Gojo Masanosuke and Kota Yamazaki, besides representing the pivotal Japanese role in the events, also introduce the work's classical and contemporary dimensions: Masanosuke performs classical *kabuki* while Yamazaki welds the aesthetic and discipline of *butoh* and Western ballet into a layered kinesiology of dance. That Masanosuke dances the *onnagata* role also subverts gender assumptions, and challenges notions of masculinity and machismo among the military. Moreover, he serves as a reminder of the performative elements of the war, where nationalism (or king and country) prescribes certain immutable roles beyond that of the intrinsically individual.

Attention to detail also accounts for the subtlety of the production. One segment has the dancers enacting the physical travails of the forced march by focusing on its dire implications on the body. In the arduous journey over hilly and jungle terrain, without food and medical supplies, some soldiers, unable to stand, begin crawling like animals. What one critic has described as 'face-pulling and melodramatic crashes to the floor'[16] are in fact representations of the traumatic state when physical bodies collapse while the spirit, transcending the trauma, rises. By defying normal muscular composure, the soldiers are rendered seemingly immortal. Another segment features Crosby as Bill Moxham who, unable to exorcize the demons of that experience, committed suicide in 1961. As the sole deliverer of the script at this juncture, Crosby succinctly captures the experience of a man trapped in his interior landscape fighting invisible demons. The final act has Masanosuke reprising the *kabuki onnagata* role as an old woman ravaged by a memory fraught with the spectre of death yet mixed with the joy of love. As Masanosuke dances before 2,000 projected images of POWs taken at the Canberra War Memorial, these photographs of young soldiers of incandescent beauty juxtaposed with the stylized aesthetics of Japanese *kabuki* reinstate beauty amid the gratuitous suffering and loss of lives.

In *Sandakan Threnody*, Ong is constantly alert to the need for balance. The spotlighting of the graceful, muscular legs of the dancer-choreographer, Tim Harvey, contrasts with the wasted physique of the debilitated soldiers in an earlier scene. Everywhere Masanosuke's dance of transcendence is counterpointed by Kota Yamazaki's hyperbolic gestures of despair. The *kabuki* presence weaves through the tapestry of war and pain like a motif, suggesting a strand of hope. This hope materializes when the *kabuki* player transforms into a bird, symbolizing flight, as if to intimate the liberating of souls mired in the horrors of war. It is also significant that the Narrator performs the role of the *kurogo* facilitating that transition. As Narrator, Lok documents and archives, ensuring that history and its lessons are not forgotten, but, as *kurogo*, she performs the concomitant and necessary act of letting go and relinquishing the last vestiges of war.

Justin Hill's austere and minimalist set features a big projection screen that wraps around the entire cyclorama and offers an audio-visual backdrop. A second stand-alone vertical structure provides yet another screen upon which other images may be projected at significant intervals to reinforce or counterpoint the audio-visual environment behind. In addition, a grid of thousands of little mirrors, serving to catch the light, is lowered periodically from the flybars. Finally, a shiny metallic square is suspended monolithically from the ceiling like a canopy, upon which the actions on stage as well as the visual projections from both screens are mirrored, and deliberately distorted in evocative intersections. As the set remains largely unchanging, the soundscapes, whether a solo violin, or snatches of piano and brass, signpost the important transitions and liminal points, as when they build up to a climax at the end of the Bill Moxham segment to correspond to his fraying psyche and eventual disintegration.

What one Australian reviewer[17] has considered an unnecessary afterthought is Ong's surrealistic projection into the future – a fantastic scenario where the last Australian meets the last Japanese while both are suspended in a spatial and temporal limbo. As Ong has explained in his director's notes, the encounter is a signal for the wounds of war to heal and for legacies of the past to be buried once and for all. Each figure is cast like the tragic clowns in *Waiting for Godot*, awaiting deliverance from their emotional impasse. The Narrator now bears witness to the possible reconciliation while the Hairy Midget adds a note of ambivalence. Indeed, the production continually reminds the audience that it is impossible to talk about war through any one culture or to designate heroes and villains or perpetrators of violence and victims in a strictly binary manner.

The documentary footage on the projection screens can be classified into five major categories serving a multitude of functions. The most fundamental is the footage from the war itself, often graphic and unrelenting. The second comprises video interviews with family members of the POWs or the Japanese soldiers. The third, interspersed throughout the visual narrative, is an extended documentary about Ong and his team's dramaturgical field research, tracing the route of the death march and video-taping interviews with local inhabitants or war survivors who have slipped through the cracks and are not commemorated, whether at Koya-San or at the Sandakan War Memorial Park. To splice the docu-drama with sporadic images of the present instils a sense of postmodern irony and critical distance while reminding one that all accounts of historical events, including the theatrical presentation itself, are always mediated. The fourth is an Australian documentary made during the war and retrieved from archival sources. It purports to teach Australians how the Japanese are groomed to hate from an early age, but ironically exposes Australian xenophobia instead. The final category of projections consists of the still images of the dead soldiers etched against the lyrical notes of Stow's 'Sleep'. In harnessing all these forms, Ong not only proffers a comprehensive and variegated canvas of factual data, but allows their collisions to spark off moments of illumination or insight.

If one were averse to the austere symbolism of *Sandakan Threnody* and its multifaceted set design, one would be dazzled by the simplicity of *Global Soul: The Buddha Project* and its all-white set. An intertextual meditation on the central theme of travel, *Global Soul* delineates physical as well as spiritual journeys, treated in playfully tangential ways. The white set is bare, except for a couple of ramps and a flight of steps leading to a raised platform which are reminiscent of the escalators and conveyor belts of airports, depots, and stations. If *Sandakan Threnody* benefits from a rational, intellectual response, *Global Soul* exhorts one to immerse in a visceral way in its holistic experience. The subtitle, *The Buddha Project,* is rooted in the idea that Buddha was the earliest traveller to have combined an internal spiritual journey towards enlightenment with the external journey of physically leaving his comfortable home and circumstances. With Buddha, the deed is everything and attendant questions of craving or desire relating to the definition and constitution of the deed are irrelevant. Ong appears to be advocating the same attitude towards his production, urging his audience to allow the production to leave its impression on each of them in different ways at different moments, without seeking to explain each phenomenon or interpret every element or stage device.

Ong assembled six collaborating artistes from different cultural traditions and genres, five to play different global souls engaged in their varying trajectories and, the last, Japanese composer-deejay, Toru Yamanaka, to provide a soundtrack with post-industrial pulsating rhythms. The five performers could not be more antithetical to one another in language, technique, or craft. Paris-based Nigerian dancer, Sophiatou Kossoko, plays Millie who speaks entirely in French and whose encounters in airport lounges on business trips are conveyed through athletically vigorous kinesics. Thai dancer, Pichet Klunchun (with a bald head suggestive, perhaps ambiguously, of an iconic portrayal of the Buddha), plays The Man, who is silent but rigorously precise and calculated in his movements across the stage. Zeng Jingping is the Chinese *liyuan* operatic performer who sings in Hokkien and is purportedly the embodiment of three different heroines in the *liyuan* repertoire, all searching for love in the guise of a singular figure, Miss Ping. Kong Kwon Soon, a practitioner of Korean court music, plays The Singer and is predominantly static in composure while she vocalizes *kagok*, a traditional operatic genre. The fifth and last traveller, simply known as The Woman, is Swedish artiste, Charlotte Engelkes, who speaks a combination of English and Swedish, sings the occasional James Bond movie theme, and recounts random tales of travel.

Underlying such ostensible disparities of form and idiom is an interconnectivity that produces surreal, epiphanic moments. For instance, the songs of the *kagok* singer find their descants in the more personalized journeys of Millie, Miss Ping, and The Woman. Millie's enactment of the inconveniences of travel (jetlag, customs, and duty-free shops) is echoed in The Woman's account of massage therapies. When The Woman sings her love songs, she mirrors the dilemma of Miss Ping searching for her absent lover. Moreover, The Woman's suggestion, through the lyrics of 'From Russia with Love', that the end is merely the beginning, is materially presented by Millie running on the spot but literally getting no further up the ramp. Similarly, when The Woman sings 'You Only Live

Twice', it seems like a retrospective reference to the *kagok* singer's operatic evocation of borrowed lives.

If the *kagok* singer is the displaced voice which articulates the common quandary, The Man epitomizes the journey towards enlightenment through pure movement. By making The Singer completely still and stripping The Man of any verbalized text, Ong renders their journey as archetypal and clearly placed on an overarching, metatextual plane. The Man in particular embodies the trials and tribulations of that difficult journey to spiritual awakening. In one scene, with arching back and controlled musculature, he makes his difficult way backwards up the ramp, suggesting the endurance and discipline needed to complete that journey. With the rest departing the platform at the end of the performance, having arrived at their respective resolutions, it is The Singer who has the last word while The Man assumes a prostrate position at her feet, transformed into the quintessential symbol of Buddhahood, 'the lotus above the water'.

The seed of Ong's inspiration for this production was his own wanderings over a period of years from South America to Africa, to source for artistes for a festival (aptly titled *In Transit*) that he was curating in Berlin. Even as the global traveller loses a familiar sense of himself in a different spatio-temporal context, and as the world gets smaller with the amplification of the global village idea, the unfamiliar often bear traces of the recognizable. Crisscrossing continents and seeing more hotels and transit lounges than home and hearth, Ong likens his subsequent creation of *Global Soul* to 'dream time ... an atmosphere of dreaming and time passing'. Audiences therefore cannot expect to be 'concretely enlightened'[18] because this last is a contradiction in itself, as true enlightenment involves transcendence of any concrete, empirical understanding.

The individual trajectories all culminate in some semblance of transcendental understanding to parallel the visual projection of the crescent moon growing to full circle, and the reduction of the overlay in Toru's soundscape at the end. Just as the lighting design casts shadows of a scale that hint at multiple lives reverberating through different planes and times, the five travellers achieve, in different permutations, a new grasp of the concepts of time, space, distance and the coordinates of the human body. Millie finally comes to terms with the physical shell of her body. The Woman becomes a child again after traversing large stretches of memories across the years, and, as she projects the lighthouse, finally appreciates the importance of being the symbol of direction herself. She then helps Miss Ping to achieve equanimity by intimating through the lyrics of her last song that they 'have all the time in the world just for love'. This reiterates what Miss Ping has already known, but needed a revised mindset to accept: that the synchronic and the diachronic are not mutually exclusive. The notion that time is not an ephemeral passage but devoid of past, present, and future renders impossible the idea of loss. The Woman is thus able to duet with Miss Ping before they exit together. The Singer summarizes the Buddhist precepts best. Caught in the wheel of *samsara*, our mortal existence is an illusion: 'borrowed lives as in a dream'. The reconciliation among the 'two or three lives' and 'four or five bodies' also suggests that perhaps the five travellers are different facets, manifestations, and paradigms of the quest of that one Global Soul.

After nearly a decade and a half of being condemned by local critics for being a pompous, self-absorbed auteur, the production for which Ong received the 2007 *Straits Times* Life Theatre Award for Best Director is, appropriately, *Geisha*. Both consistent with and yet, in terms of its codifications, a departure from Ong's usual oeuvre, *Geisha* charms with its light touch and even incorporates an element of levity.

As usual, Ong's intercultural agenda is foregrounded: he states that he wishes to debunk potential essentialisms that lurk beneath representations or receptions of culture, particularly the implications of *chinoiserie* as an external projection that resulted in a form of artistic expression.[19] He wants to convey the contention that 'there is no authenticity in art in an ever-changing and evolving world', but 'only the presentation of diverse perspectives and a multiplicity of positions'. By underlining the importance of hybridity, Ong attempts to 'explode easy categorizations that ultimately imprison cultural positions rather than liberate us from cultural hierarchies'.

But, to Ong, *Geisha* is much more than the dissection of an intriguing cultural tradition although he was, to begin with, intrigued by the myths surrounding the tradition. The *geisha* is often conflated with the *oiran* or prostitute, and consequently eroticized rather than aestheticized. This misunderstanding is compounded through such vehicles as Arthur Golden's *Memoirs of a Geisha*.[20] Misunderstood and associated with sex for barter rather than with the transporting experience of art, the '*geisha* function' or *ozashiki* is consequently made obsolete by *karaoke* bars where women entertain and provide company for male clients. The *geisha* as a 'sunset industry' or declining trade thus interests Ong, who is consistent in his campaign to prevent traditional cultures from extinction or ossification. But he is also captivated by the world of illusion upon which the world of the *geisha* is premised, a world he likens to the dream-weaving magic of theatre. Just as the *geisha* spins a world of beauty for the client far beyond discordant reality, the theatre encourages the audience to suspend disbelief and participate in its world of illusion. Hence Ong is interested in interrogating the dialectic between truth and artifice. As he says, 'Artifice plays a very important role in our social lives. We value truth, but what about the artificial?'[21]

In *Geisha*, deconstructing the illusion becomes the way to foreground it and Ong does this firstly through his casting. He selects an African-American actress, Kandel (with whom he has worked in David Henry Hwang's *Silver River*), to play the *geisha* as Dreamweaver. The ethnicity of the actress immediately challenges conventional notions of self and the other, and cautions one against cultural essentialisms. Since the *geisha* is also a male-construct of the ideal woman, Ong has a Japanese man, Gojo Masanosuke, perform the role to undermine gender assumptions. The trans-Pacific casting further dismantles the boundaries between East and West, tradition and modernity, by positioning Toru Yamanaka's electronic score in a running dialectic with the traditional stringed *shamisen* of the *geisha*.

Secondly, like Brechtian methodology which unveils its artistic armature and proffers the split subject, Ong splinters the iconic figure of the *geisha* by assigning her different aspects to contrasting performers on stage. The African-American Kandel who plays the Dreamweaver is also the voice of the *geisha*, personifying a plurality of roles from *maikos* (apprentice *geishas*) to *okamisans* (*mama-sans*). Intermittently, she also takes the gender subversions further by playing the *geisha's* clients, introducing a dash of irreverent humour to the deference that the production accords to this longstanding icon of classical Japanese culture. If Kandel is the voice, Gojo is the physical manifestation of the *geisha*, embodying her intrinsic refinement and enacting her gracefully sinuous dance movements. Traditionally, *geishas* are skilled in song and in plucking the *shamisen*. In the production, however, the live musical accompaniment on the *shamisen* as well as the occasional Edo epoch ballad is performed by Kinoya Katsumatsu. Hence, it is not only the voice and body of the *geisha* that gets splintered but also her singing and dance.

In line with this deliberate fragmentation is the postmodern pastiche of multiple texts that include interviews with actual *geishas*, the plays of eighteenth-century master dramatist Chikamatsu, David Henry Hwang's postcolonial *M. Butterfly*, and Kenji Mizoguchi's canonical film, *Sisters of the Gion*. The resulting phenomenon is as multilayered as the costume donned by Kandel at one point. Presenting the titular figure in multiple incarnations, Ong makes us see that she resists easy pigeonholing. The discrete segments are in fact a contrivance that reinforces the lack of a totalizing perspective or master-narrative of the *geisha*. The solitary consistent thread is the 'perception, not deception' that the *geisha* conjures as a trader in dreams: to make each man believe she is his heart's desire. The production ends in a kind of mischievous anti-closure by unfastening the last shred of illusion about the *geisha*: Kandel, in her modern persona, dances a waltz with Gojo, now stripped of the *geisha*'s accoutrements and looking every inch a dapper fellow. The organizing principle of the piece is reiterated at the denouement when the audience is invited, like the clients of a *geisha*, to surrender to the dream world of the stage production and participate in the illusory space of the theatre even as it pulls the last bits of blindfold from their eyes.

Ong's intercultural productions, while rewarding those open to dramaturgical and scenographic possibilities, remain frustratingly cryptic and arcane to those who need a narrative arc. Paul Rae's arguments, for what in the title of his essay he understates as a 'weak interculturalism',[22] can be said to sum up best Ong's ultimate achievements. Having sat in on a Flying Circus performance laboratory for three weeks in December 2000, and witnessed the interactions among 72 East Asian performing artists, Rae was able to infer from his documentation and observations of the proceedings that all the prevalent theories and models for understanding intercultural praxis fell short of the 'richly cross-hatched performance' that Ong's reinventions unleashed.[23] He sees these theoretical perspectives and conceptual frameworks as 'over-determining markers' that only prove counter-productive in their exegesis.[24] Rather, the productions of *Sandakan Threnody, Global Soul*, and *Geisha*, which collectively represent Ong at the pinnacle of his craft, generate what Rae calls 'the sense of possibility that attended each interaction'. The intercultural dynamic 'in process', and the 'informing rather than determining roles in the unfolding action' of various performative traditions,[25] reflect what the audience would receive from 'the experiential flow of the performance as event'.[26]

NOTES

1. Ong has received fellowships from the Japan Foundation, the British Council, the German Academic Exchange Service (DAAD) in Berlin, the Asia Cultural Council (New York); he received from the National Arts Council of Singapore, firstly, the Singapore Young Artist of the Year Award and, subsequently, the Cultural Medallion, the nation's highest accolade for contributions to culture. He has been a Visiting Fellow at the University of California, Los Angeles. His plays have premiered in cities

in Asia and in Australia, and he has directed plays and curated festivals in Copenhagen, Vienna, Berlin, Rotterdam and major cities in the USA. For more information about his work, see <www.TheatreWorks.org.sg/international/sandakan_threnody/creative_team.htm> accessed on 15 May, 2009.

2. For a sampling of papers and critiques that question the validity of his approaches, see Josephine Tan, 'Bard's play gets Asian flavour for benefit of Japanese', *The Straits Times*, 6 August 1997, p. 20; Craig Latrell, 'After Appropriation', *The Drama Review* 44: 4 (Winter 2000) 44-55; Rustom Bharucha, 'Consumed in Singapore', CAAS Research Paper Series No. 21 (May 2000); Helena Grehan, 'TheatreWorks' *Desdemona*: Fusing Technology and Tradition', *The Drama Review*, 45:3 (Fall 2001) 113-125. See also Lee Weng Choy, 'An Interview with Ong Keng Sen', in *Singaporeans Exposed: Navigating the Ins and Outs of Globalisation*, ed., Lee Geok Boi (Singapore: Landmark Books, 2001), pp. 53-63.

3. Ong told a reviewer from *The Straits Times*, Hong Xinyi, that she was 'not welcome' at the performance of *Diaspora* which he was staging for the delegates of the World Economic Forum held in Singapore in September 2006. Since admission was by invitation only, the gesture constituted a 'de facto ban'.

4. Robin Loon, 'Reading Intercultural Performance: The TheatreWorks' Intercultural Trilogy', Unpublished PhD dissertation, University of London (2004), p. 14. The Ideological Approach, according to Loon, focuses on difference and unnecessarily politicizes the performative text by 'addressing imbalances of power, the tension between cultural appropriation and cultural preservation'.

5. Loon, 'Reading Intercultural Performance', p. 22.

6. Loon, 'Reading Intercultural Performance', p. 15.

7. Rustom Bharucha, 'Foreign Asia/Foreign Shakespeare: Dissenting Notes on New Asian Interculturality, Postcoloniality, and Recolonization', *Theatre Journal*, 56 (2004) 1.

8. Clarissa Oon, 'Global Take on the Soul', *The Straits Times*, 'Life' Section, 21 June 2003, p. 6.

9. Wong's *Mergers & Accusations*, created during the first of Ong's TheatreWorks' Writers' Lab series, was produced by TheatreWorks in 1993, and *Wills & Secession* in 1995. *Jointly & Severally* was produced as part of *Invitation to Treat* in 2003 by the WILD RICE theatre company, the first time the trilogy had been staged together.

10. Ong Keng Sen, 'Encounters', *The Drama Review*, 45:3 (Fall 2001) 126.

11. Ong, 'Encounters', 132.

12. Ong, 'Encounters', 132.

13. See Clarissa Oon, 'Heart of Darkness', *The Straits Times*, 'Life' Section, 17 June 2004, p. 6. Also see Composer's Notes and Director's Notes in Programme of *Sandakan Threnody*, where detailed expositions of the production process and its rationale are given.

14. Jonathan Mills, Programme, *Sandakan Threnody*.

15. Michael Shmith, 'Father, Forgive Them', *The Sunday Age Preview*, 10 October 2004, p. 33.

16. Martin Buzacolt, 'Voices of the Dead Overwhelm the Drama', *The Australian*, 20 September 2004.

17. John Slavin, 'Horror of Sandakan March Brought Movingly to Stage', *The Age*, 16 October 2004, p. 13.

18. Clarissa Oon, 'Accidental Tourist', *The Straits Times* 'Life' Section, 21 May 2003, p. 4.

19. These statements and the quotes that follow are extracted from the Director's Notes, Programme, *Geisha*, 27-30 July, Gerald W. Lynch Theater at John Jay College, USA.

20. Charles Isherwood, 'A multi-faceted new view of a tradition built on dreams', *The New York Times*, 29 July 2006, p. 7.
21. Ong, Director's Notes, Programme, *Geisha*.
22. Paul Rae, 'Don't Take it Personally: Arguments for a Weak Interculturalism', *Performance Research*, 9:4 (2004) 18-24.
23. Rae, 'Don't Take it Personally', p. 20.
24. Rae, 'Don't Take it Personally', p. 20.
25. Rae, 'Don't Take it Personally', p. 22.
26. Rae, 'Don't Take it Personally', p. 21.

Great Singapore Sale

WAI-CHEW SIM

The message on the back of the headrest caught his attention when he entered the taxi. He gave the driver his destination and took his seat. The man grunted once, cleared his throat, gunned the engine, and drove off.

'Remember to give directions early,' the words said.

He saw white, one-inch-tall letters printed in a joined cursive hand. The tone suggested coolness and distance, and furthermore the same message was printed on the back of the driver's seat headrest.

Together they glared at Kian Ming like windows framing a doorway.

On the space above the glove compartment he noticed the same message written in Mandarin, also in white, and what seemed like Malay and Tamil. The strokes and letters were smaller in scale but clear enough even from where he was sitting.

Kian Ming assessed the situation and agreed that it made sense. Some passengers tend to give last-minute instructions. He did the same thing himself on occasion. They might say 'turn left' or 'turn right' just as the taxi reached an intersection. If the driver jerked into action without thinking, the chances were great that something horrific would happen. In a worse case scenario there would be a pile-up.

But in fact – he realized – it didn't even have to be so dramatic. Even without an accident the consequences could be appalling. A near accident was enough to do the trick: the driver might spend all his time after that cringing whenever he approached a traffic junction. The fear that a new set of directions would be barked out at the wrong moment might sink into him like fog settling over a valley. In the final seconds before he crossed into the no-man's-land in the middle of the junction his fingers might grip the steering wheel like a set of talons, his body braced for impact.

Imagine that! A cab driver cringing at every intersection, going around the whole day in a state of nervous tension! It sounded like some diabolical torture invented to torment people in the afterlife. The whole thing was vile and pathetic, and Kian Ming winced as he considered the implications.

At that moment something else about the message started to bother him and he leaned forward to examine it. He brought his nose right up to the letters, close enough to smell the upholstery. His eyebrows pulled together in a frown, he studied the letters for a while. There was something odd about them. They were fat and thickly painted in the middle but flaking and smudged at the edges.

Why were they like this? Oh, of course – the shock of recognition hit him – the message was written with correction fluid. Instead of paint or a marker pen, the man had used correction fluid!

Well, well, Kian Ming told himself. A slow, thin smile appeared on his face and he thought, okay, this is new, this is clever! That's one way to use correction fluid, he acknowledged, nodding to himself. It explained the whiff of thinner spirit in the air. The spirit must have been used to dilute the fluid, to make it less viscid.

He wondered how many bottles the driver had used. Five? Six? He felt sure that – everything considered – he must have used at least five bottles.

The figure seated across from him had a long, slack-jawed face and heavy, expressionless eyes. He saw a fleshy body in a checked turquoise-grey shirt, khaki pants and a baseball cap pulled low over what looked like a crew cut. The sleeves were worn completely rolled down and buttoned at the wrist.

Late thirties, growing thick about the waist, exactly like me, Kian Ming thought. Even the body shape was similar.

Apart from the cap he was like many of the drivers Kian Ming met on his way to work, or coming home from work. There was nothing noteworthy or distinguished about him. Told where to go, he didn't bother to murmur a reply or a confirmation. He grunted once and drove off, and that was normal as well.

With a shake of his head, Kian Ming dismissed the driver and returned to the words on the headrest.

He mulled over them.

He saw that the writing was stylish and elegant, the letters graceful and well-proportioned. The words were arranged in pairs, one below the other, with the last word printed in capital letters and positioned pointedly in the centre. Each word had an allotment of cursive whorls twirling out like tendrils from a stalk. The dark upholstery helped to set them off. To balance the feel of it, the tail of the letter 'y' in 'early' had been extended in a neat double loop so that it formed a kind of support or a base. The message seemed to rest on the elongated tail like a statue on a plinth. It came over sharp and imperious – it clamoured for attention.

Kian Ming looked over again at the driver. Only his arms and his hands stirred as he adjusted the steering wheel to keep the taxi in its lane. His eyes stayed fixed on the strip of grey asphalt illuminated by the headlights. He was relaxed, but also businesslike and aloof.

Nothing explained how this bland and businesslike person could have produced such a graceful and elegant message. It didn't look like it came from him. And the rest of the taxi was dull and sterile too. It didn't have a single item of decoration in it. There were no stickers on the windscreen or windows, no religious icons on the dashboard, no Buddhist, Taoist, Christian or Catholic inscription, no flip-page calendar, no metal bracket for the mobile phone, no notepad, no magazines in the seat pouches, no bauble or talisman dangling from the rear-view mirror.

Even the smell was of something delivered brand new from the workshop, of freshly burnished leather and newly-moulded plastic. Nothing in the taxi gave a glimpse into the personality of the driver, his desires, dreams and secret fears.

Only the message stood out, so important it had to be said a few times in different languages.

'Remember to give directions early' – written in correction fluid.

Kian Ming grinned as he pictured his wife's reaction. If Kathy was there she would scold him silly. Stop it! she would say. Why did he have to fret so much over a simple message? He should just follow instructions. He – a grown man – spent his time brooding and dissecting the world when he should learn to accept things as they were. He should learn to be practical.

More and more in recent months he could feel himself moving into a separate space, a different order of world altogether. He knew that Kathy was upset and troubled. But he didn't know how to explain his lassitude so that it didn't sound aberrant. All he knew was that every time he opened his mouth, nothingness came out. A disembodied orifice with fleshy lips opened and closed. Muscles moved in back of throat and jaw. Nothingness *emerged* into the world.

So when he got home he wanted only to watch television and take his dinner without being disturbed. If it was possible to be a hermit in a cave, he would. He knew that his actions were perverse but, more and more, the world of the imagination crowded out the world of people and connections. More and more he could sense change in the air.

With a shrug Kian Ming turned to the traffic outside the window. Maybe she was right. He shouldn't daydream so much. All that mulling got him nowhere anyway. It was sad and unhealthy.

He watched as the taxi went past two lorries chugging along in the inside lane. It put on a burst of speed and slid past a pickup truck, and then a small panel van. A motorcycle pulled away on the left, just out of his peripheral vision. It entered the slip lane and curved out of sight.

Good, good, Kian Ming told himself. He was making good time. Soon he would be home. Safe in his fortress – he laughed inwardly at the idea – he would take his dinner. He would chew every mouthful and savour every bite. 'E-a-t s-l-o-w-l-y!' he reminded himself, so that he wouldn't get heartburn. Then he would relax in front of the television. What's on today? he tried to recall. Oh, yes, the detective series – a thrill of pleasure ran through him – the one with the clever graphics! The real hero in the show was science, he thought, the fact that it could be harnessed to track down thieves and murderers. Science was brought to life in the show and the result was stunning, simply stunning.

But what happened next took his breath away. What happened next was the driver flipping his indicator lights and filtering smartly into the passing lane. He started to accelerate. Far ahead in the distance, the back of a large, boxy-looking car began to take shape. Within thirty seconds he had caught up with it. He trailed the vehicle – a Volvo – for a minute and a half, hugging its bumper. Then he high-beamed the driver once, a second time, and finally a third time.

The driver – a woman in her twenties – peered into her rear-view mirror and frowned. She filtered into the middle lane. As the taxi whizzed by, she pounded on her horn and stuck out her middle finger. The taxi driver ignored her.

Within thirty seconds he had caught up with another car in front, this time a Toyota, silver-grey, a recent model. Again he hugged the bumper. Between the taxi and the Toyota was a distance of eight, maybe ten feet.

Kian Ming frowned and reached for his seatbelt. He tugged at the loop of canvas, released it with some difficulty from its receptacle and clicked the metal tongue into place. Usually he didn't bother to belt up when he sat at the back, but this time it seemed necessary.

All at once the message on the headrest caught his attention. It came to life and reared up on a set of scaly, reptilian legs. Balancing on its elongated tail, it sneered and tittered at him, 'What are you going to do, Lim Kian Ming? What are you going to do, little man? Do you dare to tell him off?'

For the second time the driver reached for the lever controlling the indicator lights. Click – click – click went the lever, and the lights raked the back of the sedan.

In response, however, nothing happened, nothing at all. The Toyota continued on its way in a cool, unperturbed manner. It didn't slow down and it didn't speed up – it refused to be intimidated.

The taxi driver shook his head. His eyes narrowed into tiny slits. He licked his lips and made a coarse, clicking sound with the underside of his tongue. He waited.

After what seemed an eternity, he high-beamed the Toyota again. The light spurted harsh and relentless as if he were delivering an ultimatum. Each time he swept the car, the light reflected off the rear and filled the interior of the taxi. It lit up Kian Ming's broad square face and the front of his torso up to his midriff. It washed over his large protuberant eyes and he had to hood them to keep out the glare.

But again the Toyota refused to budge. It seemed to be saying, 'I'm not road-hogging, I have a right to this lane.' The two drivers raced down the highway bumper to bumper, no quarter given, squaring off like children fighting at the playground.

After a moment's thought, Kian Ming straightened up in his seat, squinted at the dashboard, and caught the reading on the speedometer. He saw, too, the set of the taxi driver's jaw, the hunch of his shoulders, and the stiff, fierce grip on the steering wheel. All softness had gone from him. The tip of his tongue protruded from between his lips, a febrile grin grew on his face. Then came a soft, almost imperceptible movement – a shift of posture – as if he had reached a decision of some kind. A catch of fear rose in Kian Ming as he watched the driver lean back into his seat, watched him straighten his arms and lock his elbows. Then he was pressing down on the accelerator and the engine growled and the distance between the two cars narrowed. The speedometer now read a hundred and twenty. They were forty kilometres above the legal speed limit and neither showed signs of relenting.

The distance between the two vehicles was down to six feet.

Now Kian Ming began to worry. He felt a tightening in his groin and his world contracted to a view of a silver-grey Toyota with two ridiculous looking tissue boxes visible on the rear window shelf. The taillights expanded to fill his vision, and any minute now he knew they would blink. The last thing he saw would be two flashing taillights, the taxi skidding wildly, and a thunderous sickening crash. Without looking, he reached for the belt buckle lying next to him. He grabbed the handle of the door with his left hand and both sets of knuckles went white. He braced his feet against the back of the front-passenger seat and hunkered down into his own.

A picture of himself trapped in a wreck came to him. Time seemed to thin out, spread, and slow down. There was debris everywhere. The chassis was crushed like a concertina into the side of a bus shelter. Broken glass sprinkled the dark asphalt and glinted when it caught the light. Then he saw, as if through the eyes of a person floating high above, his body caught in a section of the wreckage, torn and mangled. His ribcage was shattered. His right arm was fractured in several places and the white of the bone shone through. Both his legs were broken. He looked down at a piece of galvanized iron sticking out from his stomach and his mind refused to register the implication. Blood welled from the wound and, when he gasped for air, a shrill, terrified whimper escaped from his lips.

'Remember to give directions early' kept up a constant incantation in his head, like a broken-down gramophone.

'Do you dare to tell him off?' accompanied the chant in monstrous counterpoint. The tone was no longer taunting and acerbic. It was breezy and casual.

He recalled suddenly an accident he had read about in the newspapers, an incident in Malaysia where a funfair ride called the 'runaway train' had lived up to its name, had thrown off four passengers, and crushed them dead beneath the wheels of a runaway carriage. One of the passengers – a boy – was only eight years old.

This can't be happening! This can't be happening! Kian Ming told himself, the horror growing on his face. He had to warn the driver – he had to stop him!

But when he opened his mouth nothing came out. He could only manage a weak, indistinct croak, 'Carrgh … carrgh …,' then fell silent.

What if I distract him? he thought. What if he takes his attention away from the road and just at that moment we reach some roadworks or a diversion? What if suddenly he needs to jam-brake?

Then Kian Ming couldn't believe his eyes. The Toyota signalled left and filtered into the middle lane. The taxi shot into the cleared stretch of road.

Kian Ming felt the breath explode from between his lips. He blinked and gulped for air and shook his head trying to clear it. He released the belt buckle and his hand from the door handle. He wiped the sweat off his brow with one hand and checked his heartbeat with the other. The hammering in his chest dismayed him and he tried to calm himself. 'Take it easy. You've made it, Kian Ming!' he warned himself. 'You should look on the bright side of things. Stop stressing yourself out or you'll have a heart attack!'

There was a lesson here somewhere, and really he should find it, and listen to it.

Finally he leaned back and heaved a sigh of relief.

The next moment his eyes widened as the driver stomped on the accelerator and held his foot down on it. The engine roared and the taxi surged forward – again they bore down on a vehicle ahead of them.

For a while Kian Ming observed the traffic swish by on the opposite side of the highway median. He went over the options available to him. It occurred to him that they were separated from the oncoming traffic only by a low concrete bed, filled with earth, four, maybe five, inches off the ground, and two-feet wide. They hadn't got round to planting this section of the highway yet, so above the flower bed there was only air. A pocket of air separated him from disaster.

He wanted to cry, 'Hey! I have a wife and kids! Can you slow down, for God's sake!' He tried to shout the words but again his tongue betrayed him. It sat fat and sluggish at the back of his throat and refused to budge. He saw that, after all, the driver was in control, that his actions were practised and unhurried. He held his left wrist draped lazily over the crossbar of the steering wheel. His right hand held the wheel in an easy, relaxed manner, his forearm resting on a thigh. Every line of him seemed to say that, after all, this was what he did for a living. This brinkmanship was as natural as the sun rising in the east and setting in the west. Everything about his posture and his demeanour said, 'Trust me, Kian Ming, trust me.'

And the funny thing was – when Kian Ming went over it afterwards – by the time he finished going through all his options, they had caught up with the vehicle in front. Again, they hugged the back of a sedan, a black Mazda with spoilers and a vanity license plate bearing the number 4848. Kian Ming thought that he had, at any rate, found an auspicious number, that maybe he could place a bet on it in the four-digit lottery over the weekend. It was then that he noticed the small rectangular sign on the rear window, tucked low in a corner, 'If you can read this you're driving too close!' And despite himself, Kian Ming had to groan and shake his head. Despite himself, he had to acknowledge that fate could be capricious, that it had a sense of humour. He had to acknowledge his damn bad luck.

What should I do? What should I do? he thought. He slumped back into his seat and screwed his eyes shut. At once he jerked them open. No, that was the last thing he should do. There had to be something else.

He watched as the driver went through his high-beam routine again. They were so close behind the Mazda he might as well roll down the window, stick out his head, and aim a gob of spit at the license plate.

Now, more than anything else, Kian Ming wanted to humiliate the driver. He wanted to say, 'Excuse me, if you slow down and keep a proper safety distance, I'll give you an extra twenty dollars when you reach my estate.' He wanted to see the look on the driver's face. Then the irony hit home as he flinched from the mockery and the derision. The extra money he made driving like this didn't come up to the price that his passengers paid, the demons they had to endure. If it came to that, he would give him the extra cash, all of it. How much would it come up to, after all? Thirty? Forty dollars a day? Even if it were a hundred dollars, he would fork out the money happily and immediately. He would do anything, in fact, to convey to the driver that he was taking unnecessary risks. Perhaps he should tell him, 'Excuse me, if you want so much to die, why don't you go jump off a high-rise flat?'

Would it help if he said that? He pictured himself saying those words. He willed it to come about. But again they failed to materialize. He gave a low hoarse croak and again fell silent. 'Carrgh ... carrgh ...,' was all he could manage.

Again fear paralyzed him and froze him up. He studied it for a moment and realized it was the kind of fear that needed a long and carefully nurtured apprenticeship in order to bear fruit. It was the kind of fear that didn't build up over night, that you learn because ever since you were young everyone and everything around you teaches you to be cautious, to hide, to batten down the hatches and play safe, because the nail that stands out gets hammered down. Each time he roused himself for the effort a picture held up by his fear overwhelmed him. All he had to do was to imagine himself speaking, imagine the driver whipping round to confront him, imagine the tail lights flashing ahead of them. Then the momentum he had built up would start to ebb.

So he kept his eyes trained on the back of the Mazda and cursed his bad luck, riled himself inside where it was useless. An idea started to dog him. It started to jab at him in an insidious, querulous voice, saying, 'You're useless, you're useless, your opinions are worthless and your feelings irrelevant. You can't even give directions.' Again and again the invective rained on him. And in response to that, Kian Ming could do nothing except to fix his eyes on the back of the Mazda and prepare for the worst. And presently the taxi's headlights spurted yet another warning and the glare washed over his face and his hooded protuberant eyes. And it occurred to him that, all this while, the speedometer had not gone below a hundred and ten.

Meaning arises from the possibility of retrospect. With hindsight we learn to discern patterns in our lives, to pick out connecting threads in our conduct and behaviour. The moments take shape with the sleight-of-hand conjured up by memory – a job not taken up, a love affair abandoned, a cast-off friendship. With the benefit of hindsight things get pushed into a certain order, a certain causal configuration. But, in Kian Ming's mind, the certainty was already growing that this taxi ride, this encounter with this driver – this was a turning-point in his life. He was willing to understand that, if he didn't speak up now, he would never do it, that it was now or never, the conviction striking him lucidly like a full moon gleaming on a cloudless night. If he didn't speak up now he was rendered impotent. Forever and ever he would remain silent. He might as well chop off his tongue.

Finally, he had reached the stage where he wanted to dispense with irritation and sarcasm. He wanted to say, in as calm a manner as possible, keeping the fear out of his voice so that he wouldn't spook the driver, 'Excuse me, can you slow down, please? Can you keep a proper safety distance?' He would fight to keep his voice level, fight to keep out the tremor of alarm waiting in the wings.

He mouthed the opening words. 'Excuse me,' he croaked, experimentally. 'Excuse me –'

And he nearly did complete the sentence, except that they came out of a curve just at that moment, and the gantry indicating the turning-off ramp came into view in the distance, yellow letters enumerated starkly on a green hoarding. And Kian Ming thought: 'We're only a few seconds away from the exit. We'll be getting off soon anyway. In a few seconds it won't matter.' No doubt, given the way the driver operated, some unlucky passenger would, some time or other, have to warn him, to tell him off. No one should be allowed to drive like that. But it needn't be his problem. Let someone else deal with it, Kian Ming thought ... let someone else deal with it.

At that moment, the taillights came on and stayed on.

No! Please, God ...! No!

The driver stomped on his brakes. The deceleration threw them forward against their restraints. The driver swerved left to avoid the back of the Mazda and they careered into the middle lane into a cacophony of grinding brakes and squealing rubber. In the same instant the van cruising behind them peeled away. More vehicles sheared off like water passing round an obstacle in a river. Their ears filled with the whine of blaring horns, raucous and irate, and then fading away as more vehicles careened past them. They fishtailed and skidded, and Kian Ming felt rather than saw the driver pump his brakes as he fought to bring the vehicle under control. They continued to skid, burning up rubber, bracing for impact.

The world dissolved into movement, a clenched sphincter, a collection of surfaces. And through it all, the lights and the fanfare came at them like a chorus mourning an untimely death.

Somehow they came to rest on the hard shoulder of the highway, lurching hard, the engine stalling. They came to with the traffic whizzing past them, spinning away like comets, the taillights receding in the distance. Gradually the world started to slow down, stopped spinning. The Mazda was nowhere in sight; it had vanished over a rise in the road. Miraculously they seemed all right. Nobody was hurt. The world had righted itself and everything was back to normal.

Enveloped by the sweet, frangipani-scented evening air, one could even believe that nothing had happened.

The driver turned around. He looked ashen-faced and embarrassed. His words tumbled out in a rush, 'I'm sorry, I've been driving the whole day. I'm so sorry. Are you all right?' Before Kian Ming could reply he repeated in a rush of nerves, 'I'm so sorry, I've been driving the whole day.' He wrung his hands and added, 'I've only been driving for two weeks.' And then he stopped, aware all of a sudden that he had said the wrong thing, maybe even the unforgivable thing.

For a while Kian Ming couldn't register the implications. His eyes went to the laminated card mounted on the dashboard above the glove compartment. 'K.Y. Lee', the card said. Beneath it was printed the registration number of the taxi. The driver saw Kian Ming check his particulars and his face grew redder and he seemed to shrink further into himself. They both knew that Kian Ming was deliberating whether to make a police report. They both knew that they could easily have died.

As Kian Ming studied the card it struck him that the name printed there meant nothing to him, absolutely nothing. He turned to the driver. The man looked white and beaten and ready to faint. And he thought, what's the point? If I report him, he'll lose his licence, and what good would that do, depriving a man of his livelihood?

Next to them the traffic continued to whizz past, barely an arm's length away. The air conditioner had died and they could hear the wind whistle in through a crack in the window where the glass had not been fully wound up. The moon hung low in the sky and wrapped the earth in a soft, friendly glow. The stars glinted their indifference. Gradually the resentment and the fight drained out of Kian Ming. He looked down at his hands and examined the lines on his palms. He looked back again at the driver.

'Never mind, it's okay,' he said. 'Just get me home.'

The rest of the journey was uneventful except for a part where the traffic was funnelling from two lanes to one. They got through the bottleneck speedily, passing an enormous road-roller with giant drum wheels, the acrid smell of liquid asphalt burning in their nostrils. When they reached Kian Ming's apartment block, the taxi driver refused to accept the fare, but Kian Ming insisted. Then he wanted to reduce the amount but Kian Ming refused that, too. It didn't seem worth it, getting a discount after all they had gone through. The whole point would have been lost.

★ ★ ★

He was home. He must have stepped across the threshold a thousand times, tens of thousands even. But this time, it seemed, things were different. Everywhere he looked, the flat had lost something, something was awry. The objects around him seemed lighter as a result, more fragile, and insubstantial but also more solid, more like themselves. As if the scales had fallen away from his eyes, he saw things for what they were – steel, wood, leather, concrete, plastic, glass. He stood in the hallway taking in the plush sofa set, the flat-panel TV, the cabinet filled with expensive knick-knacks, the dining table, the sideboard and the picture hanging on the wall above it. He studied the cornices and the concealed pendant lights in the ceiling. Even the simple country scene depicted in the picture – lush vegetation, a bend in the river, a farmer driving a bullock cart to market – looked different.

His eyes fell on the sofa and the maroon coffee table next to it. The table was what they called a conversation piece. It was cut in the shape of a flower; the edges formed four parabolic petals and in the centre was a piece of frosted Venetian glass. But now Kian Ming wondered whether it was really worth it, the money they spent on designer furniture. All of a sudden he knew that he wanted to change his life.

On the dining table was a message from Kathy, a single sheet ripped from a yellow note-pad, stark against the heavy mahogany wood. She had taken the children and gone to her mother's place. She had had enough.

Kian Ming sighed. On the way up in the lift he had pictured another scenario. He had pictured Kathy in the kitchen tending to a pot on the stove.

'How was your day?' she asked as he walked in.

He went up to her, put his arms around her waist and kissed the nape of her neck. A shock of surprise crossed her face. She turned sideways and cocked an eyebrow at him.

'I was in an accident,' he explained.

'What! Are you all right?' She turned to face him. She looked him up and down searching for wounds. Her eyes were deep wells of pain.

'What happened, Kian Ming?' They held each other close and his eyes brimmed with tears.

But, when he opened his eyes, he saw a vacant flat, a collection of surfaces. Cornices in the ceiling, concealed pendant lights.

He sighed again, crumpled the note into a ball and threw it on the floor. He eyed it for a while, moved to the sofa and took a seat in the middle. He sank backwards into the upholstery and stretched his legs out on the coffee table, his body suspended in a gentle arch.

By now the adrenaline had worn off and the near accident – near death? – the meaning of it and its mystery touched him to the quick. As he pondered its essence, his eyes kept returning to the coffee table, to the heft of its solidly built frame, and its sleek, easy lines. His mouth was parched and his throat felt sore and painful as if he had shouted himself hoarse at some sports event. It struck him again that an ordinary coffee table would do. He didn't need a specially-designed, Italian-made extravagance. So what if it was a conversation piece? What a ridiculous thing to hanker after. His priorities were all wrong and his life was itself a runaway train. He should spend more time with his family. Surely he knew that?

All at once he sat up straight and gripped the side of the table. From the storage section in the middle he took out a set of newspapers – Kathy always kept them there. He spread the papers out on the glass-top surface and began to read, his mind still in a blur. He hadn't read the papers yet, he realized. It had gnawed at him the whole day, this break in his routine. If he read the papers, everything would be fine. The malaise that plagued him would disappear. Read this, he told himself. Everything will be fine.

On page two, it was reported that an additional eight hundred million dollars would be pumped into a factory making hard-disk drives. Singapore was the second largest maker of hard-disk drives in the world. This investment would keep it there.

On page four, someone proposed a revamp of the education system to promote greater creativity, to help students think out of the box. This way the country would produce more entrepreneurs, more self-starters and go-getters, and hopefully they would pull everyone forward into the new millennium.

On page six, someone important – a minister of some kind – warned local journalists not to *editorialize* when reporting the news. They shouldn't mix news and politics. They should just report the facts and steer clear of any political agenda. If they wished to pursue an agenda, they should come clean about it and join one of the parties and enter the political arena at election time. If they used their media platform to abuse the public's trust, to pursue irresponsible agendas, then the government had a right to step in. Indeed, it had a responsibility to do so.

In an article adjacent to this, the same person was quoted on the topic of foreign journalists. Foreign journalists should not get involved in local politics, he said. One of them – someone from the UK's *Guardian* – had recently called for press laws to be reformed, and this showed that he had crossed the line. In the minister's opinion, it was a simple open and shut case: the destiny of a country should not be decided by outsiders. The West had its values and the East had its own as well; not to say that one was better than the other, but there were differences, and these should be respected.

Kian Ming grew bored. His entire life had been a litany of arguments like this.

'Don't worry,' he murmured under his breath, as if he were speaking to an invisible interlocutor seated across the table from him. 'Nobody cares about politics or wants to get involved in it. You either get sued or go bankrupt or you get locked away by the Special Branch. You think I'm stupid or what? I'm a *gila babi*? I'm a *goondu*? Do I have to tell you that, compared to Hong Kong and Taiwan, this place is dead! That nobody in this country dares to care about politics! We couldn't care less about that kind of shit. We prefer to focus on the Great Singapore Sale – .'

'What's that you said?' he heard a reproving voice in his head. 'Remember what I told you about talking to yourself, Lim Kian Ming! You promised you would stop! It's a bad habit and it makes you sound crazy!'

'Okay, okay, sorry,' he mumbled, turning the page. 'Don't yell at me like that.'

He scanned quickly through the contents. 'World News', the section-header, said: South Korean students were demonstrating about something, getting riled up for some reason or other … Something about the presidential elections in Taiwan – some parliamentarians were up in arms about something … A campaign of some kind in India – someone trying to save a patch of forest from a planned hydroelectric dam …

Kian Ming stifled a yawn and turned the page again. A flash of red at the bottom of the page caught his eye, an advertisement for a new car. They were promoting the new Saab convertible, and right away Kian Ming saw that it was a sumptuous, splendid vehicle. It appeared to be all sweep and flow, all sexy curves, and bends with no hard edges.

He imagined himself at the wheels of the Saab, barrelling down the highway with the hood down. In such a car, people would look at him and know straightaway that he was successful, that he represented style and achievement. He wouldn't have to open his mouth or say or do anything. All they had to do was to look – to open their eyes and look – and like magic the sleek lines would say it all.

For a while longer Kian Ming dwelled on the vision in his head. Then the light went out of his eyes and he turned to the football news.

Artistic Citizenship: The Repoliticization of Theatre in the New Creative Economy of Singapore

DAVID BIRCH

The arts as new economy

The following provocative question about Singapore theatre, 'Will local artists still have as much leeway if the government decides some time in the future that arts and cultural events can all be imported?' was posed in 2002 by Tan Chong Kee, a Director of the Board of a leading Singapore English language Theatre group, The Necessary Stage. He continued, 'Will the pressure to "measure up" to imported cultural spectacles force more local art groups to imitate these productions and jettison engagement with indigenous realities?'[1] This comment implies a potentially powerful influencing role in the arts (both imported and indigenous) for a Government keen on encouraging and supporting 'cultural spectacles' as part of a push to developing a new, globalized, creative economy.[2]

Part of that push involved significant investment in the S$600 million Esplanade – Theatres on the Bay, which was completed in 2002. Its use (apart from the small studio) is well outside the realms of the budgets of all but a handful of performing companies in Singapore. Such a performing arts complex is, as I see it, a visible representation of the tension that plays out in so many different ways in Singapore between the global and local;[3] between the arts as local, indigenous expression in Singapore and the arts as global economic drawcard. Its very presence has required some companies to rethink who their audiences are and the sort of productions that can be mounted and sustained in such spaces.[4]

In this article I will explore some of the ways that in contemporary Singapore the performing arts are gradually being repositioned, redefined, and repoliticized as an industrialized component of a larger and new creative economy, and what that means for the way that mainstream theatre companies in particular[5] position and present themselves within a government-driven cultural politics which is increasingly articulating an *arts-as-new-economy* model. Esplanade – Theatres on the Bay is, if you like, the flagship for leading the theatre fleet of companies into more productive economic waters, not so much for the sake of art *itself*, but as an *active* part of a state enterprise dominated by a search for new ways of growing the economy.[6] Artists in Singapore have a clearly defined role to play in that economic growth, not so much as individual performers exploring their own creativity irrespective of their impact on the economy, but as *artistic citizens* with responsibilities to contribute beyond just their art.

Being an artist in Singapore

At a forum held in the National University of Singapore in October 2000, T. Sasitharan, Artistic Co-Director of the Practice Performing Arts School, a highly respected and significant theatre institution in Singapore founded by Kuo Pao Kun,[7] responded to then Minister of Arts, David Lim (who had argued in that forum that artistic 'social responsibility' was effectively synonymous with the maintenance of 'social peace')[8] by saying:

> I think that as an artist, as a person working in the arts, as a creative being, as someone who is a citizen of this country, as a father, as a son, as a person who sees himself having a future in this country, I demand the right to be irresponsible. I demand the right to be irresponsible when I think it is my prerogative to be so. An artist cannot work unless that right is given to them at certain points in their careers.[9]

This raises a very interesting issue for artists in Singapore, particularly those operating in highly visible, public spaces, like theatre and performing arts, namely the tension between artistic individualism and the constraints that might be put upon that individualism – in other words, the tension between *self* and *State*.[10] Increasingly it appears that it is the State that, even if not always put first, is generally omnipresent to some degree in decisions that theatre companies make on a daily basis, especially given the occasions when an artist or company putting self first has generally run foul of the authorities. Despite the view that Singapore is becoming a more open society in recent years, the dominance of a State-driven ideology seems more and more to suggest an 'appropriate' (and certainly State-acceptable) overall direction for theatre, even if only in its most benign manifestation as a discursive economic undercurrent influencing theatre groups.

Responding also to David Lim at the same forum, Ekachai Uekerongtham, a leading Director in Singapore, founding President and Artistic Director of one of the country's most prominent theatre companies, *Action Theatre*, said: 'Well, I think, when you're running a theatre company, you need to be realistic about things because by the end of the year, you will be interviewed by a panel from the NAC [National

Arts Council] who will question you why you didn't do certain things even though you had put them down on paper … It's not so easy to say, "I'm an artist, I just want to do what I want", because you're an artist in Singapore, you know.'[11] That statement says a lot, not simply about pressures on artists and companies, and varying levels of complicity with the State, but also that a major question to be asked is, 'why is it so different to be an artist in Singapore than anywhere else?' The answer to that, I believe, rests with the role of the Government, either as explicit or implicit driver of the directions for *creative* members of the arts and culture sector as active (*artistic*) *citizens* in the new creative economy.

'Culture', 'creativity', and 'citizenship' are not the strange bedfellows that some might think.[12] As the UK-based Centre for Creative Communities makes clear,

> The premise is that whilst culture seems to point in the direction of particularistic issues of aesthetics, meaning and difference, citizenship points towards universalistic issues relating to rights, obligations and belonging in the modern world. Likewise, a theory or policy of citizenship which fails to take culture into account is worthless, while an approach to culture which marginalises questions of rights and obligations is equally defective.[13]

What, then, might once have been seen as separate domains is increasingly being seen through the connections (rather than the differences) among them, not least in a Singapore actively seeking to develop as a creative, and connected economy. As Randy Martin points out, 'public art occupies a space that can confound what constitutes the clear boundary between government authority and private discretion. Controversy issues from this ambiguous border'.[14] And it does so, especially in Singapore where the arts, if not contributing directly to the financial economy, needs at least to demonstrate themselves to be a *social good* and 'not simply a personal statement or private service'.[15]

We have been witnessing a major rediscovery of creativity in recent years by governments and businesses in particular, especially, as Terry Flew points out, when that involves a 'discovery of the value of original ideas when converted into tradeable intellectual property'.[16] 'Creativity discourses' are becoming big business, as indeed is the whole globalizing push towards support of creative industries.[17] These creative industries were defined, for example, by Dr Tan Chin Nam when Permanent Secretary of the Ministry of Information, Communications and the Arts in Singapore, as 'the convergence of arts, business and technology'. This convergence is worth exploring within the context of Singapore's increasing push towards the appropriation of the arts and creativity towards the greater growth of the economy overall.

Creative industries as an economic good

A great deal has been written on the moves made by the Singapore Government to reposition Singapore as an Asian global hub for the creative industries in order to find new avenues for continuing economic growth in an increasingly globalized, knowledge-economy driven world.[18] Those moves have potentially serious implications, I believe, for mainstream theatre companies and for the development of the arts and culture generally in Singapore. For example, in a 2002 Government report, *Investing in Singapore's Cultural Capital: A New Agenda for a Creative and Connected Nation*, issued by the Ministry responsible for the Arts, creative people are defined as 'individuals who have "cultural capital inside". These are people who have a deep consciousness of the importance of culture and creativity and deploy it to their full advantage in the New Economy'.[19] This also includes consumers 'who fuel the demand for cultural activities and differentiated products and services, as well as individuals who are inspired by the arts but are creative in ways that go beyond the arts'.[20]

Lee Boon Yang, when Minister of Information, Communications and the Arts, said in an important speech in 2003 about the development of creative industries in Singapore that 'Without the arts and culture, there can be no creative industry.' He continued, 'Nurturing a dynamic arts and cultural sector is important because it is the artistic core of the creative cluster.'[21] For example, the Singapore Government has openly stated that it expects the creative industries to contribute up to 6% of GDP by 2012. So 'In order to grow the creative industry cluster, we need a growing community of creative people who are fully connected to the world of arts and who can use their artistry and innovations as important competitive tools to tap new business opportunities.' Theatre, as part of the arts, has a clear role therefore not just to attract people to spend money in Singapore (although this is one of its requirements in a creative economy) but, more subtly, to help contribute to a general climate that increases creativity overall in a new economy. In effect, this is a repoliticization of theatre from being traditionally a *civil* society player (and as such, one that might rub up against the Government from time to time) to an *industrialized active citizen*, operating, like any other economic player in the *civic* society of Singapore, for the greater good, and growth, of the Singapore economy – complicit with, rather than potentially (through creativity) interrogative of Government policy.

In 2007, Lee Boon Yang put the case for Singapore thus: 'The creative industries will not only contribute to economic growth directly but also act as a powerful catalyst for other sectors such as tourism, retail, manufacturing and education.'[22] Creativity in Singapore, along these lines, therefore, is to be put to work, *as an industry*, in order to ensure that it is economically productive, 'by extracting useful skills and values out of otherwise unproductive individuals or groups'.[23] As John Kao has pointed out, 'The opportunity for Singapore is colossal; it is to create a world-leading, not merely world-class, innovation system. It is about reaping the fruits from such investment by realising unprecedented amounts of value.'[24] But it needs to do so within a sociocultural context that has been articulated in Singapore as a distinct set of values and directions by its Government for many years: those operating in the public eye, like theatre companies, ignore these at some risk. For example, a major Government initiative, known as *Singapore 21* and announced in August 1987, established five ideals for the future Singapore will enter in the twenty-first century. They are:

1. Every Singaporean matters
2. Strong families: our foundation and our future
3. Opportunities for all
4. The Singapore heartbeat: feeling passionately about Singapore
5. Active citizenship: making a difference

It is the fifth, depending upon how one defines 'difference', that would seem to be the most difficult to interpret for artists. But it must be realized that it is these sorts of ideals which theatre companies have to engage with, even though they may not be known by heart by the average Singaporean, and which are operated by the Government – mostly through its public/civil service managers (that is, the people interpreting Government policy who often apply them more rigorously than the Ministers who make the policies and set the values intended). *Singapore 21* was very clear that every Singaporean needed to contribute to civic life, and later reports articulating the 'remaking' of Singapore all echoed this call for Singaporeans to 'co-create a "Home for All Singaporeans" in an era of change and uncertainty'.[25] What this means is that artists, as Singaporeans, are positioned by the Government to have clear responsibilities to contribute as active citizens to this creation of 'home' and its 'heartbeat'. It is, if you like, a repoliticizing by appropriation (a very familiar political tactic in Singapore) of *civil* society into *civic* society.

The political context for a creative economy

Mainstream theatre cannot escape this powerful discourse in Singapore, either artistically or commercially. This doesn't mean to say that the Government actually dictates the *content* of theatre (although it does monitor this, in various ways, for possible points of contention) but, rather, it creates a socioeconomic political climate, through its views on the arts-as-new economy model, against which theatre companies and artists inevitably (even if only implicitly) have to make their decisions about the theatre they actually create. In practice, this effectively means that theatre companies, in order to continue in business, do the Government's job of the repoliticizing of theatre to an arts-as-new economy model. They do this through their own interpretation of the prevailing cultural politics and Government discourse which, *de facto*, position theatre companies, as artistic citizens, as needing to actually share (rather than simply be just complicit with) the same language and discourse of the Government.

As part of this discourse, and in the context of an overall strategic plan, Singapore has sought variously over the years to 'remake' itself as a 'Renaissance City', as a creative and connected society, and as a 'Global City of the Arts'. In March 2000, the *Renaissance City Report* spoke of Singapore as a 'Global Arts City', and, consequently, significant investments have been made in the creative industries. The Creative Industries Development Strategy was set up in 2003 to drive this agenda, and, in July 2005, 'Creative Community Singapore' was launched with the then Minister for Information, Communications and the Arts, Lee Boon Yang, saying that 'Our future will be propelled by the creative and innovative capacity of our people.' A fund of S$10million was established for a three-year period to encourage this new creativity in Singapore.

But, in fact, this was a process which had begun in the late 1980s and was more fully developed as a concept by the Singapore Government in 1992, 'to spearhead its vision of cultivating a thriving arts, cultural and entertainment scene, not only for economic reasons (to attract tourists and foreign talents) but also for socio-cultural objectives (enrichment of Singaporeans and nation-building)'.[26] The *Renaissance City Report*, it should be noted, emerged after Singapore's worst economic downturn since separation from Malaysia in 1965,[27] and was an attempt to 'fundamentally review Singapore's strategies for survival as a nation ... an attempt to "pragmatize" and foreground the industrial-cum-economic aspects of culture'.[28] This has basically developed (and continues to do so) into a unique Singapore-branded 'equilibrium' that is loosely creative at the 'margins' but 'bears the marks of political conformity'.[29]

As Alvin Tan, founding Artistic Director of *The Necessary Stage* in 1987, and one of Singapore's leading theatre directors and commentators, pointed out a few years ago,

> The whole tenor of what is permissible seems to be changing, but will its essence be allowed a full and healthy journey? The impetus for opening up today arises out of pragmatic, economic necessity. With globalisation and the cyber-creation of alternative spaces and means of supporting multiple voices and diverse viewpoints, the authorities' only defence is to encourage critical thinking and creativity. Yet, it is still rigorous in making sure that its citizens abide within its ways of thinking.[30]

While the politics appears to have shifted from a once rampantly command and control approach, there is still, as Kenneth Paul Tan suggests, 'a politics of apprehension' in place.[31] Such a politics inevitably affects a theatre which cannot, currently, stand outside of Government-driven policy discourse. That discourse is summed up well in the *Renaissance City Report*:

> Renaissance Singapore will be creative, vibrant and imbued with a keen sense of aesthetics. Our industries are supported with a creative culture that keeps them competitive in the global economy. The renaissance Singaporean has an adventurous spirit, an inquiring and creative mind and a strong passion for life. Culture and the arts animate our city and our society consists of active citizens who build on our Asian heritage to strengthen the Singapore Heartbeat through expressing their Singapore stories in culture and the arts.[32]

What, then, does that mean for theatre practitioners and companies as artistic citizens in Singapore?

Theatre and artistic citizenship in Singapore

Given the dominant Government discourse in Singapore, it seems to be a reasonable conclusion to make that the artist in Singapore is in a more heightened state of awareness than in other parts of the world about whether they should, in Randy Martin's words, 'answer first to the muse or the State'.[33] The answer is not simply a matter of individual expression – Singaporean artists need to serve, in some way, the greater, generally economic, good of the society as *artistic citizens*. Artistic citizenship poses a very simple question which formed the heart of a symposium organized by the Tisch School of the Arts in New York in October 2004: 'What can art achieve that cannot be accomplished through conventional channels?'[34] Theatre in this sense then is public art and the question I have been interested in here is the extent to which that public art is, again in the words of Randy Martin, 'a particular kind of social good that serves as a means to bring forth ideas about our lives together'.[35] If 'such work rests on a conviction that art is not simply aesthetically enlivening of everyday surroundings but that it is civically ennobling',[36] then, unlike in some other parts of the world, the difference, I would suggest here, is that in Singapore such active (artistic) citizenship by individuals and groups is not so much the *voluntary* act described by Martin, but an *expectation* of the Government.

To speak in light of the above to one example of theatre in Singapore. The Necessary Stage (TNS) is a non-profit theatre company with charitable status founded in 1987. Using the dominant language of creativity and citizenship developed by the Government, its mission is 'to create challenging, indigenous and innovative theatre that touches the heart and mind', and to commit itself 'to developing new works, international exchange and collaboration and reaching out to new audiences while maintaining high standards of production'.[37] Over the years the company has created numerous indigenous productions, often using the voices (and people) of the Singapore 'heartland' to explore serious social issues, such as health, education, mental health, ageing, marginalized peoples, homosexuality, HIV/AIDS and so on.

More recently, however, there is clearly an anxiety to broaden the internationalism of its productions in Singapore. For example, *The Good People*, written by Haresh Sharma and directed by Alvin Tan for TNS in 2007 featured well-known actors – Rody Vera from the Philippines, Sukania Venugopal from Malaysia and Siti Khalijah from Singapore. In 2006, the TNS production of *Mobile* was a collaboration featuring actors and writers from the region – from Thailand, the Philippines, Japan and Singapore – and dealing with stories about men and women affected by the movement of migration, very much a regional/global theme.[38] Similarly, *Separation 40* (2005) was a collaboration between TNS and Malaysia's well known Dramalab, and *Boxing Day: The Tsunami Project* (2005) involved actors from Singapore, Malaysia, and Thailand, and was performed in English, Malay and Thai with English subtitles. The reproduction and revision of the 2002 *godeatgod* (2004) also involved non-Singaporean actors, including Rody Vera from the Philippines and Eriko Wada from Japan. While not all of these productions were multimedia, many were. Internal collaborations also feature, as in the *100 Years in Waiting* (2001), the bilingual (Mandarin and English) Theatre Practice company. The first international staging of a TNS play was *Still Building* in Cairo, in 1992, and since then a total of 15 original Singapore plays by TNS have been presented in over 25 international venues.

The work of TNS raises some very interesting issues about how active citizens in a society – which Haresh Sharma, resident playwright with TNS for many years, once described as a 'Don't Say, Don't Say society'[39]– can function in socially responsible ways while still exercising their independence and exploring creative boundaries as artists within Singapore.

Among other notable theatre companies in Singapore, there is TheatreWorks, established in 1985 as a not-for-profit theatre company and registered charity. It says of itself that it is 'known for its reinvention of traditional performance through a juxtaposition of cultures ... Its works reflect a concern with cultural negotiation and artistic exchanges with artists, through a network of traditional and contemporary artists from different disciplines'.[40] This is clearly a strong reflection of the dominant Government discourse of the sort of theatre aimed at positioning Singapore as a regional artistic hub. Thus, under its Artistic Director Ong Keng Sen since 1989, TheatreWorks has actively developed both a Singapore and International Wing 'to facilitate its growth both in Singapore and in the international arena'.[41] In doing so, it seeks to promote and produce Singapore writing, 'thereby creating a theatre that is Singapore and with a Singaporean voice'; and at the same time, through meaningful regional collaboration, to contribute 'to the evolution of an Asian identity and aesthetics for the 21st Century'.[42]

Wild Rice founded in 2000 by Ivan Heng is, like TNS, a company limited by guarantee with charity status in Singapore. It is 'inspired by the multicultural societies that make up Singapore and modern Asia celebrating their diverse cultures and performance styles and bringing them together in creative collaborations that inspire, challenge and entertain'.[43] Ivan Heng makes the point on the website that

> In order to understand our world, to effect change, to respond to issues with compassion and integrity; our society must be able to see beyond the limitations and inevitable biases of our own perspectives. We need to imagine other possibilities. We need a larger vision. We need Art, because the vision to see other possibilities is the gift art gives to society. And live performance gives art a connecting energy parallel to none.

Theatre Practice was formed in 1986 by Kuo Pao Kun as Singapore's first fully bilingual theatre company. It says of itself that, within its multiracial environment, 'its sensitivity to social differences has captured the essence of an emerging culture in Southeast Asia – harmony amidst diversity'.[44] It underlines its approach to theatre-making as one which 'reflects the intense struggle between tradition and modernity' and 'while it provides access to global influences through international collaborations, The Theatre Practice remains true to its assertion of local identity.' Clearly the central issue of global versus local, so prominent a part of the Singapore Government's own policy positions, is highly influential here, as indeed it is to the way *WILD RICE* positions itself.

Teater Artistik was likewise established in 1986 and at Pasir Panjang Community Centre by a group of bilingual (Malay and English) theatre enthusiasts 'with a strategic mission to expand Singapore's theatre to the Southeast Asian region and the rest of the world in the near future'. Its vision and goals are:

1. to regard TA as a socially responsible theatre group; via our pursuit to be the best and most sought after Malay theatre management group in Asia
2. to maintain our responsibility by giving back to the community
3. to encourage young adults to discover their full potential to create awareness of social issues; encourage critical thinking and self reflections so as to discover who we are, where we stand and how we can make a difference
4. to increase the collective impact of local theatre groups in Asia collaboration, encouragement of Singapore writing and to invite established artists and practitioners both local and abroad.

While not considered to be a mainstream company (in the sense that the Malay community is relatively small in Singapore), this established and dynamic group has nevertheless adopted the language and discourse of a Singapore Government which emphasizes internationalism and collaboration.

Similarly Drama Box, formed in 1990, is a professional, Mandarin language, non-profit company with charity status. It has, according to its publicity, 'gained a respectable reputation for its acute sensitivity and perception in heightening social awareness and civic responsibility'. Significantly, one of its stated objectives is to 'contribute to Singapore's presence as an artistic force in the region and internationally', declaring that 'We believe that we live in a big global village, not in terms of economic scale, but one of collective humanity and human concerns. We believe that what happens in other countries affects us as well and hence we have a lot to share and learn from international collaboration.' As such, Drama Box began an International Outreach programme in 2003, and as an example of this approach, collaborated in a multidisciplinary play, *Drift* (from an original story by Shanghai's Nick Yu), with the Shanghai Dramatic Arts Centre, bringing together artists from Singapore, Shanghai, and Hong Kong under the direction of Singapore's Kok Heng Leun and

Koh Hui Ling. The play was premiered in Shanghai in November 2007. Clearly, as with other theatre companies in Singapore, Drama Box picks up on official language and discourse, positioning itself through concepts and issues such as social responsibility, internationalism, collaboration and globalization.

Finally, there is Ravindran Drama Group (RDG), a leading Tamil language theatre company, founded in 1988 'by a group of youths who wanted to continue the torch of Tamil theatre in Singapore'. Adopting the commercial language of retail, it says of itself that 'Today RDG has successfully weaved itself into the hearts of the Singapore Indian Community and has become a one-stop centre for theatre productions and talents.' It positions itself, albeit perhaps a little more tentatively than some other theatre companies, in a language reflecting the dominant cultural politics I have outlined in this paper, saying that

> [it] has also gained its recognition in the Singapore art scene through many independent and collaborative productions. RDG has made its mark in many of the theatre festivals and carnivals organised by various national organisations like the National Arts Council (NAC), Tamil Language Society (TLC), Singapore Indian Development Association (SINDA), People's Association (PA) and many other prestigious organisations since its inception.

Perhaps not unnaturally, there is an anxiety here, as we have seen with other companies, to prove its credentials *beyond* what it does on stage, not least of which (like the Malay group Teater KAMi in years past with literary and classical Malay) is to establish its credentials as an important vehicle for ensuring the continuation of literary and classical Tamil, including, for example, productions like the 1999 *Pathy Vathy* in literary Tamil; Shakespeare's *Macbeth* (2000, 2001) in classical Tamil, and *Kuralovium* (2004), which was a contemporary production of nine plays based on the writings of the great Tamil Sage-Poet Thiruvalluvar. In November 2007, the company collaborated with Miror Theatre to present *Thondan*, a Tamil adaptation of Shakespeare's *Titus Andronicus* in the Esplanade Theatre. Like all the other main theatre companies in Singapore, RDG positions theatre in education as an important part of its work (and in fact such activities are often a major means by which these companies develop a regular source of income). *Ali Baba* (2005) and *Asuran* (2006), for example, were staged with (and for) young school students. Overall, there is a strong positioning by the company as having a social responsibility 'to serve the society through theatre'.

Though not explicitly stated on its website, the mission of RDG, as well as promoting Tamil culture and language, is to bring Indian community issues to English-speaking audiences, both in Singapore and, less frequently, overseas.[45] Its current Artistic and Deputy Artistic Directors, G. Selvananthan and Puva Arugumugam were both trained in universities in Australia and have developed a strong commitment to exploring local issues of specific reference to the Indian communities in Singapore.

Corollary

What I have tried to argue here, through selected examples of some mainstream theatre companies operating in the four official languages of Singapore, is that they are not only positioned by the Government to be part of an arts-as-new-economy model, but in varying ways they also position themselves to be complicit with this over-riding economic discourse. More often than not, they seek to leverage credibility by a rethinking of what they do as companies in order to better concentrate on government-driven performance indicators, such as international-ization, professionalization, and intercultural collaboration as a means of helping Singapore (through its Government-led discourse) towards achieving its vision of being a creative and connected 'renaissance' society, one that is leading the way regionally towards a globalized new creative economy. The way that all the companies present themselves reveals, if not exactly an anxiety, a definite preoccupation with being part of the larger, *corporatized* model of the Singapore economy. The language of their positioning of themselves is not what would generally be considered the language of artistic expression of 'self'; it is the language of the State.

NOTES

1. Tan Chong Kee, 'Can the Co-opted Speak? A Brief History of One Theatre Company's Negotiation in the Singaporean State', *focas*, 3 (2002) 329.
2. See Terence Lee and Denise Lim, 'The Economics and Politics of "Creativity" in Singapore', *Australian Journal of Communication*, 31: 2 (2004) 149-65.
3. See Kenichi Kawaski, 'Cultural Hegemony of Singapore Among ASEAN Countries: Globalization and Cultural Policy', *International Journal of Japanese Sociology*, 13 (2004) 22-35.
4. See T.C. Chang and W.K. Lee, 'Renaissance City Singapore; A Study of Arts Spaces', *Area*, 35: 2 (2003) 128-41.
5. The National Arts Council website lists 25 English language theatre companies, 13 Mandarin, 2 Tamil, and 3 Malay language theatre groups, although there many other much smaller groups in existence.
6. The rise in ticket prices for theatre in Singapore in recent years is a good indicator of this new arts-as-economy model. For example, *The Toy Factory Productions'* 2008 production of Raymond To's *Shanghai Blues The Musical* in the Esplanade Theatre had tickets ranging from S$48 to a top price of S$128, whereas the *Singapore Repertory*

Theatre's 2007 production of Martin McDonagh's *The Pillowman* in their own theatre, the DBS Arts Centre, had tickets set at S$35, rising to S$50 for a Friday and Saturday performance. Ticket prices for *Action Theatre*'s 2007 production of Desmond Sim's *Postcards from Rosa* in their own theatre space in a converted house in Waterloo Street were set between S$35 and S$45. By comparison with London, New York, and Sydney these prices are low, but they do still limit the range of people prepared to pay these prices to go to the theatre. *The Necessary Stage*, for example, recognizes this and has often set ticket prices as low as S$3 for community theatre productions in order to educate audiences into going to the theatre by enabling them to afford a ticket. But such pricing is not sustainable: even if set within price ranges of S$35 upwards, theatre companies in Singapore (as elsewhere) are continually seeking corporate and other sponsorship. Fundraising inevitably goes hand in hand with theatre in Singapore. For example, the 2008 production of *La Traviata* by Singapore Lyric Opera in the Esplanade Theatre had tickets starting from just S$25 peaking to S$150 for a box seat (very cheap by world standards for a full opera) but for the opening fundraising Gala night, a box (with 8 seats) cost S$8,000, with the cheapest seat at S$300.

7. See Quah Sy Ren in this issue, pp. 148-61.
8. See Ruth Bereson, ed., *Artistic Integrity and Social Responsibility: You Can't Please Everyone!* (Singapore: Ethos Books, 2001).
9. Bereson, ed., *Artistic Integrity and Social Responsibility*, p. 52.
10. See James Gomez, *Self Censorship. Singapore's Shame* (Singapore: Think Centre, 2000), p. 68.
11. Gomez, *Self Censorship*, p. 40.
12. See Nick Stevenson, ed., *Culture and Citizenship* (London: Sage, 2001) and his 'Cultural Citizenship in the "Cultural" Society: A Cosmopolitan Approach', *Citizenship Studies*, 7: 3 (2003) 331-48.
13. <www.creativecommunities.org.uk/essays/72.html> accessed 18 December 2008.
14. Randy Martin, 'Artistic Citizenship. Introduction', in *Artistic Citizenship. A Public Voice for the Arts*, eds, Mary Schmidt Campbell and Randy Martin (London: Routledge, 2006), p. 4.
15. Martin, 'Artistic Citizenship. Introduction', p. 3.
16. Terry Flew, 'Creativity, the "New Humanism" and Cultural Studies', *Continuum: Journal of Media and Cultural Studies*, 18: 2 (2004) 162.
17. See John Howkins, *The Creative Economy: How People Make Money From Ideas* (London: Penguin, 2001).
18. See Terence Lee, 'Creative Shifts and Directions. Cultural Policy in Singapore', *International Journal of Cultural Policy*, 10: 3 (2004) 281-99, and his 'Industrializing Creativity and Innovation', in *Renaissance Singapore? Economy, Culture and Politics*, ed., Kenneth Paul Tan (Singapore: NUS Press, 2007), pp. 45-67; Audrey Yue, 'Cultural Governance and Creative Industries in Singapore', *International Journal of Cultural Policy*, 12: 1 (2006) 17-33; and Can-Seng Ooi, 'Free the Mind. Mind the Free: The Creative Economy and Limits to the Freedom of Expression in Singapore', in *Communication and Human Rights*, ed., Mike Hayes (Bangkok, Mahidol University, Office of Human Rights Studies and Social Development, 2007), pp. 44-68.
19. See also MITA *Renaissance City Report: Culture and the Arts in Renaissance Singapore* (Singapore: MITA, 2000).
20. MITA, *Singapore Global City for the Arts* (Singapore: Singapore Tourism Board & MITA, 2000), p. 4.

21. Lee Boon Yang, Welcome Address to the Second World Summit on the Arts and Culture, Singapore, 24 November 2003.
22. *The Straits Times*, 29 August 2007, p. 7.
23. Petrina Leo and Terence Lee, 'The "New" Singapore: Mediating Culture and Creativity', *Continuum: Journal of Media and Cultural Studies*, 18:2 (2004) 206.
24. John Kao, 'Can a Communitarian Society Nurture Creativity and Innovation?', in *Perspectives on Singapore 2002*, ed., Chong Li Lin (Singapore: Institute of Policy Studies & Times Academic Press, 2002), p. 81.
25. Tan Tay Keong, 'Social Capital and Singapore Society' <www.spp.nus.edu/sg/docs/wp/wp51.pdf> p.5 accessed 18 December 2008.
26. T.C. Chang, 'Renaissance Revisited: Singapore as a "Global City for the Arts"', *International Journal of Urban and Regional Research*, 24: 4 (2000) 819.
27. Leo and Lee, 'The "New" Singapore', p. 205.
28. Leo and Lee, 'The "New" Singapore', p. 206.
29. Terence Lee & Denise Lim, 'The Economics and Politics of "Creativity" in Singapore', *Australian Journal of Communication*, 31: 2 (2004) 149-65.
30. Alvin Tan, 'Theatre and Cultures: Globalizing Strategies', in *Renaissance Singapore? Economy, Culture and Politics,* ed., Kenneth Paul Tan (Singapore: NUS Press, 2007), p. 79.
31. Tan, 'Theatre and Cultures', p. 2.
32. Tan, 'Theatre and Cultures', p. 3.
33. Martin, 'Artistic Citizenship. Introduction', p. 1.
34. <www.nyu.edu/publicaffairs/newsreleases/b_tsoa_hiphop_10082004.shtml> accessed 18 December 2008.
35. Martin, 'Artistic Citizenship. Introduction', p. 3.
36. Martin, 'Artistic Citizenship. Introduction', p. 3.
37. <www.necessary.org> accessed 18 December 2008.
38. See Harish Sharma, *Eclipse*, in this issue, pp. 135-45.
39. David Birch, *Haresh Sharma, The Cultural Politics of Playwriting in Contemporary Singapore* (Singapore: Ethos Books, 2007), p. 10.
40. <http://theatreworks.org.sg> accessed 18 December 2008.
41. For a detailed account of the achievements of TheatreWorks, see K.K. Seet in this issue, pp. 92-106.
42. <http://theatreworks.org.sg> accessed 18 December 2008.
43. <www.wildrice.com.sg> accessed 18 December 2008.
44. <www.ttp.org.sg> accessed 18 December 2008.
45. In 2001, for example, the company collaborated with Melbourne-based Avant Theatre and Language in productions in Melbourne.

Eclipse

HARESH SHARMA

ONE

Son: My father used to say, there are too many people in the world. Some have to die. It's in the books. It's been happening, he says, for thousands of years.

Tomorrow is the Festival of Lights. Tomorrow's celebration is a triumph of good over evil. When the demons wanted to rule the mortal world, the gods had no choice but to allow it. However, there was a condition: the demons could rule anywhere in the world without light. So for days and nights, everyone lit lamps. The whole world was bright. There was no darkness anywhere, and the demons could not rule.

My father used to say, when it is time, everything will come together. There is a reason for violence, a reason for suffering.

Tomorrow is the Festival of Lights. But today ... today I am holding my father, taking a journey with him, back to where he was born: Hyderabad Sind.

In 1947, my father was forced to leave his birthplace. The word they used was 'partition' – a word I would use of that which separates my living room from my kitchen. 'Partition' made my father's neighbours throw stones at him and his family, asking them to bugger off. 'Partition' turned friends with similar beliefs into enemies with different gods.

He fled. He had to go to the station several times because the trains were filled with people trying to escape death. There was hardly any space on top of the train, let alone inside it. But he was lucky. Many on the trains before and after his had been raped, tortured, killed. He was lucky to have escaped that silly 'partition'. And, since that day in 1947, he has not gone back. He never again saw the neighbourhood where he grew up, the friends he played cricket with. He never again saw the house where he was born.

I cremated him. Three weeks ago. As mourner after mourner shook my hand and offered me condolences, I thought ... a holiday would be nice. I've been working too hard. I need a holiday. I deserve one, dammit.

And in a moment of total selfishness – and selflessness – I decided. Take your father home, I told myself. Scatter his ashes where it really matters.

[*slight pause*] And get a tan.

My father was born in 1929, in Hyderabad Sind.

PAUSE

Father: I am born in 1929 in Hyderabad Sind. I go to Hindu High School in Hyderabad and learn Sindhi for first five years and after that I learn English, Maths, Science. I learn about all the gases. I know oxygen and carbon dioxide and I pass my matriculation in '46 and work as salesman here and there until '47. There is partition, so all of us we must leave.

My father is in Japan but we never hear from him many years so my mother is always crying and thinking what to do.

We leave Hyderabad in 1947. It is very difficult time during partition. We settle in Bombay. I don't want to stay there. I try and I am lucky because I find job in Singapore. I have good job and I am happy. But few years pass and I think I want to start a family. So I go back to Bombay. There I get married. My wife is my neighbour. Every day I see her, she is on her bicycle, laughing, and very happy. I tell my mother I like her. It is love marriage.

The priest say her chart is very strong. It is love, a good match ... but the astrology is not good. I don't care. I am happy. We have pooja and she change her name and we get married.

I don't want to be like my father. He never come back. I don't want to promise and make people wait and worry. That is why few days after wedding, I straightaway bring her to Singapore. It is 1959. We rent one small room. Very polite Christian family at Lavender Street. I pay $40 every month. I work with Singapore best textile company, and stay with them until I retire.

We want family but we try for many years no success. Then we ask priest to pray to Mother God and finally we have child. After 13 years ... one son. He is not my son. He is my wife's son.

PAUSE

When my wife die, my son he cry a lot. His aunties they scold him, why you cry so much, it is no good. If you cry, your mother will not have peace of mind, she will not go. When I see he is crying, I think about my mother. She also cry very much during wartime and partition when we don't know where my father is.

My son ... we don't talk much, just a few words. He ask me how are you, I say I am very good. It is OK, he is grown man. Once your son is grown he is not your son, you treat him like grown-up. You cannot command him, you can only suggest him. Same thing, I never see my father. He travelled lot. All the time he is in Japan, in foreign country. He is born in 1898.

PAUSE

Grandfather: I am born in 1898 in Hyderabad Sind. After school, I am doing textile business for few years. My boss, he ask me to go Japan with him. There is plenty business there, he say. We can sell textile. We can open factory, do export, all that. This is 1928. I am 30 years old. My wife is only 25 but I still go because I don't want to stay in Hyderabad.

From Hyderabad, I go to Karachi by train. From Karachi I go to Bombay, and then by ship to Osaka. In total, it take one month about. I work in Osaka lot. We open factory, make good business. Japanese also I speak very well. Few years I stay in Japan, few months I go back to Hyderabad.

It is no problem for me. Sometimes I think about my wife, my children. But that is woman's duty, no? Everything is mother. Mother is main part of the house, the heart. Father is busy with work. It is mother who raise them and love them and teach them respect.

But during war everything change. They don't want all this import export. The factory, the textile, all we must close. I cannot do anything, cannot go back Hyderabad, nothing. I want to go Singapore, but they say Japan is fighting there. It is not practical. It is best to stay in Osaka only.

I meet a woman. She is very kind and gentle lady. We stay together and have family. It is war everywhere in the world, but I am most happy. Aray, I cannot think about Hyderabad. What is happening there, how they are coping, all I cannot control. What I can do? Past is past. Now I have small tailoring shop with my wife. I have family. I have responsibility. Now I am here. My life is here.

[...]

THREE
Son: They call it ashes. But there are actually quite a lot of bone fragments. Like everything else in the world, the high octane incinerator at the crematorium is not perfect.

I am now at the border town of Munabao, in India. One more stop, and I'll be in Pakistan. I could have easily taken a plane there and made my way to Hyderabad. I am, after all, a fortunate citizen of Singapore. Pakistan and India are just a visa away. My red passport is my trump card.

But my father took this journey in 1947. And as much as I'm slowly regretting this insane notion of retracing his footsteps, I do feel rather daunted about the whole affair. So much for my holiday.

I feel my ancestors' history channelling me, especially after having googled 'partition' and reading countless accounts of the largest population movement ever recorded. Even Gandhi said, 'My whole soul rebels against the idea that Hinduism and Islam represent two antagonistic cultures and doctrines. To assent to such a doctrine is for me a denial of God.'

But that's Gandhi. And Ben Kingsley truly deserved the Oscar. I, however, am badly in need of a shower, let alone a spa treatment. Needless to say, I have doubts.

It's almost sunset. If I catch the right train, I should be in Hyderabad by morning. The morning of the Festival of Lights. I don't know where I'm going. I have a destination but no address. I long to hear an Indian voice yelling, 'we will handle everything, you don't worry, you just come and we will settle everything.'

I don't know where I'm going. I feel trapped in the crossfire of history. I have ashes and bones. And the sun is setting.

PAUSE

Father: During Second World War my father is in Japan and for many years there is no communication with us and we don't know where he is. When we try to locate him, there is no news. They say he is in Singapore. But if you are in Singapore, why you never send news to us … to your family?

'Baba, when are you coming back? Many years we are waiting and you never come. Mummy every day she is crying. Every day she is asking for you. Baba, where are you? We need you. There is partition and we must go. Baba, I am leaving this letter here, on your favourite chair because I know you will come back. You are my hero. Baba I must go now because there is fighting.'

1947. I write letter to my father. I cannot have light because it is dangerous, so in the dark I am writing. I don't know if he will read. I don't know if he will come home. But I put my letter on his chair and leave Hyderabad.

At train station, I meet a man. He is Muslim, just coming from India. They are beating us over there, he shout at me. The Hindus want to kill us! Bhaiya, over here also there is fighting. Over here also they want to kill me, kill my family. You must leave your house, we also must leave ours. He is crying. He say to me, I am free now … I have no home but I am free.

1947. I am on the train to Bombay. There is hardship but I am smiling. I think of my father, all the sacrifice he has made. He is a good man. Like my father, I will be good man. I will have my son and I will teach him everything. I will give him everything. He will not have problems of war. His neighbours will not kill him. His country will be his home and his home his country. No fighting, no torture, no corruption, no nothing. He will be happy. My son will be happy.

I never hear from my father. Until today ... we don't know what happen. They tell my mother to wear white sari, but she say no. I am not widow, she say. I am not widow. He will come back. Very soon he will come back. I am not widow.

PAUSE

Grandfather: I am happy in Japan. Seven years pass by, the war is finished, I have my wife and daughter ... I am very happy. Then one day in the evening, when we are closing our shop, she say to me, don't switch off the light. I want to talk to you. She talk to me and I listen. Few days later, I leave Japan. I leave Japan to go back to Pakistan.

It is 1947. When I arrive in Hyderabad, there is already partition. I go to my house, but there is no one. My neighbours, they don't even want to talk to me. They say I am Hindu, they are Muslim, we cannot be friends. They tell me go away, leave Pakistan. My old friend, he is also Muslim, but he take me inside his house. Are you mad, he shout at me. Why you come here? All Hindus have left. You must quickly go or they will kill you. But where is my wife, I ask him. Where is my family?

I go inside my house. Nothing has changed. I sit on my chair. I am thinking I will hear my wife, her voice ... any time now she will come back from the temple and ...

Grandmother: And then Jyoti came round and I had to make tea, so I was busy whole morning entertaining her. I gave her Prasad from the temple and she took a little bit and was very happy and left. Then I am thinking what to cook for dinner ... Yes, you like mutton but ...

PAUSE

Grandfather: I am sitting on my chair. But I hear nothing. They have left. They have all left. I sit on my chair. There is no light, no sound. I sit in the darkness with only my heart beating.

And then I see his letter. And I smile. Jhoole Lal. I always say Jhoole Lal.

FOUR

Son: My father died in the morning. We kept his body overnight at home before he was brought to the crematorium. I stayed up with him – it was the least I could do. They say that a moth is a dead relative coming home. It is the soul or spirit of a loved one. The moth will naturally go towards any source of light or a flame, even if it may be burnt.

As I look at my motionless father, I think of my mother. Her feet were my world. I would touch her feet before an exam. I would touch her feet before a trip. I would touch her feet during a religious festival. Her feet were my temple. When she died, my faith was shattered. I had no beliefs. God was a joke. [*slight pause*] As was my marriage.

My marriage was a glorious union of man and woman – the wedding was a celebrated affair involving crates of duty-free alcohol. The whole world was invited. It was a night of hilarity – finally, your son is a man – and lament – your wife would have been so happy, but the mother of the groom is not here with us!

My wife was a decent soul who I believe truly loved me. I don't know why I proposed. She was there – a friend. Someone I could speak with, open up to. I guess I felt ... it was my duty ... my obligation. I was the son, the only son ... a blessing and half. I had to ... marry ... have kids ... it was the right thing to do.

When we divorced, I think my father was secretly happy. He was ecstatic about the fact that his son was married ... but he wasn't quite ecstatic about her. He immediately mobilized the aunties.

Father: He is still young. They have no children. All that is the past. Now he needs a decent girl, a simple girl from India. The girls there have morals, they have Indian culture. The Indian girls in Singapore go to discos and come home at two in the morning.

Son: I go to discos ... with my boyfriend.

PAUSE

Grandfather: I am happy in Japan. Seven years pass, the war is finished, I have my wife and daughter and I am very happy. Then one day, when we are closing our shop, she say to me ... don't switch off the light. I want to talk to you. She ask me ...

Japanese Wife: You don't want to go back?

Grandfather: No. Why go back? I will send letter to say all is well and I am now happy here. [*slight pause*] She look at me with shame.

Japanese Wife: That is not correct. You are not such a man. They are also your family. You don't want to know if they are OK? You don't care if your wife is crying? If your son is missing you?

Grandfather: I don't understand this woman. She is now my wife. She is now my family. But she look at me. And she tell me go … go settle everything and come back. But how can I leave her? How can I leave my daughter?

Japanese Wife: If you are a man who will abandon his wife, if you are a man who will abandon his family, then I do not know you. If you don't go, I will take our daughter and I will leave you. But, you must promise … you must promise you will come back.

PAUSE

Father: My mother wait for him. Long time she wait. In wartime, in partition … she still is hoping he will come home. What can she think? That he abandon her and the family when they need him? What can she do but make up her own story …

Grandmother: Some people they say he is in Singapore during war and was killed. Some say he settle in Japan with new family. They tell me to wear white sari. No. I am not widow. Why I must wear white? He will come back. Very soon he will come back.

PAUSE

Father: My son … he never meet his grandmother. She die before he even born. I don't want to tell him how much she suffer. I myself also don't have the full picture because I leave her to come to Singapore. People always tell her, you are strong, forget about him. Have faith in God's grace. But she is stubborn.

Grandmother: What is faith? You can tell me? Where is the answer? All my dreams, all my hopes are gone. When he looks for me, I am no longer there. It is finished. [*slight pause*] I am his wife and now I am leaving him.

PAUSE

Son: I no longer have a wife. I have boyfriend. A partner. What do I call him … a husband? My father calls him 'the second son'. My father adores him to bits. When is your Muslim friend coming again for dinner, he would ask. No, it is late, he must stay here tonight, he can sleep on your bed. Dad … dear daddy … the man I share my bed with is my true love. And the woman I used to live with was … just my wife.

Tomorrow is the Festival of Lights. My father is not sure whether he wants to go to the temple. He asks if I want to go. I tell him I want to go to New York. Only $600 for a return flight on North West Airlines. My father tells me not to go. And frankly, I don't really want to go. It's 2001, and not the best time to travel to New York.

I'm going because my boyfriend wants to. It's so cheap, he says. We'll never get this special offer ever again! And it's New York! We can hold hands and walk down the road! We can walk down the road here as well … Serangoon Road! [*slight pause*] He smiles … I look at his sweet eager eyes. In my mind, I'm thinking … I don't want to die. I'm willing to die. But I'm not ready for him to die. If he does, what will I do? Leave the country? Start a new life? Where? The world is full of darkness. I want to find a place with some light. But I don't know where that is.

Tomorrow I'm leaving for New York. I am not asleep because I am writing a will. I am leaving everything equally to my ex-wife, my boyfriend and my father. No one will hate me then.

I look around my room. There are four lamps. One is fluorescent, which I never use. One is a table lamp, which I only use when I need to read. One is a standing lamp, which points to the ceiling. The last one, the only one I use, is orange. That way, the room is still dim, but atmospheric. Not bright and gaudy, not dark and scary. Just dim. My room will attract neither gods nor demons.

This is the room I slept in, the night my mother died. I was asked if she appeared to me that night. She did not. We kept a fire burning for twelve days after her death. On the twelfth day, early in the morning, the flame was brought to and left at the sea. She stopped existing after that. She is neither in heaven nor hell. She just stopped existing.

When my father died, my boyfriend – my 'Muslim friend', my father's 'second son' – stayed up with me, always making sure the flame was still burning. As we sat there, looking at my father's body, I turned to him. I smiled and said, I am now an orphan. [*slight pause*] I didn't cry.

PAUSE

Grandmother: That day when I leave my home, I am thinking how he will find me? I am not choosing to leave. It is force. Everybody is saying go, go, go. I don't want to go. This is my house. This is my family. My whole life is this. If I go, how he will find me? How my husband will find me? [*slight pause*] We cannot change the world. We can only bring up our children. I thought I will have a happy life. I thought I will die with the sound of my family crying and praying for me … That is my dream. Now, it is all finished. But I will not wear a white sari. I will still not wear a white sari.

FIVE

Son: The train has stopped. It is morning and I'm in Hyderabad. The people here are as friendly as one can expect in such conditions. Give them a few bucks and they'll take you anywhere. I'm no longer the enemy but a welcome tourist – one of many who have attempted to 'visit the home of their ancestors', as we say in the East.

I am here, in a land devastated by that silly word 'partition'. I have retraced my father's life, and the life of his father. I am here, sixty years later. But I don't see anything. I don't hear anything. I don't feel anything. This has been a total fuck of a holiday.

'Hello!' A Pakistani man greets me. I explain my situation, and he kindly invites me to his home. Over a meal we begin talking. He tells me stories and shows me photographs of the land. He plays me songs from his collection of cassettes. As I listen to the songs, he tells me stories of partition that he had heard.

One Muslim man was attacked because he was mistaken for a Hindu. He had many Hindu friends. He had even sheltered some of them in his home during the riots. One Pakistani woman said her Hindu neighbours asked the women to slit their throats and jump into wells.

By this time, more of his friends have gathered in his home. Apparently, word has spread of this Indian slash Hindu slash Pakistani slash Singaporean slash idiot who has arrived with his father's ashes. Everyone wants a piece of the action.

They all speak in Urdu, but I can understand. Partition was only the beginning, they say. There was war between India and Pakistan, there was fighting between Hindus and Muslims … Mothers lost children, children lost fathers, wives lost husbands … families lost homes … everything was lost.

One woman holds my hand and says … we all look the same. We all speak same language. But we are not the same. Your god is different. My god is different. You cannot eat this, I cannot eat that. We are not the same. You have different heaven. In my religion, your heaven is hell.

Another man … We are proud of our country. Pakistan is our mother and our child.

And yet another man … What we are trying to say, my son, is that in 1947 … in 1947 … 1947 …

I'm beginning to feel a little nauseous.

… 1947 is the year Pakistan is born! It is different from India. India only become independent, separated. But Pakistan is born! God is great! Pakistan is great! Pakistan is freedom! Freedom for all!

I can't breathe. Their hospitality is suffocating me. I tell them I have to make a phone call. At a corner of this increasingly crowded room, I call my boyfriend. I speak to him in whispers in case they stone me for being a homosexual.

Hello? Hello? Honey? I'm in Pakistan! They're all Muslims here, just like you, but with more baggage ... No, I haven't scattered his ashes ... Yes, I still have it ... No, I haven't found his home. I just got here a few hours ago! Honey ... listen ... I love you ... I said I love you! No, it's not the TV, there're a lot of people around. But did you hear what I said ... I said? Hello? Hello? Honey?

I got a little upset by this time. Poor network connection, in this day and age ... I'm sorry, I'm not buying it. Thankfully, I received an SMS which read: I love you sweetie. Do what you have to. Just come home soon. Miss your kisses and cuddles.

I wanted to show all of them the text message my love sent to me. I wanted to scream at them, THE TIMES HAVE CHANGED. GET ON WITH IT.

But instead I show them my father's ashes. I tell his story. I tell the story of his father ... his mother, his wife. I share everything I have, everything I know. Then I tell them I want to scatter my father's ashes here. Suddenly, there is complete silence. Everyone looks at me stunned. After what seems like forever, someone says, 'Why do you want to leave your father here?'

PAUSE

Son: My father was born in 1929 in Hyderabad Sind.
Father: I am born in 1929. My father was born in 1898.
Grandfather: I am born in 1898. I live in Hyderabad until I go to Japan.
Father: The mother must teach them. Everything is the mother. Mother is the main part of the home.
Grandfather: Father is busy with the work. The mother must love them and teach them how to behave. Teach them to be respectful. Mother is the light.
Son: Yes ... the mother is the light ... But the husband ... the husband ...

PAUSE

It's dark. I've spent a day here, in this man's home. And as I look at his smiling face, I find it difficult to fathom that just 60 years ago the family of this lovely Muslim man forced my family to leave. 'Are there still

Hindus here? Do you celebrate the Festival of Lights?' He turns to me and says, 'Hindu, Muslim, we all live together. We all celebrate. We all speak same language, no?'

No. Not all of us. My language is my home. And this, I'm sorry, is not my home. Neither is it my father's home. Not any more. And then I realize what I have known all this time ... Why would I ever want to leave my father here? Here, in Hyderabad Sind.

Dad, you told me little about Partition. But when I googled, I learnt a thing or two. I learnt that on 14 August 1947, the new Islamic Republic of Pakistan was born. The next day, at midnight, India was freed from colonial rule, ending about 350 years of British presence. I learnt that about 15 million men, women, and children had to uproot themselves, crossing borders to regions completely foreign to them. Whether they were Muslims or Hindus, their true identity, their true home, was where they were born, where their ancestors were. I learnt that 60 years after Partition, India and Pakistan are still trying to heal the wounds left behind.

But as you said, all that is unnecessary history.

Suddenly, I hear the crackling of fireworks. I go outside. The sky is ablaze with light. I look at the dark sky intermittently set afire with colourful and rather dangerous fireworks. It's a lovely sight, but far from grand. After a while, I stop looking at the fireworks. I stop looking at the sky. I look at the people around me. And every time the sky is set ablaze, their faces light up. Men, women, children ... Their faces light up. There are smiles, there is laughter ... There is light.

PAUSE

Today is the Festival of Lights. A triumph of good over evil.

And I'm going to have a whiskey with my dad ... if it's the last thing I do on earth.

HENG SIOK TIAN

Stairway
(157, Neil Road, Singapore)

A spiral stairway
joined the backyard to a third floor.

There was no ghost there
to receive me.
I would not have minded,
would have asked about
the tear-stained walls,
cracked light bulbs
and bloodstained smell
of rooms.

157 Neil Road is the Peranakan 'Baba House' in Chinatown, a conservation project.
Dilapidated and abandoned, it has been restored by the National University of Singapore
Museum to its former glory as the family home since 1860 of six generations of wealthy
Straits Chinese.

Meeting Crow at Karakorum Highway, Pakistan

I crashed onto a moon
to wake up to a Crow screaming.

White was Crow's tongue,
white were Crow's feet,
yellow my crayon moon,
yellow my skin.

My lineage was both a Crow scream
and Red-Indian howl.
In the beginning was
a word,
then a string from a zither,
then a note from a beat,
then a psalm from a river
then a pain from within
then black emptiness.

Meeting Crow on Karakorum
was accidental.

Representing Idealism and Activism: Kuo Pao Kun's Theatre in the 1960s and 1970s

QUAH SY REN

Kuo Pao Kun (1939-2002) was one of the most important dramatists and cultural activists in Singapore. Effectively bilingual in Chinese and English, he left a substantial legacy of plays, theatre productions, and a considerable body of cultural criticism unrivalled in intellectual engagement and insight when he passed away at the age of sixty-three. Besides writing, translating, and directing more than forty original plays in both Chinese and English between 1966 and 2001, Kuo also co-founded the Singapore Performing Arts Studio (1965), the first private arts education institution in Singapore; founded the Practice Theatre Ensemble (1986); the first multidisciplinary arts centre, The Substation: A Home for the Arts (1990); and co-founded the Theatre Training and Research Programme (2000) – all of which have survived him. While others have detailed and discussed his wide-ranging achievements and influence,[1] I will focus on his rarely examined activities and achievements before his arrest and detention as a political detainee from 1976 to 1980 under Singapore's Internal Security Act. These tend to be unfamiliar to English-language readers as most of the primary materials are in Chinese.

During the 1960s and 1970s, Kuo became inspired by the socialist idealism and activism in the newly established People's Republic of China and the anti-colonial struggle in many Third World countries. He created a theatre that provided an alternative discourse of identity and belonging, urging audiences to be proactive in the building of an ideal home and nation within the context of Singapore. An understanding of the key role social activism played in Kuo's earlier artistic creations enables us to perceive his work of the 1980s, not as a departure, but as making up one continuum with the beginning of his professional career in theatre. While his earlier works appear to pose a direct challenge to the political status quo, his post-1980 works did not retreat from the political but persist, albeit more obliquely, even allegorically, in provoking reflections on the relationship between the individual and the State and to interrogate the State's ideology.

The notable lack of critical attention in English to the early years of Kuo's creative engagement with theatre is mainly due to his then exclusive involvement in Singapore's Chinese-language theatre. Furthermore, all his plays and writings were in Chinese and not available in English translation. Consequently, what the English-educated audience knew and wrote about Kuo only followed upon his first play written in English, *The Coffin is Too Big for the Hole* (1983).[2] As the cultural critic, Janadas Devan, has noted, the English-speaking audience and public, both nationally and internationally in the Asian world, knew little about Kuo before then, beyond the fact that he was a leftist writer whose plays were in Mandarin and reflected his belief in social realism, that he was detained without trial, and that, upon his release from prison, his writing in English meant he had turned his back on politics. But Devan argues otherwise:

> This chronology distorts Kuo. There is nothing in his post-1980 works that suggests accommodation, nothing that suggests the internalized censor.
> Kuo undoubtedly used the experience of detention to work on himself, and emerged from it refined and spare, stripped of superfluities, but he did not, in the process, abandon his ideals. He did not, to use a stark word from those times, break.[3]

Undoubtedly, life before 1980 was to Kuo of much significance, more than can be imagined by most people. Firstly, Kuo's character and his art were closely related, and consistent with his life, and cannot be defined solely by the events of 1976 or 1980. Secondly, despite the cultural and critical prominence that Kuo achieved as a dramatist in his later years, his earlier life should not be regarded as peripheral or merely secondary in importance to his entire existence. In fact, the opposite is true.

Early multicultural representations

Born in 1939 in a village in Hebei Province, northern China, Kuo Pao Kun moved to Peiping (now Beijing) when he was eight, to Hong Kong when he was ten, and to Singapore in the same year, to be reunited with his father, a businessman. In Singapore, he attended six different high schools. In a chronology of his life, he highlighted political events, such as students' demonstrations and strikes, suggesting their deep imprint on his mind as a young adult.[4] Such activism among Chinese-medium school students was much influenced by revolutions in China in the first half of the twentieth century. At the time, most Chinese in Singapore and Malaya (with the exception of English-educated Peranakan Chinese, who had lived in the region for three generations or more, and generally perceived themselves as loyal British subjects) had strong emotional and family ties with China, and looked upon China as their homeland. They were thus deeply concerned about, and many were actively involved in, the Nationalist revolution led by Sun Yat-sen at the turn of the nineteenth century and the Chinese Communist revolution dating from the 1930s. At the same time, the Chinese-educated intelligentsia in Singapore was, historically, strongly influenced by Chinese political ideologies and inspired by the May Fourth Cultural Movement (1919) in China. Influences from China included the mass awakening to China's social problems in the 1920s, the propagation of socialism in the 1930s, and the anti-Japanese resistance movement in China in the 1930s and during World War II. These ideologies and activist movements particularly affected, and were associated with, the Chinese-language literary and theatre scenes.[5] Kuo's political awareness and inclination, which began to emerge in his theatre practice towards the late 1960s and early 1970s, were clearly influenced by this tradition.

Between 1959 and 1965, Kuo worked and then studied in Australia, these five years proving to be crucial to his development as an artist. Kuo originally went to Melbourne to work for a Chinese-language radio station, supporting financially Goh Lay Kuan who was then training at the Victorian Ballet Guild, and who was later to become his wife. In 1963, Kuo enrolled in the Theatre Production Programme at the National Institute of Dramatic Art (NIDA) in Sydney and was exposed to Greek drama, the works of Shakespeare, Chekhov, Ionesco, and Beckett, among others. Meanwhile, the training at NIDA and his involvement in the productions of its Old Tote Theatre Company demonstrated to Kuo the importance of professionalism in theatre practice. Upon his return to Singapore in 1965, he co-founded the Singapore Performing Arts Studio (SPAS) with Goh, the first of what were to be a number of professional theatre and arts institutions mentioned earlier.[6] From the inception of SPAS, Kuo and Goh envisioned an artistic practice that was strongly underpinned by professional training, an artistic belief which he always upheld such that his theatre practice was neither merely amateurism nor merely political activism.

1965 also happened to be the year Singapore separated from the Federation of Malaysia, just two years after merging with it. It was thus a time when Singaporeans experienced a troubled uncertainty with regard to their identity – being firstly British colonial subjects, then Malaysian, and eventually Singaporean. Multiculturalism as an ideology under various names and in various forms was claimed by all political parties and cultural groups. In the State's discourse, the term 'multiracialism' was preferred and is in use still.[7] In a 1967 speech, *National Culture in a Multi-Racial Society*, Lee Khoon Choy, a first-generation leader of the ruling People's Action Party (PAP), which came to power in 1959 and has retained it since, declared that 'we should seek for unity of content out of the diversities [*sic*] in the forms of cultural expression ... but the content of this expression must be directed to a Singapore loyalty'.[8] A cultural variety show called in Malay – the national language – *Aneka Ragam Rakyat* (Variety Concert of the People), and featuring songs and dances of the different ethnic groups, was launched by the PAP government and regularly staged by performing arts groups.

However, this form was not an invention of the PAP government. Since the 1950s, such variety shows, aimed at promoting 'healthy literature and arts' in connection with students' political activism, were commonly staged in Chinese-medium schools to send off graduating students. The intimate relationship between theatre or dance activities and student activism was evident from the coincidence of the two in terms of manpower, organization, and ideology.[9] Indeed, in the early years of SPAS, at least one such concert was produced each year, showcasing strong cross-cultural and cross-ethnic consciousness. Although Kuo's directorial debut with the arts institution was in 1966, a year after its formation, and the first play he wrote was produced in1968,[10] he had been active from the first in moulding SPAS's artistic direction as both co-founder and partner to Goh Lay Kuan, then Principal and Head of Dance. Programming of SPAS in those years was obviously imbued with a multicultural ideology, crucial among artists and practitioners, such as Kuo, Goh, and their contemporaries in Chinese-language theatre, in their imagining of an integrated society.

Forms of collectivism
From the late 1940s up to the early post-Independence years in Singapore, Chinese-language theatre and the social and political activism of Chinese-educated students were always closely related. Although Kuo was not directly involved in the student movement of the 1950s, he was engaged in the imagining of a multicultural Singapore through his involvement in dance and drama performances in the mid-1960s. Because these expressions of multiculturalism were generally perceived to be in line with or even versions of the State's discourse, the subversively interrogative nature of Kuo's social consciousness may not have been very obvious then. However, in the late 1960s when Kuo started to write and direct plays, his theatre became a medium for fierce political and social criticism.

Kuo's first full-length play – *Hey, Wake Up!* – was staged in December 1968. Before that, he had directed three plays, including *The Caucasian Mother* (a translation of *The Caucasian Chalk Circle*), and thus was the first to introduce in Chinese translation the German dramatist, Bertolt Brecht, to Singaporean audiences.[11] He had also directed a play in Mandarin, *The Eruption of Life* (1966), written by the Singaporean playwright, Chen Bo Han. Beginning with *Hey, Wake Up!*, Kuo's theatre was moving in the social and political direction of student activism and becoming more intense in its criticism of the developmental path chosen by the Singapore government.

Between 1968 and 1975, Kuo brought out four plays. Apart from *Hey, Wake Up!* these were *Struggle*, *The Sparks of Youth*, and *Growing Up*. *Struggle* and *The Sparks of Youth* were in rehearsal and scheduled for public performance in December 1969 and December 1970 respectively, but were banned by the licensing authority.[12] After revisions over several years, *The Sparks of Youth* was renamed *Growing Up* which was successfully staged in January 1975 by the Selatan Arts Ensemble, a theatre company established in 1972 by the theatre trainees of SPAS. These plays were distinctive for being the 'collective creation' of members of SPAS under Kuo's leadership. And *Hey, Wake Up!* may be seen as the transitional piece. The play, published in 1969, was described as a collective effort, with Kuo named as the 'scribe' who had put the play into words. In contrast, all subsequent plays were unpublished, existing only as cyclostyled scripts and programme booklets (as in the case of *Growing Up*) and attributed solely to 'collective creation'. Such attribution of authorship was a marked feature of a period when collective effort was celebrated over the individual's. This was quite different from the works of the 1980s, each of which Kuo had led the cast to create through improvisation.

In the volume which contained the script of *Hey, Wake Up!* there is a detailed exposition of this unique artistic process.[13] The process would start with a chosen topic to which members of the artistic group would contribute their life stories and personal experiences. Furthermore, to involve the community beyond, a writing competition would be held to invite real-life accounts from the public. A first draft based on this material would be sent to other members for comment. After several rounds, the resultant final version would be used for rehearsal.

Kuo, the writer, obviously did not play a passive role in simply incorporating the thoughts and narratives of others as is implied by the label of 'scribe'. On the contrary, he was the key person responsible for the script who developed each concept and idea, and decided upon characterization and representation. The participation of other members happened prior to the drafting stage when initial research was carried out and various ideas were considered, and not during the creation of the script as such. This creative process is quite different from Kuo's later use in the 1980s of the method of collective improvisation. In plays such as *Mama Looking for Her Cat* (1988) and *0Zero01* (1991), Kuo mostly functioned as a facilitator, leading the cast members to create dramatic situations and dialogue or what is commonly described as a 'devised play'. The key difference is that, in the earlier period, the initiative of creating the play lay with the playwright, while, in the later, it lay with the cast members. Evidently, the artistic process of *Hey, Wake Up!* articulated a well-regarded ideology of the 1960s, which was collectivism. Using *Hey, Wake Up!* as the first model of collaboration, Kuo and his team then embarked on more collective creations.

Challenging the State's ideology

Major socioeconomic changes after 1965, in the first decade after Singapore became independent, precipitated a departure from the PAP's thinking prior to the forced separation from Malaysia. The loss of the Malaysian hinterland, and thus a large domestic market, followed by the withdrawal of British troops, resulted in substantial job losses. PAP leaders thus concluded that Singapore's immediate post-Independence challenge was economic and national survival. The PAP government consequently departed ideologically from other then newly independent nations in eschewing a purely socialist or nationalist agenda for a pragmatism that saw Western capitalism, technological advancement, and industrial development as the primary engines of economic growth and development.[14] Kuo Pao Kun's plays during this period reflected and responded to these economic directions. *Hey, Wake Up!* depicted the people's anxieties and attitudes towards the attendant social changes, while *Struggle* and *Growing Up* exposed the increasingly obvious social divisions caused by the State's economic policies. These works exemplify the playwright's vision of an ideal future society which starkly differed from that of the government's.

In *Hey, Wake Up!* the protagonist, Xiao Mei, fresh out of school, finds a job as a tour guide to help her family lead a better life. However, her innocence and wilful refusal of well-meaning advice from her family and friends led to her being taken advantage of sexually by the tour agency manager. The play opens with a chorus, expressing the playwright's unease about developments in Singapore society:

All our young people are schooled but no one can guarantee that they have been educated. After a number of years in the classroom, they all end up with some form of qualification. But it remains to be seen if any of them will succeed in society.

In the cry for 'free competition,' there is much room for strange things to happen. In the name of 'job creation,' any lucrative deal no matter how suspect may also be permitted.

What happens when an innocent child is placed in this kind of social environment? Xiao Mei may very well become the answer to the question above.

The observations of the Chorus and the action of *Hey, Wake Up!* reflect how Singapore society was beginning to alienate its members, causing the protagonist to become an exploited victim without any means to defend herself. The mottos of national development, such as 'free competition' and 'job creation', were echoed in the play, only to be interpreted ironically.

The government's notions of economic and national development and the social attitudes entailed were opposed by Kuo in light of his own vision of the ideal society. At the opening of Scene 7, the Chorus is blunt in its criticism:

Making money is a principle of our society,
To live without greater purpose is nothing to be ashamed of.
…
These are the origins of corruption,
They are the very things that lead to degradation.

In the play, 'corruption' and 'degradation' are respectively represented by the people who run the tour agency and the victim. Against the government's enthusiastic promotion of tourism to accelerate economic growth, *Hey, Wake Up!* ironically transforms official modes of thought into targets of dramatic satire, as in the dialogue between the manager of the tour agency and the tour guides:

Manager Lian: Remember, our job is to make our customers' stay here satisfactory by giving them the holiday experience that they want. However we also have to achieve two other objectives. Miss Tan, what is the first objective?
Miss Tan: To convince the customer to stay in town as long as possible.
Manager Lian: Good. Miss Lam, what is the other objective?
Miss Lam: To create a lasting impression on the customer so that he will return.
Manager Lian: And Miss Lu, tell us why?
Xiao Mei: The longer he stays, the more he spends. And a favorable impression is in fact an investment of the future.

While the lines above represent the views of the tour agency, they so exactly mimic official views and language that the playwright's ultimate target is obvious.

Hey, Wake Up! belongs to the intellectual tradition inherited from modern Chinese theatre, which aims seriously and responsibly to address the real problems of society. Indeed, the play marks the beginning of Kuo's leaning towards the leftist movement which, since the end of World War II, had spread worldwide, influencing anti-colonial activism in the region. Moreover, prompted both by the launch of China's Cultural Revolution in 1966, and by the Chinese modern intellectual tradition of enlightening the people to save the nation, Kuo and his artistic partners increasingly mounted a strong confrontational challenge to the ideology of the nation-state implicit in the Singapore government's blueprint for development.

Anticipating social activism

Nonetheless, the oppositional thrust of *Hey, Wake Up!* seems much less insistent, when compared to Kuo's later plays, such as *Struggle* and *Growing Up*. Theatre performances by SPAS became more resistant and oppositional to the State's ideology such that several plays were banned by the government. Flush from the accolades received by *Hey, Wake Up!* Kuo Pao Kun and his team returned to the collaborative production process and completed *Struggle*. But SPAS received an official order to cancel the performance a fortnight before the opening in December 1969.[15] The production team immediately put together a variety show of short dramatic pieces and ten poems ingeniously titled *Struggle: An Evening of Poetry and Short Plays*, and a performance was staged as scheduled. This episode, signifying the team's perseverance and responsiveness to challenges, has been fondly and proudly recollected by Kuo in an unpublished personal interview with this author in 2001.

Struggle was never to be publicly performed. In December 1970, SPAS prepared to stage another play, *The Sparks of Youth*, but that, too, was banned. Revised and renamed *Growing Up*, it was however successfully staged in January 1975. The banning of the two plays was obviously occasioned by their oppositional nature. In *Struggle*, a family of farmers, despite their resistance, are eventually forced to leave their rented land to make way for a factory. To support her family, the farmer's daughter, Ah Long, finds a job in the factory, but is unjustly treated when negotiations over worker welfare fail. The factory manager ignores safety regulations, causing a machine to explode. While Ah Long rushes to help rescue the injured, the manager flees the scene. After this incident, she realizes that the workers are her real allies.

The revised *Growing Up* shows a more intense class consciousness than *The Sparks of Youth*. Lin Zhigao, a young man from a working class background, returns from further studies in Australia and turns his back on his family. He marries his boss' daughter, abandoning his former girlfriend who had selflessly sponsored his studies, and uses his position to bully his friends and colleagues. Other capitalist figures, represented by the supervisors of the factory, attempt to destroy unity among the workers through bribery and intrigue. In contrast to the capitalist group is a group of upright and loyal youths who not only donate blood to victims of the factory explosion but also lend money to workers in difficulty. They shelter young people who have run away from home on account of differences in ideals, fervently educate the workers, start a magazine, and earn a living at the same time as pursuing their studies.

In contrast to Xiao Mei's progress from innocence to degradation to eventual self-realization in *Hey, Wake Up!* the protagonists and antagonists in *Struggle* and *Growing Up* are largely two-dimensional – either good or bad – and are obvious vehicles for representing the inevitable conflict between opposing classes. Indeed, the synopsis of *Struggle* opens with a statement resembling a manifesto:

> To survive, one needs the most basic of conditions and the essential right to existence. But when we look at the blood-stained reality around us, do we realize just how many people have been forced out of their beloved homelands? So many are forced to work themselves to the bone, yet without assurance of a warm bed and food enough to fill their bellies. Are we even aware that some are subjected to the greatest bullying and oppression just to get by? Ever so often, we hear of those who are turned out of their homes and forcibly displaced, those who are fired by their employers, those who take their lives, those who meet with mishaps when rushing to meet deadlines at work, those who are injured or dead. There are even more poor people, especially those stuck at the lowest social level who struggle to survive and teeter dangerously on the edge of life. They stubbornly hold on to whatever livelihood they can in defiance of oppression. Such people have paid an unspeakable price, even their very lives, to trace their stories and woes in blood and tears.[16]

This statement demonstrates a primary characteristic of the social-realist tradition in modern Chinese literature and arts with its deep sense of oppression and injustice. The manifestation of this tradition in their theatre practice signalled that Kuo and his fellow artists are no less committed in their art to addressing social inequality than those who engage in mass demonstrations and political activism.

Unlike socialist countries that are opposed to multinationals and foreign investment, Singapore's pragmatic economic strategy from the mid-1960s was to attract international investors. Agricultural land was high-handedly appropriated by the government for industrial development and farmers were forcibly resettled, an injustice which Kuo has dramatized as originating in social inequality. While Xiao Mei in *Hey, Wake Up!* experiences an awakening to the dark social reality which she inhabits, such a realization comes too late in *Growing Up*. In pin-pointing social inequality as the source of suffering, the playwright's message is that those who are oppressed must unite, and fight for their rights. A couplet at the end of *Struggle* serves as a self-motivating motto: 'When there is unity no one will be vulnerable to bullying. When there is unity an unjust society can be transformed.' On the one hand, a consciousness of the need to struggle and fight was obviously inspired by leftist ideology; on the other, it also showed the playwright's overwhelming sense of social responsibility in placing his hope in social activism, reflecting the idealism of the intellectuals of the time.

Idealism and its defeat

A rapidly industrializing and urbanizng Singapore is like many other countries in having to face such social consequences as economic exploitation, inequality of wealth distribution, problems of overcrowding, and popular unrest. Through their work, Kuo Pao Kun and his contemporaries expressed or dramatized the anxieties and urgencies of the times. The ideology and the issues represented in Kuo's plays offer the kind of idealistic solutions to social ills similar to those put forward in China since the late nineteenth century by Chinese intellectuals and the literati. Inspired by leftist ideology and movements, Kuo's idealism radically departs from the State's ideology that is averse to and fears Communism.

Kuo's plays usually have a working class setting typified by limited or non-existent personal space. Such restriction is countered by a communal space shared by a group. Xiao Mei of *Hey, Wake Up!* lives in such a shared space or workers' quarters, alongside cleaners, washerwomen, construction workers, carpenters, hawkers, newspaper boys and apprentices. Indeed a motley group of Chinese working class people coexisting under one roof was not uncommon at the time. While the living conditions of such tenements were bad and families did not enjoy much if any privacy, and while conflicts were liable to occur as a result of opposing class consciousness, there tended to develop as well a shared closeness and camaraderie within the community.

For example, when Xiao Mei returns home in high spirits with gifts paid for with part of her salary and hands over the rest of the money to her mother, not only does she fail to make the latter happy, but the older woman and the neighbours give her a earful because of the nature of her new job. Their views are echoed by Ah Chun, a fifteen-year-old newspaper boy, who self-righteously insults Xiao Mei's profession, declaring that tour guides are merely glorified social escorts and that the tour agency is nothing but a prostitution den in disguise. But Xiao Mei's distress at Ah Chun's insults is soon overtaken by a spontaneous collective flurry to raise money for a neighbour who has injured herself on the job. Such communitarian values however are often shown to be fragile. In *Struggle* disagreement easily arises among the workers over whether or not to accept delayed payment and a cash reward from their employer for working longer hours. As the play progresses, it becomes apparent to the audience and readers that the capitalist employer has all along intended to deceive the workers with false promises of rewards. The illusion of material gain ironically causes division among the workers.

Kuo further defines and explores the importance of social cohesion in *Growing Up*, his last full-length play before he was arrested and detained. Li Guiyu's father is the managing director of a company that exploits workers. But she turns her back on the social class that her father represents and allies herself with the working class. One of the workers, Zhou Xia, derides Li for opposing her father because of her naïve belief that the interests of the group should come first. Towards the end of the play, the belief that social responsibility takes precedence over family ties is articulated by Li:

> The workers are closer to me than my parents. Having lived in this new environment for two years, I don't miss home at all. In fact, I feel that I belong here and that the previous place was merely transitional. I feel estranged from my parents and sister. Other than sharing the same bloodline, we do not seem to have anything in common … Only those bound by a similar fate can be considered family!

Li's rejection of blood ties and material comfort symbolizes her disassociation from her previous belief in a class-based society. Earlier in the script, the terms 'blood ties' and 'material comfort' have been redefined. A pregnant worker, Aunty Zhang, has a fall and loses a lot of blood. Those around her immediately come forward to donate their blood and scrape together whatever money they have to help her. By overturning and then redefining key ideas, Kuo establishes the ideals essential to a community. Compared to Ah Long in *Struggle*, Li's character is more heroic and subversive. Li's decision shows her eagerness to jettison outmoded notions of society and to work towards building a new community.

My purpose in this article has been to demonstrate that Kuo's plays of the 1960s and 1970s were forceful expressions of the idealism he and his contemporaries shared. In the early years of post-Independence Singapore, Kuo and members of SPAS continued to propagate the idea of a unified, multiracial, and multicultural Malaya, a community grounded in a strong 'Malayan consciousness'. Their notion of multiculturalism was non-threatening and non-antagonistic. Rather, it complemented the government's own plans for nation-building. From 1968 onwards and beginning with *Hey, Wake Up!* Kuo's artistic focus turned away from representing and advocating multiculturalism towards a leftist-inspired social idealism. Such a move thus marked the departure of Kuo's ideological path from the PAP government's. While the latter focused on economic development to achieve social progress, Kuo and his artistic partners strove to give a voice to the underclass which they believed was being progressively marginalized in the national pursuit of economic success. Although his primary mode of expression was the theatre, Kuo's advocacy of the suppressed underclass and his representation of an alternative image of Singapore as home, with evident similarities to the left-inclined intellectuals and social activists of the era, led to his arrest during a nationwide hunt for political dissidents. That was the price that Kuo paid, and his fate was not unlike that of other social and political idealists.

NOTES

Some parts of this article were originally written in Chinese and translated into English by Kao Jong-Ee. I would like to express my heart-felt appreciation to Koh Tai Ann for her time and effort in editing this article. This final version has been revised and written by the author who bears full responsibility for its deficiencies.

1. See Kwok Kian-Woon, 'Remembering Kuo Pao Kun (1939-2002)', *Inter-Asia Cultural Studies*, 4: 2 (2003) 193-201; and the commemorative volume, Kwok Kian-Woon and Teo Han Wue, eds, *Kuo Pao Kun: And Love the Wind and Rain* (Singapore: Cruxible, 2002).

2. Articles on Kuo's works in the 1980s, which only started to appear in the late 1980s and early 1990s, include Krishen Jit, 'Kuo Pao Kun – The Man of the Future in Singapore Theatre', in Kuo Pao Kun, *The Coffin is Too Big for the Hole and Other Plays* (Singapore: Times Books International, 1990), pp. 7-28; K.K. Seet, 'Critical Untranslatability as Dramatic Strategy: A Speculative Look at the Different Language Versions of Kuo Pao Kun's Plays', in *Prize Winning Plays, Volume VI, 1992: Beyond the Footlights – New Play Scripts in Singapore Theatre*, ed., Thiru Kandiah (Singapore: UP, 1994), pp. 243-55. As Kuo's role in Singapore's English-language theatre scene

increased and his influence became more strongly felt, especially after his death, more was published about him: see Jeanette Ng, 'Of Coffin and Parking Tickets: Social Mythology and the Singaporean Everyman in two Kuo Pao Kun Monologues', in *Interlogue: Studies in Singapore Literature, Volume 3: Drama,* ed., Kirpal Singh (Singapore: Ethos Books, 2000), pp. 37-51; Quah Sy Ren, 'Evolving Multilingual Theatre in Singapore: The Case of Kuo Pao Kun', in *Ethnic Chinese in Singapore and Malaysia: A Dialogue between Tradition and Modernity,* ed., Leo Suryadinata (Singapore: Times Academic Press, 2002), pp. 377-88; a chapter on Kuo's *The Coffin is Too Big for the Hole* in Jacqueline Lo, *Staging Nation: English Language Theatre in Malaysia and Singapore* (Hong Kong: Hong Kong UP, 2004). See also fn 1 above. Surveys and analyses of Singapore's English-language theatre since the 1980s, invariably include substantial coverage of Kuo's work.

3. Janadas Devan, 'Reading Kuo Pao Kun Loud and Clear', *The Straits Times,* 21 September 2002.

4. Kuo Pao Kun, 'Chronology', in *Images at the Margins: A Collection of Kuo Pao Kun's Plays* (Singapore: Times Books International, 2000), pp. 386-88.

5. See Lynn Pan, ed., *The Encyclopedia of the Chinese Overseas,* 2nd edn (Singapore: Editions Didier Millet, 2006) on the relationship between the Chinese overseas and modern China.

6. The Singapore Performing Arts Studio was to change its name twice: first, to Practice Theatre School in 1974, and then to Practice Performing Arts School in 1984.

7. 'Multiracialism' as a political concept first appeared in the *Report of the All-Party Committee of the Singapore Legislative Assembly on Chinese Education* (Singapore: Government Printer, 1956). I have discussed the emergence and use of this term, especially in relation to theatre performances: see Quah Sy Ren, 'Form as Ideology: Representing the Multicultural in Singapore Theatre,' in *Ask Not: The Necessary Stage in Singapore Theatre,* eds, Tan Chong Kee and Tisa Ng (Singapore: Times Edition, 2004), pp. 27-42.

8. Lee Khoon Choy, *National Culture in a Multi-Racial Society* (Singapore: Government Printing Office, 1967).

9. Little research has been done, especially in the English language, on this very important chapter in the political and cultural history of Singapore. A brief account in Chinese may be found in Zhan Daoyu, *Zhanhou chuqi de Xinjiapo huawen xiju (1945-1959)* [Singapore's Chinese-language drama in the early post-World War II period (1945-1965)] (Singapore: The Chinese Department, National University of Singapore and Global Publishing, 2001).

10. The first play Kuo directed under the auspices of SPAS, and which was staged in February 1966, was *The Test,* a translation and adaptation of *The One Day of the Year* by the Australian playwright, Alan Seymour. The first play Kuo wrote and directed was *Hey, Wake Up!* in 1968, discussed in the following section.

11. Other adaptations which he directed, besides *The Test,* were *Black Spirit* (March 1967), adapted from *A Raisin in the Sun* by African-American Lorraine Hansberry, and *The Caucasian Mother* (December 1967), adapted from Brecht's *The Caucasian Chalk Circle.*

12. These plays in their original Chinese language are now collected in Quah Sy Ren and Pan Cheng Lui, eds, *The Complete Works of Kuo Pao Kun, Volume 1, Plays in Chinese, The 1960s and the 1970s* (Singapore: Practice Performing Arts Centre and Global Publishing, 2004). No English translation is currently available.

13. Guo Baokun [Kuo Pao Kun], *Wei, Xingxing!* [Hey, wake up!] (Singapore: Biaoyan

yishu chubanshe, 1969). This collection also contains four other parts under the title 'Our Words' – an account of the process of creating the play; a section showing stage design sketches; scenes from the plays; and a collection of reviews and responses, demonstrating the importance Kuo and members of SPAS placed on documenting the details of 'collective creation'.

14. See C.M. Turnbull, *A History of Singapore 1819-1988*, 2nd edn (Singapore: Oxford UP, 1989), pp. 288-99.

15. The banning of public performances did not happen only to SPAS but was common experience in the 1960s and 1970s among Chinese-language theatre and arts groups with a strong leftist inclination. While *Struggle* was their first play to be banned, it was not the first time that a SPAS public performance was banned. In September of the same year, *Evergreen*, a dance-drama written by Kuo and choreographed by Goh Lay Kuan, was banned, as was another dance-drama, *Story of the Old Mason*, also written by Kuo and choreographed by Goh, in April 1971.

16. Although *Struggle* was banned, this statement, synopsis, and an account of the play's creation were published in the programme booklet of the variety show which replaced it. See p. 155 of this essay.

'A Star-Lovely Art'

GOH POH SENG

I first met Patrick Kavanagh by chance when we both shared a tiny table at the Coffee Inn, a popular establishment off busy Grafton Street. This area crawled with undiscovered writers, artists, actors and dancers, and their hangers-on. Dilettantism was rife then.

I was one of a small number of foreign students in Dublin. We were conspicuous and exotic, like rare orchids. I felt different, accepted my difference, if not also exaggerated it. Furthermore, although I had written nothing yet, I considered myself a poet. I was somewhat self-conscious about this, as if I had made a wrong claim. But I felt the thrill of mutual recognition whenever I was with another poet. I believed then a poet was special although I would be hard put to define what that was.

So when Patrick Kavanagh came into the Coffee Inn one mid-afternoon and took a seat at my table, I was so overwhelmed, I became quite speechless. Of course, I recognized who he was, one of the finest living poets in Ireland. The man who called poetry 'A star-lovely art'! Just think, I was sitting across the table from a true master of poetry, a man I venerated. Such a God-given opportunity to have a heart-to-heart talk with this angel of a man in the flesh. But I was struck dumb. That brilliant profound conversation I had wanted to conduct with Patrick Kavanagh remained only in my head. I was so ashamed. What must Kavanagh think of me? An idiot for sure!

For the two of us to sit in such close proximity and not address each other would be unnatural. So we did talk but only about the weather, where we came from, and other inconsequential chitchat. It was obvious he was bored. I yearned to open up, to reveal myself and my poetry to the poet. I was sure he would understand me.

I studied Patrick Kavanagh closely that afternoon, throwing stealthy side glances at him now and then. The place was packed, and the collective voices trapped in that small room made conversation difficult. One had to raise one's voice in order to be heard. It even affected one's brain, making thinking difficult. That may be part of the reason our conversation was rather casual.

The most noticeable feature about Paddy was his hat, which sat on his head all the time, a brown, battered thing, time-worn, sharing all the vicissitudes gone through by its owner. Like a pet dog, it followed him around loyally. I found it peculiar that he kept it on his head all the while he was in the Coffee Inn, and wondered whether he kept it on all the time, even in bed or when bathing. My curiosity was piqued as to what his head really looked like beneath his hat, the structure and shape of it, its physiognomy. And his hair. Was it plentiful and untidy, or thinning? Was he going bald?

Another peculiarity was his eyes which were somewhat obscured by the reflecting quality of a pair of cheap plastic spectacles. Behind the lens, his pupils swam about like fish in a fishbowl. In spite of this, his eyes could penetrate your soul. Or so you suspect.

He had a two-to-three-days growth of beard which looked a little rough. His clothes were crumpled and a bit threadbare. When he spoke, his voice was gravelly, as though he had chronic laryngitis.

After about half an hour or so, Paddy took his leave. I stood up stiffly and formally shook his hand. I felt a little absurd and could not help feeling dissatisfied with myself. I looked after his retreating figure as he stepped out into the mild sunshine and was soon swallowed by the traffic. I sat down again musing on our meeting. What a waste to have let such an opportunity pass, to spend precious time mouthing inanities when I could have bared my soul! I don't think I even gave the poet my name. He continued to know nothing about me!

Dublin was a small city then, and it was easy to bump into acquaintances on the streets. In the months following that first encounter, I met Paddy again three or four times. Whenever I greeted him, he would turn to me and ask, 'Do I know you? What's your name?' Each time, I was put off by this rebuff, and went away thinking, 'It's your loss, you arrogant bastard!'

Once I was reading at the Coffee Inn when Paddy entered. I stood up to greet him. He seemed to be in a hurry and brushed me aside. My face turned red as a beetroot, and I spent the next hour devising devilish ways for his demise. An hour passed. I felt a hand on my shoulder. It was Paddy. He said, 'Sorry, me lad. I was grappling with the muse, you see.'

Then, one late summer afternoon, I was relaxing on one of the colourful canvas chairs at St Stephen's Green, watching the world go by. I was guffawing at Myles Na Gopaleen's column in the *Irish Times* when I saw Paddy approaching. He was alone, moving slowly through the pedestrian traffic. I went to greet him full of trepidation. Why did I torture myself for this bastard? It was because he was a fine poet and his poems celebrated the ordinary in our mundane life:

A road, a mile of kingdom, I am king
Of banks and stones and every blooming thing.

Paddy was making his laborious way, head bent, looking weary and in pain. I greeted him and he acknowledged me after a second's hesitation. We stood there exchanging small talk again, until I blurted out that I wanted to write poetry. Instead of words of encouragement, Paddy gave me a disapproving, even contemptuous look. He said gruffly, 'And why on earth would you want to do that? Don't you think there's already more than enough fools wanting to write poetry? Tell me, what makes you think you can write?'

One barrage followed another, like machine guns going rat-tat-tat! I was flabbergasted to be attacked like this. I didn't know what to say. I was speechless with anger and humiliation. He must have noticed the effect on me although he still carried on, but in a perceptibly gentler voice, a father's voice. Quoting the lines,

Why do you want to go
Into the dark places of the soul?

he went on, 'I say these things in the hope of dissuading you from a life that could be filled with pain and poverty. Take me for instance. I am often penniless, sometimes I don't have money to eat, and have to importune friends for a few shillings to get by.'

'I don't care whether I am rich or poor, as long as I can write poetry.'

'My God! How green you are. How juvenile, and stupid, too. Think of it. Our man here has no fear of poverty. Just listen to him! Doesn't care if he's rich or poor, sez he. What utter rot he's sprouting. Bet you when proper hunger gnaws at your guts and the larder's empty, and your wallet too, you'd not be so casual about poverty. When you have no money for the rent, and the landlord's at your tail, and you fear being thrown out into the street, homeless, you'd not likely dismiss poverty. There's nothing romantic or redeeming about poverty. It hurts both body and soul. And poetry, why you will throw poetry out of the window if, in exchange, you can eat.'

'I didn't say poverty is desirable, or that one can only write when one is sunk in poverty. I meant that a poet can write under adverse circumstances, under any circumstances.'

'Is that so? This I would like to see.'

'Why are you so hostile? If you believe in what you just said, why do you continue to write poetry? Why don't you bloody give it up?'

Paddy gave a hearty laugh, 'Testing ya, you see. Yes, you are a green one, indeed you are. Don't you know by now that one's advice is for others to follow, not for one's own consumption? Why, if we only follow our own advice, we'd be far better off today instead of being so messed up.'

'You're condescending, or you're taking the mickey out of me.' I turned away and started walking towards the exit near Grafton Street.

Paddy followed me, saying, 'And you my son, your pride's too easily hurt. Must toughen up if you're going to be a poet.'

'There, you are making fun of me again.'

'Thin skin will not do ya any good. And you misread my intention, which is not to hurt but to prevent ya from being hurt. I, too, was laughed at in my youth when I came to Dublin town, a country bumpkin. I was raised on the stony gray soil of Monaghan. That was another world altogether. I've been a cowardly exile now for many a year.'

'Why do you say a cowardly exile? I would think the reverse is nearer the truth?' I said, quickening my steps.

'Are you running away from me?' he asked, changing into a merry note, a twinkle in his eye.

'No, I'm not. This is my usual walking pace.'

'Well, slow down, will ya. You're out walking with an old man, with bloody arthritis in his joints, and a weak heart. Every step I take gives me pain. Slow down, if you want to talk to me.'

'I'm sorry. Wasn't thinking.'

I stopped and waited for Paddy to catch up. I noted he was dragging his right foot, and that sometimes he winced in pain when a footfall was particularly heavy. At times I noticed a shadow passing over his face like that thrown by a cloud upon a hillside. Of course, there was talk in town about Kavanagh's poor health, that he had diabetes, hypertension, and a bad heart. Someone should be taking better care of him. However, even in those early days of our acquaintance, I knew that one must not pity the old fella. Imagine a volcanic blast of hot burning lava erupting over you if you dare try. Yes, best keep the pity to oneself.

We continued our slow stroll. I was very proud to be walking alongside the poet, conscious of the privilege. I fancied that something of his poetry making would accrue to me somehow. I was so young and superstitious then that I believed Patrick Kavanagh would simply pass some of his poetical nature to me, that there would be a kind of effortless osmosis flowing through invisible pores, from the one to the other through the skin, through the air. That there would magically be a transference such that I would write, at last, the poems that would give meaning to my life and my death – poems that would shake and transfix the whole bloody universe, no less.

I asked my superior and elder practitioner of the art of poetry why he regarded exile as a cowardly act. Paddy heaved a sigh, then took a deep breath in order to tackle this young nuisance, this foolish aspiring poet.

'Speaking solely for myself and no other, I should have had the guts, the integrity, to live where I was born. Placed there originally by an incredible act of Providence, I had to run after the imagined glitter of the city, the suspicious glamour, the fake power and glory. I should have stayed put among my own people, the dirt-poor farmers of Monaghan, unique and special. To be a poet, and not accept this true locale, this true source of inspiration, is as bad as to be a poet and not know his trade. And I have done that to myself, turned away from my birthplace, my ancestral land, and daily I am punished for that.'

'I know what you mean,' I said, with temerity. 'I can empathize with you, being a kind of exile myself, so far away from my home.'

'Sure as sin, I wake up each morning haunted by the simplest memories. I start by thinking how it was, approaching the farm, going through the narrow lane-paths leading to it, how crowded with ripened blackberries in the summer time, the sheer overgrowth rendering difficult the passage into a leafy tunnel, the fat black berries just about everywhere, and good for the eating, for jam making, wine brewing. I remember how it was like, as children, tearing off fistfuls and stuffing the goodness, delirious into our ardent mouths. The taste of it. And I also remember the air dancing from the grassy headlands up to the bald mountains, the wind sometimes churning, turning violent and moving like a gigantic blade, scything across the fields and meadows, the heads and stems of tall grass swaying like the sea waves, and the yellow cornfields resisting the prevailing wind, agitated, their brown tassels drooping like moustaches through the entire summer. Aye, I remember, running with a pack of village kids, running after the sheep, to dispel them across the land, avoiding the hazards which cause many a child to stumble with their hidden unevenness. Such bruised knees and elbows, and the occasional wailing from a young 'un. I remember too, the dungy smell when we laboured in the stables, or played with the farm animals, the sheep and cows and ponies, and the chicken yard loud with the ceaseless cackling of the fowl, all these creatures regarded almost as family. Oh yes, I remember, remember all that and more. To bursting!'

'Your childhood seems idyllic and rural! I was brought up in a big town and hardly related to nature at all.'

'Perhaps the setting was idyllic, but I know my childhood was almost crushed by my family's poverty. As a young child, my day was made full: attending school, doing homework, and the myriad farm chores as well as housework. I worked ceaselessly but no matter how hard I tried, it was never finished. When I was thirteen I gave up my formal education to work on the farm. I would say my life was hard, but not more so than our neighbours'.'

'Yes, your early poems in *Ploughman* depicted the grim poverty of the peasant so vividly.'

Paddy looked at me and recited,

> I broke away, yet
> Wherever I turn I see
> In the stony gray soil of Monaghan
> Dead loves that were born for me.

He asked, 'You have read my poems?'

'I have enjoyed your poems immensely.'

I watched a smile grow into full bloom. Paddy was just like the rest of us, susceptible to praise and flattery. 'No point chasing after me my lad. I don't take apprentices.'

'That's all right. I never intended to be an apprentice to you. I think that a poet must struggle alone. Discover for himself.'

'What an arrogant bastard you are, bejesus. You better be good, or I'll trash your hide till it reaches your bones!'

'I know that I have not written any decent poetry, but I shall.'

'Ah, so you are only a potential poet, a future poet. Then I think you should carry yourself in humble measure. But why do you come to me when you say you can do it alone?'

'For pleasure. I've come to you for the pleasure we can share in poetry.'

'Let's wait till you've written some decent stuff. Then we'll take it from there.'

'As I've said, I like your poetry about ordinary people and their ordinary lives which is a new direction for poetry in Ireland. Right now my country is struggling for independence. The role of a poet in that society will be complex and dangerous.'

'You talk about poetry as though it's some big Hollywood production. The role of the poet in society, the function of poetry in the cause of nationalism, all these sound false to me. I am just a simple versifier. I don't understand what you are saying. You probably will dismiss me, for the kind of poet I am has no room for haughtiness and arrogance.'

I felt chastened for being so ill-mannered and boastful. To make matters worse, I really had no evidence of my worth as a poet. I did feel like a poet although I couldn't explain it.

'My son, only time will tell what you can do. In the meantime, you're right. You alone can learn the hard way. But here we are. We must part, go our separate ways.'

'Well, goodbye then. I shall think of what you've said. At any rate, thank you.'

'Get on with your writing. I hesitate to say good luck to ya.'

He crossed Dawson Street, and I went down Grafton Street. I felt in great need of a comforting pint of Guinness.

Over the course of the next few weeks, I pondered over Paddy's words. One night, unable to sleep, I rose and paced my room. I thought I was going crazy. After an hour or so of nervous pacing, I sat down and wrote in a frenzy. Words flew out of the air on to the page of the exercise book, me being only the instrument. I wrote, burning with the creative process. When I finished writing, I calmed down and slept.

The next morning, I read the two pages of verse. They were quite good. I had succeeded in writing my first poem. I felt drunk. I folded it, put it in my pocket, and wherever I went, be it on the bus, or while listening to a lecture at school, I would read it and edit it. I worked on the poem for about three weeks.

One evening at the pub, I had the audacity to show it to a friend. He seemed surprised, congratulated me, and said it was not too bad.

'What do you mean, not too bad? Is that good or bad, goddamn it?'

'It's ... not bad. What can I say?'

'You are a lover of literature, so you must know.'

'I know there are things in it that are interesting, even impressive. And there are things that are difficult to say. It's a bit of a puzzle.'

'Damn you!' I said, and stormed out of the pub. My first work of creation, and what did I do? Show it to an ape!

I carried the bloody poem with me as though it were a valuable piece of jewelry. I could have walked into the path of a bus. I was that intoxicated. Then Heaven smiled on me. I met the editor of the college magazine. He said he'd like to have a look at my poem. The upshot was that St Stephen's magazine published it. My first poem which filled the sky over all the denizens of Dublin!

The day it was published, I peered surreptitiously at groups of people drinking coffee and imagined they were discussing my poem. I was so high I could have forgotten my name. Then I heard my name being called. It was Paddy. He congratulated me, and I asked him for his opinion. He would only say, 'Not bad.'

I grilled him that whole afternoon, and bits and pieces of his opinion danced dizzily in the smoky air of Davy Burns. By 'Not too bad', did he really mean that it was not good? Somewhere, among his words, was his opinion. He got me very confused. Did he mean to say 'Not too bad' or 'Not too good' or 'Bad' or 'Good' or 'Not bad' or 'Not good'?

Finally, although I felt my life depended on what he said, what he did say eventually did not merit my dying in the most exhibitionistic fashion. At length, another friend came and patted me on the shoulder. I did not know whether it was in commiseration or admiration, but he bought me a pint. Then Paddy became very excited and exclaimed that we were going to have a wonderful night to celebrate the debut of the new poet.

Paddy took over. In the course of that night, we crawled through all our favourite pubs. Once we entered, Paddy would barge his way through the crowd and, standing in front of the counter, clear his throat and announce to all and sundry that they must congratulate me on this night, my debut as a poet.

'A toast to the poet!' and some drunken fella would order a round for Paddy and myself. After half a dozen pubs, we ended up at Mcdaid's. Paddy repeated his performance at the counter, albeit in a slurred voice now. But he got the message across. This time, he pulled me by the hand and pushed me in front of a skinny middle-aged woman who was perched on a folded rug on top of the radiator. She was puffing on a cigarette at the end of a long holder, a la femme fatale. She had a glass of wine in her other hand and was obviously holding court in that corner of Mcdaid's.

'What did you say Paddy?' she asked through a drunken fog.

Paddy repeated his introduction, 'Goh Poh Seng is a new poet!'

'I see.' She looked me up and down, then pronounced curtly, 'Too bad I can't read Japanese.'

This was greeted with rollicking laughter. When it died down somewhat, Paddy rode to the rescue, 'You are wrong Anne. Poh Seng writes in English, and his work, singular in number, shows he's got some musical talent.'

The woman gave me a second appraisal, a closer scrutiny, and said, 'Well then, he can't be any good.'

'He has promise,' Paddy urged in defence. Later, Paddy informed me that the woman was Anne Yeats, the painter, and daughter of W.B. Yeats.

All that was in 1958.

I did see Paddy now and again after that night at the Baggot Street pub, but our friendship did not go beyond what has been described here.

Paddy Kavanagh died in 1967. I heard that he was given a state funeral which included a guard of honour with volleys of rifles fired in the air. I grieved for Paddy and imagined how he would have enjoyed all this pomp and circumstance. Now and then I would recall Paddy reading and singing:

> If ever you go to Dublin town
> In a hundred years or so
> Inquire for me in Baggot Street
> And what I was like to know
> O he was a queer one
> Fol dol the di do
> He was a queer one
> I tell you.

'The 1960s: Being the Second Generation': A dialogue between Lee Tzu Pheng and Robert Yeo

Chair: *Koh Tai Ann (KTA):* The 1960s in Singapore produced a remarkable crop of writers in English, a 'second generation' to the 'pioneers' of the preceding decade, such as Edwin Thumboo, Goh Poh Seng, Lim Thean Soo, and Goh Sin Tub.[1] While the 'pioneers', many of whom began their literary careers at the University of Malaya, were preoccupied with the struggle against British colonial rule and the domestication of the English language in writing against the empire, the 1960s writers found themselves writing in a Singapore that had gained Independence in 1963 through merger with and then separation from Malaysia in 1965. The new nation's focus was economic development and the fostering of a national cultural identity. Malay was the National Language and English became one of four official languages which included Chinese and Tamil. Notwithstanding the language policies of the post-Independence government, the new writers, many of them poets, chose to work in English, and to reinvent it by means of their creativity as the language of Singaporeans. Like the pioneering generation and, perhaps more so, they were, even as undergraduates, writing and publishing in the small literary magazines such as *Focus* (1961-2000) and the anthologies they themselves edited. A lively cohort, these young poets included Robert Yeo and Lee Tzu Pheng, both speaking today, Arthur Yap, Wong May, Chandran Nair, Yeo Bock Cheng, and the Malaysian writer, Muhammad Haji Salleh.

I'm delighted that Robert Yeo and Lee Tzu Pheng, two among Singapore's best known writers, are here today to share with us their beginnings and development as poets who have lived through that turbulent period of the 1960s.

Robert Yeo (RY): First of all, I'd like to thank Tai Ann and her team for organizing the symposium. Looking at the programme, I was particularly pleased to see that the symposium is not only about Singapore literature but also about the teaching of Singapore literature, which seems to me to be a very important part of the making and development of the subject today.

I'd like to start off with some questions that Tzu Pheng has very helpfully suggested. Her first question is: 'When did you start writing seriously and why did you start writing?'

As with most people, I started 'scribbling' when I was in school. Serangoon English School, located in Simon Road, now called Serangoon Secondary School, was a small and, educationally speaking, an impoverished school in many ways. But I was fortunate to be able to study Additional Literature as an O Level subject. I don't know if any of you have heard of it. Additional Literature exposed me, at the age of fifteen, to John Dryden and the early Romantic poets, Wordsworth and Coleridge. It was like a baptism for me, because I started scribbling verses after that. I went next to St Andrews School and then to the University of Singapore, and continued to read Literature as a subject, and to write.

To answer the second question: 'What started me writing?' Two things, actually. I think most of you may have shared my experience in that you began by writing about Death and Love. You write poems about death because it is so wrenching and memorable. Here I was, alive, young, vital and emotional and I see people I know die, some prematurely, and I wondered why. And secondly, love – or unrequited love to be exact – and all those adolescent crushes! I have a theory about that – which is, if you want to write poems in particular, it's better to suffer from unrequited love because if you are loved, you will never write. But if you were to suffer from unrequited love, you will look inside yourself and ask questions of yourself – am I not good enough? am I not capable of relating with passion to the other person? And out of that self-questioning, it is possible that poetry may come.

Nonetheless, I was surprised, looking again into my first book of poems, *Coming Home, Baby*, which was published in 1971, to see that the first four poems were about Death and the next three about Love. I will stop here and invite Tzu Pheng to join me in this dialogue.

Lee Tzu Pheng (LTP): Since Robert has talked about his earliest writing, I will also say a little about how I started. I guess – for most of us – our interest in writing comes from our reading and it's likely that those who are writing now started early in life. I know I did – and in primary school! It was a kind of love affair with language. I still remember the first poem I wrote. It had nothing to do with my life or anything that I knew about life. It was very much the sort of thing that you will have encountered in a 'Peanuts' cartoon strip: 'It was a dark and stormy night' kind of nonsense! In fact, the first line was: 'The lightning streaks across the sky, and seabirds to their nests do fly.' Look at the syntax of the lines ... the whole thing was absolutely awful! But writing it was exciting. I sent it to the school magazine, and it was printed. Imagine that! I don't know if that issue of the Raffles Girls' Primary School magazine still exists as I haven't a copy.

Anyway, I think that interest persisted into secondary school. I would say that Literature was one of my first loves as a subject. Unfortunately, I treated it only as a subject. It was not until Pre-University, the equivalent of Junior College now, that I went for some of the English writers in a big way. Our exposure then was not very great. My 'first love' of an English poet was Tennyson – quite a disaster again, for me as a writer, because what I attempted to write then was very, very derivative; and really quite bad!

But I do remember the exercise that I forced myself to do when I realized that I was writing a lot of rubbish. To get away from Tennyson, I deliberately set out to write a poem about a rubbish dump! It was a good exercise, and I learnt quite a bit from it – but I also don't have that poem any more. Wish I did! I enjoyed writing it and I think it was not a bad poem actually; but it was a child's poem.

I must say that, despite my love of Literature, I muddled my way through A Levels. We studied T.S. Eliot, Yeats ... but I found them difficult and I got the very lowest marks that you could get for Literature in my A Level exams – an E grade. So it was quite a risky decision for me to take Literature at University. I was in two minds about that, but I went with what I loved. I was a very late developer.[2]

It was at University that I had a kind of epiphany. In those days, we had to take three subjects in our first year and I did three that I liked. They were a strange combination: Geography, Economics, and English Literature. And I did equally well for all three at the end of the first-year exam. When, in our second year we were streamed into one- or two-subject 'majors' for our degrees, I very nearly chose to read Geography, but decided instead on Literature. From the second year onwards, I was totally immersed in the literature that I loved. At that time, too, I discovered in the wonderful library of the University of Singapore, the works of the French symbolist poets, Rimbaud and Baudelaire, 'A Season in Hell' and 'Flowers of Evil'. That was so great an eye-opener for me! I was discovering a very different kind of poetry.

When I was reading English in my second year, I met D.J. Enright, who was Professor of English at that time.[3] We students were 'terrified' of him, but I would say he was really one of the kindest men I've ever met. He had a strange way with his students, his manner being quite playfully frightening! But very soon we knew he had a very good heart and always had our interests in mind. We were all in awe of him. Till this day, I think he was the only person on campus who *looked* like a poet! – that was something that captured our imagination!

I started writing seriously when I was in that second year at university, partly out of inspiration from meeting a person like Professor Enright. Besides, in those days, the one-subject English class was very, very small. If memory serves me, I think there were just twelve of us. While there, I had a classmate who, I discovered one day, had a huge portfolio of poems – Muhammad Haji Salleh, who went on to become a distinguished writer in Malaysia. He is Malay, but he had this huge portfolio of poems in English, which he had written over the years. When he showed me that collection of poems, I was really, really blown away by what he had written![4] That was the first time I had come across someone from my part of the world, and whom I knew personally, whose first tongue was not English, writing wonderful poems in English. Someone once said that we always find it very difficult to write about our own landscape, our own part of the world. Muhammad's poetry *certified* the landscape for me. Seeing what he did, and what he had achieved, gave me a greater confidence to write about what I knew.

It also happened that because our class was so small, we were all on very good terms, and under Professor Enright's influence we were very interested in writing. The sense of good companionship in writing has been and still is very important to me.

RY: I want to go on now to describe what it was like writing in the 1960s, and this is an attempt to answer another question that Tzu Pheng has posed: 'What did you find in the creative environment of the 1960s and 1970s that spurred you on as a writer?'

I graduated in 1961 and became a teacher in my old school. Let me say that at the time I wanted to write as well as to promote writing. One of the things I did therefore was to get into the business of editing. I managed to persuade the then University of Singapore Society to enable me to start and edit a magazine. *Impressions* appeared in 1965, but only one issue was published.

Significantly, the early 1960s was also the time when Goh Poh Seng returned from his medical studies in Ireland and became a literary activist. He directed and produced his first play,[5] and then founded, produced, and edited a magazine called *Tumasek* in 1964. Goh published three volumes of *Tumasek* in two years, an achievement. He also started a publishing company which brought out his own first novel.[6]

Edwin Thumboo joined the English Department at the University of Singapore in 1966 as a lecturer. A poet himself, he was also active in promoting Singapore writing, producing a magazine, called *Poetry Singapore*, which however was also short-lived, there being only two issues.[7] These publications provided opportunities for young writers like myself. If you look back at the 1960s, it was a period when writers and activists like Poh Seng, Thumboo and myself produced poetry magazines – these were brave attempts to become promoters of writing. One other initiative on Goh's part was the formation of a cultural group, Centre 65, that met in a bungalow near Newton Circus. Centre 65 was very exciting. We would meet regularly once every two months – we produced broadsheets, had readings of poetry and plays, followed by discussions, and so on. I must mention that one of the leading figures and the president of the Centre was Lim Kok Ann.[8] So I found the early sixties very exciting. However I left for London in 1966. So over to Tzu Pheng for her views of the latter half of the decade.

LTP: It was during one of the meetings at Centre 65 that I first met Robert and Poh Seng. Arthur Yap was also active at that time. Edwin Thumboo who helped us a lot was very new then as a lecturer and one of my teachers.

As for the creative environment – as I said, I started writing in my second year at university, and that would have been in 1966 . Well, '*the times, they were a-changin* ''! I was trying to recall the period in preparing for this dialogue session and, while I can't remember a lot of the details, the *feeling* about that time persists. I think a great deal of it has to do with some of the things that were happening then, not just in Singapore but also in the rest of the world.

It was a time for the young. As young people, we listened to Bob Dylan and others with their songs of social conscience and protest. News from all over the world told of university students being in active, anti-establishment protest. There were riots on campuses and, in America, the rise of the civil rights movement. All this resonated with me.

There was a sense that so much was possible! A lot of things were happening, were being questioned, and challenged by the young. And there was tension in societies all around the world. In post-Independence Singapore, following upon our separation from Malaysia, there was a call by the government that we should be self-conscious of our identity as Singaporeans. We had just became a sovereign state and nation, we were asked to *be Singaporeans*. For me, at that time, being brought up in a mixture of cultures, it was difficult to understand what being Singaporean meant and what it was to have a 'homogeneous' identity.

My first serious poem was therefore called, '"My Country and My

People'". It became, for a long time after that, an albatross around my neck. But I had to write it, because it was for me a poem of self-discovery. What I discovered in that poem was that I felt the call to *will* oneself a Singaporean was not very authentic. What I discovered about the real authenticity were the contradictions which made up what I was. I think my poem expressed it well for me.

I was quite surprised and gratified that, after the poem was published and read, a lot of strangers came up to me to say that it spoke for them as well. It was not just people my age, but also older and younger people. Some saw it as a jingoistic, nationalistic piece, but I never meant to write it as that. In fact – this is not known to many people – before the poem was published, I had read it to people at lunchtime readings and so on, but it was not allowed to be read over radio! For some reason, it was banned! Till this day, I do not know why.

RY: This type of censorship is more commonly experienced by playwrights, but this is the first time I've heard of such censorship of poets. It's very interesting.

KTA: I believe I'm one of the readers who saw the ironic and interrogatory tendency of the poem because it basically questions nationalism and patriotism, and somebody at the radio station might have also noted that.

RY: "'My Country and My People'" is a very interesting poem and deserves the intelligent readers it's had. I mean, if you knew what happened to my first play, and how I had to deal with the Ministry of Culture to get it performed – it was just incredible![9]

But for me and many others, the most exciting event of the 1960s was the separation of Singapore from Malaysia. Most of us, I think, have a separation poem. Mine was called '9th August 1965' and Edwin Thumboo wrote two.[10] Did you have a separation poem, Tzu Pheng?

LTP: No, I don't think so. I felt that it was very ironic for us to be separate from Malaysia. In fact, when the announcement was made, I was in Malaysia with my family. There was some tension in the air. I have relatives in Malaysia and I still do; my mother's relatives are there. The ties have been very close all this while. It seems a bit artificial that we have to distance ourselves from such a close neighbour. But no, I didn't write about the separation as such.

RY: I have a separation story actually that was personally wrenching. On the 8th of August, two colleagues and I decided to drive to the east coast of Malaysia. We broke journey to spend the night in Kuala Lumpur. At 10 o'clock the next morning, I went to visit a friend, Lawrence Ferrera, the son of the owner of a bookshop on High Street, and we started to banter.

'What are you doing here?' he asked. 'I thought we had kicked you out'. I replied, 'I don't know what you are talking about. You need us, you cannot do without us.' So we went on in this sort of way and suddenly he said, 'You mean you don't know? Singapore is no longer part of Malaysia' and held up the front page of the day's newspaper. 'So what are you doing here?' Then it hit us – that Singapore had been ejected from Malaysia. We had slept through the night and we hadn't known about it! Of course, we couldn't continue with our journey to the east coast and returned instead later in the afternoon. That was my separation experience. Out of it came my separation poem and other things related to it.

LTP: I will read aloud "'My Country and My People'". If you can see why there should be something objectionable about this poem, please let me know, because to this day I still do not know why it was banned from the radio waves!

(Reading of "'My Country and My people'")

RY: I was going to ask Tai Ann: What you think about the poem? What do you think could have instigated whoever it was, who first read the poem? When was it published, Tzu Pheng?

LTP: Now, the strange thing is this. This poem was written in 1966. My first collection was the writing of a very young person but it was published by Heinemann only in 1980. I delayed publication as I never felt confident about the collection although a lot of people liked it.[11]

KTA: I had included this poem in the syllabus of the course on Malaysian and Singapore poetry which I was teaching at the National University of Singapore and subsequently published an analysis of it in the 1980s.[12] My reading differed radically from the critics who saw it as a patriotic poem. One of the features of the poetry in English published in the 1960s was its ambiguity and irony. Given racial sensitivities, the poem's suggestion that one's ethnicity, birthplace, and hence citizenship, are all quite contingent, might not have been appreciated or understood. The poem also satirically describes the country's economic development in terms of the skyscrapers and 'milli-mini-flats' which 'made the tourists feel at home' (but presumably, not the inhabitants) at a time when tourism was being promoted to provide jobs. In the end, whoever decided that the poem should be banned probably could not accept so much interrogation of the then official line. It would not have suited the mood of the State which was trying then to foster national identity in Singapore, particularly after separation from Malaysia. As you have suggested, Tzu Pheng, it is very often in Singapore read as a patriotic poem. Bernard Tan, for instance, has set it to music in that patriotic spirit too.[13]

RY: I think that is a very good explanation as to why the poem attracted the attention of the bureaucrats. The issue of national identity was to become closely linked to Singapore's survival. The politics of survival, which was enunciated by Prime Minister Lee Kuan Yew and the Minister of Foreign Affairs, S. Rajaratnam, called for tremendous effort and self-sacrifice on the part of Singaporeans if we want to make the new nation succeed. Under those circumstances perhaps Tzu Pheng's quietly idealistic poem was seen as not tonally strong enough for the fostering of a national identity.

LTP: There was a lot of anxiety about becoming a nation. Technically we had become a nation; but for a people to grow together takes time. And we were really anxious to get things done fast. I recall also an anxiety to preserve our traditional cultural identities against unhealthy external influences. I do remember a lot of vetting or banning of pop songs – the protest songs and so-called 'drug lyrics' of the 1960s from the West. The sixties was the time of the hippies as well, with the men sporting long hair. Some of you would remember the posters found at immigration check-points, post offices, and on the walls behind government service counters which actually stated that men with long hair 'will be served last'. We loved Peter, Paul and Mary! 'Puff the magic dragon' was such a lovely song; but it and others, like 'Lucy in the sky with diamonds', were seen as 'drug lyrics'! To many people at that time, it was incredible, mind-boggling labelling!

RY: Also there was the campaign against so-called 'yellow' cartoons that some of you might remember – against drugs, hippies, foreigners but not foreign investments (which was encouraged). If you have long hair, were hippie and unwashed, you are not welcome. Thus long-haired Western pop band members were prevented from entering Singapore.

I remember writing a long poem which had the line, 'Oh, the demands you make on us, Singaporeans'. And it was quoted by Jim Minchin in his book about Lee Kuan Yew, *No Man is an Island*.[14]

KTA: The sixties were remarkable for the emergence of many young writers in English, and I think the word we were looking for is 'fervent' to describe much of the writing and how you all felt. But most of the young writers active in the 1960s and early 1970s were to stop writing. What kept the two of you going, despite lack of official support and public readership?

RY: I think I would divide my 1960s into two halves – before and after London and my studies in comparative education. I wasn't terribly interested in studying as such but was looking forward to the life in London. 1966 to 1968 was the period of mini skirts, Beatles, demonstrations, and anti-Vietnam War protests. I was interested in the war in Vietnam because I had followed the developments in American politics. When I was growing up, I was an admirer of the American counter-culture. I grew up with American pop music, movies, and comics.

I initially became politically engaged through attending courses which civil servants had to take at the Political Studies Centre run by George Thompson and Gerald D'Cruz. The two lecturers were very inspirational, and contributed to my political awakening. London contributed further to that. So if you asked me how it is that I have persisted as a writer, I think it's because of London – what I saw, what I experienced, what I did as a result.

However, to answer another question which Tzu Pheng posed – 'What specific events influenced you and the forms you wrote?' – the London experience was something I could not distil poetically. Instead what I went through in London was distilled in my first play, 'Are you there, Singapore?' Written in 1968, it was not produced until 1974, because of the unfriendly circumstances as far as the English-language theatre in Singapore was concerned. So to answer your question as to what kept me going – it was political consciousness, living abroad, and being able accidentally to find another form of writing, which was plays.

LTP: Well, if you're talking about the 1970s, I didn't write in the 1970s. (I'm not a prolific writer anyway.) But what was happening in my personal life then was getting messier and messier, and sometimes one can't write if things get too messy. As mentioned earlier I published in 1980 one collection of poems most of which were written in the sixties, and within a span of two to three years, my undergraduate years, in fact. I don't think I wrote *a line* in the 1970s. Instead I was helping Edwin Thumboo edit *Poetry Singapore* and I did some work for *SAYA* magazine which published work by school pupils. Mrs Marie Bong was responsible not only for *SAYA* – and went on to anthologize the poems in a collection of the same title[15] – but also for popularizing poetry readings. She got her girls from Katong Convent School to perform choral readings of works written in Singapore and they performed in concerts and were very good. I was more involved with those activities than with actual writing.

RY: They performed a very successful collection of nursery rhymes called, 'Sing a Song of Mankind'.

LTP: It was a very 'Sixties' collection. I was brought up on British nursery rhymes, but I felt the time was ripe, in the late 1960s, to do a contemporary version of nursery rhymes, and I called it 'Sing a Song of Mankind'. But they have never been published.

RY: Actually, I was instrumental in getting them published in a magazine that I edited. It was called *Magazine Pendidik* (Educators' Magazine), and I think I have it somewhere. I was with the Teachers' Training College at that time and was very struck with your rendition of nursery rhymes to take on contemporary issues and wondered why you didn't publish it. I thought that was wonderful stuff and ought to be published and read again, publicly.

KTA: On that buoyant note, and because our time is up, I would like to thank Lee Tzu Pheng and Robert Yeo – two of Singapore's highly regarded writers and literary activists – for honouring us with their presence and sharing with us their memories of the 1960s and their thoughts on what that era has meant to them. Both writers, as is known, have gone on since that time to publish significant bodies of work.

May I invite you to join me in showing them our appreciation.

NOTES

This article is an edited transcription of a 'dialogue' conducted during 'Seeking An Audience: A Symposium on Singapore Literature in English', on 7 November 2008, at the National Library, Singapore, in conjunction with the launch of *An Annotated Bibliography of Singapore Literature in English,* compiled and edited by Koh Tai Ann. The Symposium was co-organized by the Centre for Liberal Arts and Social Sciences of Nanyang Technological University and the National Library of Singapore.

1. That 'pioneer' Singapore-Malayan generation included writers, such as Wong Phui Nam, Ee Tiang Hong, and Lloyd Fernando, who later became Malaysian nationals. Singapore became part of the Federation of Malaysia in 1963 and left it in 1965.
i2. Lee Tzu Pheng graduated with First Class Honours in English at the University of Singapore in 1968.
3. D.J. Enright, poet, teacher and mentor, was Johore Professor of English from 1960–1970. For an account of his run-in with the Singapore government in 1960, see D.J. Enright, *Memoirs of a Mendicant Professor* (London: Chatto & Windus, 1969). Also Koh Tai Ann, 'The Mendicant Professor: a Self-confessed Liberal in Singapore, 1960–1970', in *Life by Other Means: Essays on D.J. Enright*, ed., Jacqueline Simms (London: Oxford UP, 1990), pp. 20-28.
4. This was to become Muhammad Haji Salleh's first and only published volume of poems in English, *Time and its People* (Kuala Lumpur: Heinemann Educational Books (Asia), 1978). He has since only published poems in Malay or in English translation. Salleh also appeared with seven other poets in an anthology published in the 1970s.

See Edwin Thumboo, ed., *Seven Poets: Singapore and Malaysia* (Singapore: Singapore UP, 1973).

5. Goh Poh Seng, *The Moon is Less Bright*, first staged in 1974; unpublished.
6. Goh Poh Seng, *If We Dream Too Long* (Singapore: Island Press, 1974).
7. *Poetry Singapore* announced three issues for 1968, but the first contained a poem, 'nat.cult' by D.J. Enright which referred to 'the arsehole of Kobe/there's your national culture'. This led to the National Theatre Trust withdrawing its sponsorship and the magazine ceasing publication after its second issue that year.
8. Lim Kok Ann (1920–2003) was Professor of Bacteriology at the University of Malaya (subsequently University of Singapore). Son of Dr Lim Boon Keng, he was a leading Peranakan or Straits Chinese public figure and father of the novelist and playwright, Stella Kon.
9. It took 18 months of interviews by and negotiations with the authorities for Yeo to obtain a performance licence to stage his first play, 'Are You There, Singapore?' in 1980. For his account of the experience, see 'Interview: Ban Kah Choon talks to Robert Yeo', in Robert Yeo, *The Singapore Trilogy* (Singapore: Landmark Books, 2001), pp. 27-33.
10. Edwin Thumboo, '9th of August – I', and '9th of August – II', published some years apart, are reprinted in Robbie Goh, ed., *Memories and Desires: A Poetic History of Singapore* (Singapore: UP, The Centre for the Arts, National University of Singapore, 1998), pp. 62-63.
11. Lee Tzu Pheng, *Prospect of a Drowning* (Singapore: Heinemann Educational Books, 1980.)
12. See Koh Tai Ann, 'Literature in English by Chinese in Malaya/Malaysia and Singapore: its origins and development', in *Chinese Adaptation and Diversity: Essays on Society and Literature in Indonesia, Malaysia and Singapore*, ed., Leo Suryadinata (Singapore: Singapore UP, 1993), pp.144-47
13. Choral piece, first performed by the Singapore University Madrigal Singers in 1977.
14. Robert Yeo's 'Leaving Home, Mother' was quoted in full in James Minchin, *No Man is an Island: a Study of Singapore's Lee Kuan Yew.* (Sydney: Boston: Allen & Unwin, 1986), p. 238, as was Lee Tzu Pheng's '"My Country and My People"', pp. 99-100.
15. Marie Bong, *Saya* (Singapore: Educational Publications Bureau, 1979).

'A way of happening, a mouth': Public Transactions and Interior Spaces in the Poetry of Singapore

NEIL MURPHY

A deep fascination with issues pertinent to national discourse in Singapore clearly marked the poetry of earlier generations of its writers, in particular Edwin Thumboo, Lee Tzu Peng, Robert Yeo, Oliver Seet, Dudley de Souza, Goh Poh Seng. While a specific focus on issues of nationhood and national identity has largely receded in the work of more recent poets, many remain strongly engaged with the sociopolitical complexities of the city-state. Even in comparison with that of other postcolonial nations, Singapore's literary tradition has at its centre a deeply felt sense of the poet's self in relation to his/her complex social reality, to such a degree that it has become almost habitual for many poets and critics to assume that the private and the political are complex interdependent aspects of a locus-inspired poetic that, in Patke's words, 'voices its own tension'.[1] There are many possible reasons for this interdependence, as there are in any specific cultural frame, but the purpose of this essay is not an exploration of the potential relationship between art and the nation-state. Rather, this essay seeks to consider the nature of poetry, particularly that of Arthur Yap and Boey Kim Cheng, in the context of the inward-looking potential of their work. While it is clear that social-responsiveness is not tantamount to ideological statement, there is, as I will illustrate later, a sense in which the poetry of Yap and Boey sought to avoid explicitly social and political issues, in an attempt to retreat from any potential ideological posturing in the Singaporean nation-state. However, more fundamental to this essay is the logic that their lack of attention to political issues (relative to the earlier generation of poets mentioned above) derived from a deeper commitment to the craft of poetry than to any grand anti-political gesture. The silences, and interior musing, the self-reflexive fascination and sophisticated grasp of the lyric mode that are all obvious throughout the poetry of both authors, were derived first and foremost from an aesthetic sense of the form in which they worked.

At the heart of this essay lies a difficult question: how much ideology can poetry carry within it before it topples over into rhetoric? And an attendant question: is ideology relevant in any sense to the success of a poem? In addition, two related poetic credos have repeatedly insinuated their way into the writing of this essay:

> We make out of the quarrel with others, rhetoric, but of the quarrel with ourselves, poetry.[2]

And

> For poetry makes nothing happen: it survives
> In the valley of its making where executives
> Would never want to tamper …[3]

Finally, yet another related, parallel observation was present during the composition of this essay, and I believe that its significance will become apparent as we proceed: Cyril Wong, in an essay entitled 'Creative Writing in Singapore: Diminishing Horizons', suggests that W.H. Auden, 'ignorant of his own readers', was wrong to say that 'poetry makes nothing happen'.[4]

Implicitly, of course, the above three quotations are connected by an obvious thread reaching from Yeats to Auden's eulogy, which is in turn dismissed by Wong. Wong's citing of the Auden poem is clearly connected to its persistence in this author's mind during the writing of this essay but, more crucially, Wong's reading of Auden alerts one to a feature of much of contemporary cultural criticism. In his desire to use Auden's observations on Yeats to facilitate a discussion on Singapore poetry, he stresses the point that poetry does in fact make things happen, and proceeds to offer an extremely literal reading of a fragment of a line of a poem. Had the line been read through to its partial conclusion, Wong would have reached the following statement that poetry 'survives,/A way of happening, a mouth', pointing to the interior imaginative integrity of poetry, as opposed to its existing in servitude to places where 'executives/would never want to tamper'. Auden, of course, was simply testifying to the fierce inner logic of Yeats's poetry (and his own, one might argue) and refuting the idea that poetry is somehow subservient to the logic of pragmatic social discourse. In Wong's rejection of Auden's phrase, he reveals at least a part of his own poetic logic, which is clearly different to that of Auden, in that he desires that poetry actively 'improves' people's lives; but even if a poem does improve the quality of a life simply by virtue of its being read, it cannot be a motivation behind great poetry without the poem fossilizing into a congealed ethical blueprint; this was Auden's point, and he in fact suggests in the same poem that Yeats's poetry was damaged by 'mad Ireland'. This conflation of the ethical and the artistic, the functional and the poetic, is a condition of much of sociopolitical analysis, but very rarely a *condition* of great poetry.

Acts that make things happen, rhetorical acts, are what occupy many poets' attention in Singapore. A desire for self-definition, for the expression of national identity that one finds in many postcolonial nations was, as elsewhere, inevitable among Singapore's post-Independence poets, but the desire to make things 'happen', to object, to declare one's position on sociopolitical realities are still potent forces in the work of the younger generation of poets, such as Alfian Sa'at, Ng Yi-Sheng, Cyril Wong, Gwee Li Sui, and Felix Cheong.[5] It emerges occasionally as critiques of environmental and cultural destruction even in a lyrical, meditative poet like Madeleine Lee. An example is her 'raintree' sequence,[6] in which the poet registers her quiet anger and sorrow at the 'gangrape' of the raintree 'by three men wearing balaclavas/riding big black well-oiled horses', and wearily concludes by telling us that 'thus the rain fell'. And yet, on the whole, the poems reveal Lee's disdain and sadness without offering a sociological treatise. This is the way it is: 'same old same old/same new'. The world is interiorized and becomes part of her private ruminations.

Similarly the critical reception to Singapore poetry has been largely dominated by sociocultural ideological matters, and the way in which the nation's history intersects with its literature. For example, in his introductory comments to the *Interlogue* collection of essays on Singapore poetry,[7] Kirpal Singh foregrounds 'the self-evidencing nature of the intimate fusion between history and literature', an observation which is both a critical commonplace in certain branches of literary studies and, in recent times, a scholarly template for reading literature exclusively through the medium of history (or what that history is often composed of: nation, identity politics, race, gender, class, sexuality). In fact, in Singh's extremely valuable collection, twelve of the fourteen essays (Patke's and Hasnain's being the exceptions) offer one or more variations on this kind of reading strategy. Among them, Leong Liew Geok observes that, for a poet like Thumboo, 'too much dwelling on the personal and confessional details of one's private life was inappropriate, given a more reticent and less individualistic cultural register than [one which] obtains in the West'. Leong in effect suggests that poetic sensibility is primarily linked to cultural register.[8] On his part, Tope Omoniyi premises his discussion of Singapore literature on Peter Berger's and Thomas Luckmann's thesis that 'reality is socially constructed',[9] with obvious implications for the poetry that emerges from that social reality. Similarly, Anne Brewster prefaces her introduction to Arthur Yap's *the space of city trees: selected poems* with a quotation from the sociologist, Chua Beng Huat, again drawing our attention to the primary significance of Singapore's national culture in the analysis of Yap's work that follows.[10] The specific focus of each of these claims, or approaches to Singapore poetry, is beyond the scope of this essay but suffice it to say, for now at least, that the dominant critical apparatus that is brought to bear on the poetry is, and has been, social and cultural. Apart from a few exceptions, an evaluation of the poetry as poetry does not feature emphatically. The critical apparatus has, of course, been informed by, and has simply responded to, the proliferation of social poetry, but one has a sense that the anticipated subject matter of Singapore poetry, and its contextual frames, have become rather too closely aligned with social or ideological readings.

While a consideration of a broad selection of post-1980s poets confirms this general interdependence of the private life and the nation, it is also clear that poets like Boey Kim Cheng and Arthur Yap, arguably two of Singapore's finest poets, cannot be so easily contained within such a critical rubric. It is necessary to look beyond a poetics of nation and identity to offer them adequate assessment, as poets first and foremost, and all that this entails. Even a brief consideration of their work will show that much of it will simply not yield to the familiar ideological critical approaches, without extraordinary feats of critical inventiveness. This kind of discourse is simply not always appropriate and it can be argued that some of the most significant poetic achievements of these two poets remain relatively muted because of the critical persistence in viewing them as poets of the national or poets who form significant components of a national discourse. For example, Shirley Lim has argued that Yap's 'denial of social and political presence' in his poems is 'problematical', though she goes on to note that, while he may not be 'self-consciously' seeking to comment on society, he nevertheless satirizes 'particular social types and situations', which in effect renders the poems social.[11] Later, in the same essay, Lim suggests that Yap's approach is different to that of Thumboo, the 'public spokesman', who actively 'seeks to establish the culturally positive in his society'.[12] All of this suggests that a poet such as Yap who insists that the poem 'must be private ultimately' was in fact a social critic. It is difficult to reconcile these two positions, the one clearly stemming from a desire to trace the fingerprints of national discourse in the work, the other intent on preserving the privacy of the poetic mind or on shrugging off 'any postcolonial agenda or nationalist politics', as Boey Kim Cheng observes of Yap's poetry.[13] Perhaps it is time for an adjustment of perspective and a reevaluation of both Yap's and Boey's work as major lyrical poets rather than in the context of national discourse.

Rajeev Patke has argued that the 'poet in Singapore bears an over-determined relation to the development of the state into nation',[14] which he associates, among other things, with 'the preoccupation with self-definition [that] has made it difficult to reach the path we have seen described by poets from other cultures in terms of the transcendence of self'.[15] Patke's observations are clearly accurate when one considers the majority of Singaporean poets writing in English since Independence, though of course the preoccupation with self-definition, in relation to, for example, nation-state (or country), ethnic grouping, class, sexuality is expressed in diverse ways. Patke also points out that the short lyric is the most commonly used poetic form in Singapore literature,[16] a curious fact considering the traditionally introspective usage of the lyric. Northrop Frye, for one, claimed that 'the lyric is the genre in which the poet, like the ironic writer, turns his back on his audience',[17] and, in a variation of this position, Denis Donoghue has observed that in the lyric poem 'the poet's mind is communing with itself'.[18] Of course it would be absurd to suggest that less introspective lyric poetry is necessarily bad poetry but there is a clear connection between the lyric form and the innate private emotional or song-like quality of the tone. When one uses such a form (as opposed to a prose narrative form, for example) to write of ideological matters, a curious rupture between melody and subject can occur, and the poetry is forced to house unfamiliar matters; while this does not necessarily produce a negative effect it does change the inward gaze to an outer one, or at very least forces the inner gaze out into the light, to contextualize it in a concrete situation. It is doubtless that social poets, and their readers, seek to reveal or to discover the nature of that 'situation'. Nevertheless, when the poem performs referential acts only, it limits words to their situational meanings, to mere signification, erasing their other capacities and relations; their role as poems, one might suggest. Denis Donoghue has argued that

> in the most accomplished lyrics, we have the impression that the poet has become oblivious to himself through the single-mindedness with which he has submitted to the language in which he is working – the poem is not realistic or denotative – it is a performance among the words of a particular language, a movement of tropes and figures. It is more like dance or music, and it is there – like in the other arts – only to be perceived.[19]

Of course, in this, the accusation of retreating from the social, itself apparently a social gesture to many critics, will arise but Donoghue is drawing one's attention to the self-absorbed nature of the creative-linguistic act, an act which is fundamentally different to that of the sociologist, whose eye is clearly trained on the social energies and realities of his/her subject. Helen Vendler's observations on the lyrical poem perhaps clarify this by acknowledging the presence of the material reality of the poet's situation, but by also stressing the intellectual and lexical embodiment of the poetic consciousness:

> Although in the usual lyric the speaker is alone, this solitude does not mean that he is without a social ambiance. It means only that his current social conditions are presented as they are reflected on in solitude, embodied not in 'live' interaction with other persons but in lexical and intellectual reference.[20]

To separate the social from the private (or indeed the poetic) usually entails a diminishing of the work of art (and very likely the political and social significance too) and Vendler's observation is a useful reminder of the complex intellectual interplay between the inner and outer lives of the poet. This interplay is frequently apparent in Boey Kim Cheng's lyrics. For example, 'Past Midnight' opens with a startling merging of the inner and outer: 'I turn on the light to see I am still there', and proceeds to offer testimony to how the inner life is compromised by the external 'discordant' noise and 'perpetual unrest'.[21] It ultimately closes with a turning inward, both to the self and to the imagined centre of stillness which the poet associates with art:

> Where is the point of stillness
> Mature art directs us to?
> My mind veers crazily.
> I turn the light off.
> The light goes on burning inside.

The referential quality of language is its first calling. It has always been so – we need to name, to denote, to find a way to speak of ourselves in relation to the world and each other. But language, too, is more than that, especially when one works with abstractions, emotions, matters beyond simple reference; while such usage is still, to some degree, denotative, there is a sense in which language exists within and yet beyond its referential functions, a point at which language becomes both referential *and* its own subject of attention, a point at which the words are at play with themselves. If not in poetry, where else does this happen? Robert Graves offers us a sense of this when he alludes to the extra-referential quality of poetic language: 'True poetic practice implies a mind so miraculously attuned and illuminated that it can form words into a living entity'.[22] There is little doubt that an ideological or social observation can survive perfectly well without an illuminated form of words, but it may also be true that great poetry, almost by definition, must attain something of this quality to fully achieve its status as a work of art. It would also appear to be the case, to echo Yeats's distinction between poetry and rhetoric cited earlier, that the language of poetry is essentially different to that of rhetoric in which there is always an aim, a desire to influence, and many rhetorical devices reach towards such an effect. Donoghue argues that the difference between rhetoric and eloquence is gratuitousness:

> A speech or an essay may be eloquent, but if it is, the eloquence is incidental to its aim. Eloquence as distinct from rhetoric has no aim … It is a gift to be enjoyed in appreciation and practice. The main attribute of eloquence is gratuitousness: its place in the world is to be without place or function, its mode is to be intrinsic. Like beauty, it claims only the privilege of being a grace in the culture that permits it.[23]

Far from suggesting that poetry is of no tangible significance, the suggestion is that the purpose of poetry lies precisely in the fact that it is a non-didactic form. Its value lies in its status as an important cultural form, that is aptly defined by Umberto Eco when he notes that a literary tradition, that 'network of texts', has several significant functions which are produced not for practical ends 'but, rather, for its own sake, for humanity's own enjoyment – and which are read for pleasure, spiritual edification, broadening of knowledge, or maybe just to pass the time'.[24] One might add that literature at its best is a permanent record of the extraordinary capacities of language, figurative or otherwise, a kind of record of human communication of every kind. And poetry achieves one particular effect that all other linguistic forms do not: it shows us what happens to language when it becomes its own source of fascination, when we witness the mind of the poet in communion with his/her chosen elaborations of language, and the sophisticated adventures into both language and mind that this entails.

A profoundly important example of this quality is catachresis, or what occurs when language is torn from its normal usage in the service of new meaning, new linguistic explorations; words lose their moorings, their referential anchors, and enter into curious dialogue with each other to generate new meanings. This is a delicate creative act and failure is common, but when it works it produces extraordinary effects that appear to characterize poetry at its most powerful, akin to the oddness or 'strangeness' to which Bloom refers as a condition of great literature.[25]

For example, in Louis MacNeice's 'Snow',[26] the transposition of images of snow and roses upon the great bay window is disorientating when witnessed from within the room: 'The room was suddenly rich and the great bay-window was/Spawning snow and pink roses against it/ Soundlessly collateral and incompatible'; and the world is, at once, 'suddener', 'crazier', and '[i]ncorrigibly plural', as a result of the tension generated by the conjoining of the 'incompatible' images. MacNeice proceeds to observe the 'drunkeness of things being various', but the things are various in part because the words take leave from their usual lexical usage and force us to go beyond normal, routine comprehension, resulting in both an adventure into words, and into the imagining eye of the poet.

One finds a similar desire to free language from its habitual usage in many of Arthur Yap's poems, particularly in the more mature work. An example is the poem 'nightjar'[27] where we witness a clear disruption of the familiar night-time landscape:

> here, in the night, trees sink deeply downward.
> the sound of moonlight walking on black grass
> magnifies the clear hard calls of a nightjar,
> its soliloquy of ordered savagery, little intervals.

Moonlight, of course, doesn't generate sound in the referential world, nor does sound walk on grass, and while trees may appear to sink into the darkness of evening, they don't actually do so, in the sense that Yap's image evokes; here, words take leave of their referential moorings and another realm emerges, a realm that is entwined with the act of revelation of the poet's meditative moment. Similarly, in 'paraphrase',[28] located referentially in Japan, words hang from trees, words are brown moss, and mellow sunlight, and on the lake. The world becomes words, so powerfully that they swallow the world, and own the world, at least for the here and now of the poem. Thus language becomes its own medium and subject simultaneously and, whatever its relationship with referential reality, the words are in the process of furiously transforming the ordinariness of things into extraordinary moments in language, and, in turn, moments of intense life.

A similar fascination with the transformative power of the poetic image is apparent in Boey Kim Cheng's 'Her Hands'.[29] After initially offering a brief tableau of a kitchen scene in the first stanza, which is rhythmically punctuated by the sounds of a cleaver on a chopping block, and a 'percussive stone on mortar stone', the word 'detonating' erupts in the midst of the carefully placed referential lines that precede it, and with a momentary switch the 'hands disappeared into these deeds', and words shake loose of their situational moment, because the sheer energy of the recollection being reshaped into words demands it. In the second stanza, the descriptive act turns into a whirling play of words, a joy in themselves, which arguably echoes the twirling fingers that once played with his grandmother's jade bangle. So the words themselves are in play, as words, as poetry, with themselves:

> My fingers travelled around
> The jade bangle that she wore,
> A wrist of deep green water
> Veined with milky echoes.
> It cooled my hot hand
> To twirl it round and round
> And shimmy it up and down
> The solid stem of her wrist,
> A rope of emerald dream.

Here, the play becomes every bit as significant as the jade bangle that they appear to serve, and part of our satisfaction is clearly derived as much from witnessing the formation of the image as from witnessing the bangle, what ultimately dissolves (or, poetically, forms) into a 'rope of emerald dream'.

In both Yap and Boey, we also repeatedly encounter moments of self-reflexive awareness in which the difficulty, and/or the significance of the poet, is unveiled. In Yap's poem 'in the quiet of the night',[30] for example, the imagining mind of the poet is situated in the 'quiet of the night', only to slip, via 'alert ears' into a consideration of the poet he was earlier reading. This in turn allows Yap to think of poetry, and its core value, until it closes with an acknowledgement of what it is the poet does. We watch him witness himself as poet:

> i do not know him
> or any other, or myself, or that any poetry
> is the public transaction that it must be.
> & it must be private ultimately.

The curious partial paradox that poetry is not a public transaction, but must be, is finally undone in the closing line; the transaction must, ultimately, be private for Yap. This is a point echoed again in the late poem 'the shisen-do',[31] in which the poet negotiates a way to imply the significance of poetry, or art, by drawing a verbal scene of a woman in a

Zen garden in Kyoto, tending plants in an 'intrinsically still' tableau. The woman's silent presence in the scene is 'never once' affected by words. She does not speak, the tableau is silent and perfect, 'it is always the same & one can see/it had always been, will be'. This sense of quiet certitude, or perfect form and harmony clearly lies at the heart of both the scene and the poem, and it requires very little license to assign poetic significance to the woman's quiet patient work. Likewise, Yap's own patient rendering of the scene is not simply a literal copying; he is 'no photographer to record the scene'. The deeply felt awareness that he is performing a transformative act is central to the motivation of the poem.

Boey Kim Cheng, too, allows us to glimpse how the poet, almost not there in the opening line of 'Past Midnight', tries to locate his own texture in a world of external distraction, noise, clutter, unrest, but the way in which we gain insight to the inner private rituals is the source of the fascination. The poet turns inwards away from the clutter in search of his own hidden centres. And, in the 'Art of Seeing',[32] Boey again invites us on a journey into poetic insight as he foregrounds how changes in perspective transform the world:

> Learning to read the day like Braille,
> Learning to trust the groping steps of night,
> Something in us was brought to light, the print
> Shifting into focus, the book
> Of seeing begun.

The self-referential desire that is apparent in a significant proportion of Boey's and Yap's poems testifies to their turning inward into the philosophical conceptions of their art, and the innate problems of seeing and knowing that are inevitably a part of such inward deliberations. Their work invites a consideration of such essentially introspective fascinations, and perhaps, somewhat ironically, it may well be that only through a consideration of their private journeys will we ultimately be able to make comprehensive commentary about the poetry of the nation – as opposed to national poetry.

It is clear that poets like Arthur Yap and Boey Kim Cheng have the power to take us back into the world of poetry, a world not of reduced but of enlarged meaning and sentiments, into the words, and the fraught energies that command them, the energies that define these poet's humanity. This is a point made in 1989 by Lee Tzu Pheng in her Foreword to Boey's collection, *Somewhere-Bound*, convincingly reminding us that it is in 'the country of the spirit that the poet finds himself wandering'.[33] She goes on to conclude that Boey's work might well encourage us to refocus our critical imaginations on the core elements of poetry.

> At a time when the evolution of a national literature has become in many hands conscious attempts to shape an identity, it is good that this collection of poems reaffirms that art must first be convincing in the revelation of the human at its heart.

How much ideology can a poem take? Perhaps not much at all, if it repeatedly anchors us back to the public transaction. It is increasingly a theoretical commonplace that the non-social is an act of limitation, a closing, a narrowing, but it is evident that poets, like Yap and Boey, offer enlargement, an opening, a way forward. In fact, Boey himself has implicitly offered commentary on this way forward. In his analyses of Arthur Yap's poetry Boey recognizes that it is shielded from 'the pressures of nationalist poetics', by the poet occupying a 'liminal outsidedness',[34] which inherently offers a critique of what Patke refers to as the 'project of self-definition'.[35] From Boey's assessment of Yap, it is clear that he too shares some of that desire for 'liminal outsidedness', for the discovery of the spaces 'between words and silence, where poetry happens'.[36] Alternatively, a continued filtering of the poetic achievements through sociopolitical models represents a limiting of the poetic achievement, and for all the hurly-burly it appears to generate about the concept of a national literature, or the process of national discourse, it tends to detract from the poetic achievements of major poets like those discussed here.

NOTES

1. Rajeev Patke, 'Voice and Authority in English Poetry from Singapore', in *Interlogue: Studies in Singapore Literature, Volume 2: Poetry*, ed., Kirpal Singh (Singapore: Ethos Books, 1999), p. 100.
2. W.B.Yeats, 'Per Amica Silentia Lunae', in *Mythologies* (New York: Macmillan, 1959), p. 331.
3. W.H. Auden, 'In Memory of W.B. Yeats', in *Another Time* (London: Faber and Faber, 2007).
4. Cyril Wong, 'Creative Writing in Singapore: Diminishing Horizons', in *Argot 2: New Stories and Poems* (Singapore: NUS Literary Society/Singapore Press Holdings, 2008), p. 10.
5. As observed by Jeremy Fernando, this would seem to be true of much of Singapore film. See Jeremy Fernando, 'The Spectre of the National that Haunts Singapore (Cinema) or You Can Only See Ghosts if You are Blind' in *borderlands e-journal* (5:3). <www.borderlands.net.au/vol5no3_2006/fernando_spectre.htm> accessed 02 October 2009.
6. Madeleine Lee, *fiftythree/zerothree* (Firstfruits publications, 2004).
7. Kirpal Singh, 'Introduction', *Interlogue: Volume 2*, ed., Kirpal Singh, pp. 9-17 [p. 9].
8. Leong Liew Geok, '"We must make a people": The Lyric Enterprise of Edwin

Thumboo', in *Interlogue: Volume 2*, ed., Kirpal Singh, pp. 35-49 [p. 37].

9. Tope Omoniyi, 'Island in verse: constructing identity from Singapore poetry', in *Interlogue: Volume 2*, ed., Kirpal Singh, 51-67 [p. 51].

10. See Anne Brewster, 'Introduction', in Arthur Yap, *the space of city trees: selected poems* (London: Skoob Books, 2000), p. xi.

11. Lim, Shirley Geok-Lin, *Nationalism and Literature: English-Language Writing From the Philippines and Singapore* (Quezon: New Day Publishers, 1993), p. 132.

12. Lim, *Nationalism and Literature*, p. 156.

13. Boey Kim Cheng, 'From the Tentative to the Conditional: Detachment and Liminality in the Poetry of Arthur Yap', in *Sharing Borders: Studies in Contemporary Singaporean-Malaysian Literature II*, ed., Gwee Li Sui (Singapore: National Library Board Singapore, 2009) pp. 22-35. [p. 22]

14. Patke, 'Voice and Authority in English Poetry from Singapore', p. 90.

15. Patke, 'Voice and Authority in English Poetry from Singapore', p. 91.

16. Patke, 'Voice and Authority in English Poetry from Singapore', p. 100.

17. Herman Northrop Frye, *Anatomy of Criticism: Four Essays* (Princeton: Princeton UP, 1957), p. 271.

18. Denis Donoghue, 'Congenial disorder: *Why should we look for comfort in poetry?*', *Harper's Magazine*, Web 25 September 2009. <http://www.harpers.org/archive/2008/09/0082175> accessed 06 October 2009.

19. Donoghue, 'Congenial disorder'.

20. Helen Vendler, *Invisible Listeners: Lyric Intimacy in Herbert, Whitman, and Ashbery* (Princeton: Princeton UP, 2005), p. 5.

21. Boey Kim Cheng, *Another Place* (Singapore: Times Editions, 2004), p. 49.

22. Robert Graves, *The White Goddess* (Manchester: Carcanet Press, 1999), p. 481.

23. Denis Donoghue, *On Eloquence* (London & New Haven: Yale UP, 2008), p. 3.

24. Umberto Eco, *On Literature*, trans. Martin McLaughlin (New York: Harcourt Books, 2004), p. 1.

25. Harold Bloom, *The Western Canon: The Books and Schools of Ages* (New York: Riverhead Books, 1994), p. 4.

26. Louis MacNeice, *Louis MacNeice: Poems Selected by Michael Longley* (London: Faber and Faber, 2005), p. 18.

27. Arthur Yap, *the space of city trees: selected poems* (London: Skoob Books, 2000), p. 128.

28. Yap, *the space of city trees*, p. 129.

29. Boey Kim Cheng, *After the Fire: New and Selected Poems* (Singapore: Firstfruits publications, 2006), p. 22.

30. Yap, *the space of city trees*, p. 118.

31. Yap, *the space of city trees*, p. 131.

32. Boey, *After the Fire*, p. 97.

33. Lee Tzu Pheng, 'Foreword', in Boey Kim Cheng, *Somewhere-Bound* (Singapore: Times Books International, 1989), pp. 7-9 (p. 7).

34. Boey, 'From the Tentative to the Conditional', p. 33.

35. Cited in Boey, 'From the Tentative to the Conditional', p. 33.

36. Boey, 'From the Tentative to the Conditional', p. 34.

The Singapore River

AVIJIT GUPTA

Rivers are known to be fickle, prone to changing their form and behaviour. The stream that picturesquely flows past your house tends to rise at times and threaten with brown floods. The Singapore River however does nothing of the kind. Its banks are paved, its course is fixed, the level of its water fluctuates very little, and it ploughs a very reliable furrow through an urban landscape. It also probably flows under the highest number of bridges in the shortest distance possible.

A tourist boat entering the river from Marina Bay passes under eleven bridges in sequence: Anderson, Cavenagh, Elgin, Coleman, Read, Ord, Clemenceau, Alkaff, Pulau Saigon, Robertson, and Jiak Kim, the first eight of which are shown on the cover image of this issue. The next upstream bridge is the one that carries Kim Seng Road. A transformation occurs underneath this bridge. The waterway arrives from upstream as Alexandria Canal and emerges downstream as the Singapore River, a duckling of sorts turning into a graceful swan.

The waterway continues upstream in a series of concrete channels and progressively becomes smaller until, beyond Portsdown Road and Ayer Rajah Expressway, it reaches the foot of Kent Ridge Hill. Here the river originally started as a stream that drained the southern slopes. It now carries out the same function more efficiently through a series of concrete tunnels and canals, keeping this part of Singapore clean and safe from floods. About 20,000 years ago, during the last of the ice ages, the sea level was much lower and the sea at least a hundred kilometres away from where it is today. The river was longer, continuing beyond the present coastline along a now submerged valley between ridges whose tops at present form a series of islands south of Singapore. At the end of the ice age, the sea level rose with the melting of glaciers in colder parts of the world. Singapore became an island, and the river ended up with its lower part as a wide estuary and its upper part as a narrow stream. This also happened to a number of streams of the Malay Peninsula and the Indonesian islands south of Singapore.

The river has always been important to Singapore. The earlier rulers of the island looked down from the top of Canning Hill towards its mouth, keeping an eye on traders and troublemakers from overseas. It is interlinked with the arrival of Stamford Raffles and his entourage in 1819, and with the imperialist history of Singapore, as reflected in the names of the bridges that cross the lower river. It has been associated for a long time with mercantile commerce, ferrying boats laden with goods from ships offshore, porters struggling up steps, warehouses lining its banks. Gradually much of the commerce left the river, leaving behind only the derelict charm of abandoned warehouses and a long stretch of broken steps with bumboats carrying a limited supply of goods and tourists on its not too clean stretch of tidal water.

The next transformation came in the late 1970s and early 1980s with a massive cleaning up of the river and removal of the sources that polluted its water – a project still used as a teaching example on how to improve a small estuarine stream. The warehouses were converted into a series of restaurants; the repaired steps, specially along the quieter sections, became popular with people in the evenings; and the restaurants opened umbrellas on the bank to shield alfresco diners from the Singapore sun. Starting from Cavenagh Bridge, long reserved for pedestrians only, such changes spread upstream, and the river is a heaving mass of happy people in the evenings as well as a refreshing sight for bureaucrats, bankers, and business men and women looking down from high-rise buildings at different hours of the day. The IKONOS satellite image – taken from a height of 680 kilometres, processed at the Centre for Remote Imaging, Sensing and Processing, National University of Singapore, and reproduced here on the covers of *Moving Worlds* – shows all this and more to a discerning eye, and also the promises of further development with time. The Singapore River has always been a river that encourages changes.

Jahan Ramazani
A Transnational Poetics
Chicago and London: University of Chicago Press 2009
ISBN: 978 0 226 70344 2 hb 240pp $29.00

Rajeev S. Patke
Postcolonial Poetry in English
Oxford: Oxford University Press 2006
ISBN: 978 0 199 27564 9 pb 280pp £20.00

Ashok Bery
Cultural Translation and Postcolonial Poetry
Basingstoke: Palgrave Macmillan 2007
ISBN: 978 1 403 93310 2 hb 240pp £45.00

As Jahan Ramazani edited the third edition of *The Norton Anthology of Modern and Contemporary Poetry*, he noticed a persistent friction between the custom of identifying poets by nationality and the border-crossing character of many poets' lives and works. In his recent work, *A Transnational Poetics*, therefore, he strives to answer the question: 'How would modern and contemporary poetry studies in English – an area now largely subdivided along national lines – look if this transnationalism were taken to be primary rather than incidental?' Ramazani's critical strategy is to employ in each chapter a different lens, such as decolonization, diaspora, or modernity, and to focus that lens on an international array of poems. At the same time, Ramazani insists that to de-emphasize the nation is not to embrace a uniform global culture; he points instead to the 'translocal' qualities of many poems, their juxtaposition of specific cultural locations, as when Lorna Goodison's 'Country Sligoville' overlays Jamaica's Sligoville on W.B. Yeats's Sligo and A.K. Ramanujan's 'Chicago Zen' slides between a Himalayan river and Lake Michigan.

A Transnational Poetics builds on Ramazani's earlier innovative study, *The Hybrid Muse: Postcolonial Poetry in English* (2001), in which, devoting individual chapters to W.B. Yeats, Derek Walcott, A.K. Ramanujan, Louise Bennett, and Okot p'Bitek, he investigated how these poets hybridized local cultural materials with those of earlier poetry in English. While Ramazani, based at the University of Virginia, has been the leading voice in the US for cultivating postcolonial poetry as a field of study, Rajeev Patke's *Postcolonial Poetry in English* and Ashok Bery's *Cultural Translation and Postcolonial Poetry*, both published in Britain, strengthen this field's presence beyond the US.

Patke's volume provides an ambitious overview of English-language poetry from Britain, Ireland, South and Southeast Asia, the Caribbean, sub-Saharan Africa, and the settler countries (Canada, Australia, New Zealand, and South Africa). It introduces readers to an astonishing variety of poets, from Nourbese Philip, born in Tobago and resident in Canada, to Agha Shahid Ali, U.S.-based elegist of his native Kashmir. Despite Patke's appreciation for poetic language and form, the introductions to each geographic region that take up the heart of the book allow him little space for in-depth analyses. In the more extended case studies that conclude the book, though, he goes beyond summarizing salient themes and offers particularly appealing discussions of, for example, Arun Kolatkar (India) and Ee Tiang Hong (Malaysia/Australia). By contrast with the breadth of Patke's volume, Bery's *Cultural Translation and Postcolonial Poetry*, like Ramazani's *The Hybrid Muse*, gives chapter-length attention to a handful of poets: Walcott, Ramanujan, Judith Wright, Les Murray, Louis MacNeice, and Seamus Heaney. While touching on translation theory and some of these poets' interlingual translations, such as Heaney's *Beowulf* and Ramanujan's *Poems of Love and War* (from classical Tamil), Bery mainly deploys translation as a flexible term for in-betweenness, as in Clifford Geertz's definition of the anthropologist as a kind of translator 'located between identification with a culture and analytic distance'. Tending to read double movements in the poems under discussion, Bery does not advance a pointed argument so much as explore postcolonial poetry's complexity.

A Transnational Poetics surpasses the afore-mentioned books by Bery, Patke, and Ramazani himself in that it highlights cross-cultural dynamics not only in postcolonial poetry but also in work by Euromodernist, Harlem Renaissance, black British, and contemporary American poets. Thus, Chapter 3, 'Traveling Poetry', reads Ezra Pound alongside Langston Hughes, Elizabeth Bishop alongside Okot p'Bitek. And Chapter 5, 'Modernist Bricolage, Postcolonial Hybridity', energetically contends that postcolonial poets, such as Kamau Brathwaite, Agha Shahid Ali, and Christopher Okigbo have appropriated tactics from modernists such as Eliot, Pound, and Yeats, 'the first English-language poets to create a formal vocabulary for the intercultural collisions and juxtapositions ... of globalization'. An example is Okigbo's 'Lament of the Masks' which, Ramazani argues, adopts Yeats's own mythical syncretism in order to Africanize Yeats. Ramazani joins his dazzling range of references with close focus on poetry's formal features: 'because poetry is such a long-memoried form, it is enmeshed – even when stridently nationalist in ideology – by a complexly cross-national weave in its rhythms and tropes, stanza patterns and generic adaptations'. This argument, then, is less about specific poets or poetic traditions than about contemporary poetry as a whole.

Optimistic about the possibilities for poetry in a globalizing world, Ramazani draws inspiration from theorists of transnational culture, such as Homi Bhabha, Arjun Appadurai, and Kwame Anthony Appiah. The only critic substantially discussed, however, is Edward Said, whose openness to literary complexity and commitment to transnational humanism Ramazani stresses. He acknowledges the unequal economic and political prospects offered by globalization but does not engage with critiques of the academy's cosmopolitan turn, such as Timothy Brennan's *At Home in the World*. As a result, though Ramazani evenly notes that nationalism comes in many forms, 'dissident or alternative' as well as 'state-sanctioned' or oppressive, he pays very little attention to the potentially darker sides of transnational connection. His gravitation toward the language of poetry also pulls him away from examining the institutions – friendships, periodicals, publishers, universities – that underpin poetry's transnational character.

While the canon implied by *A Transnational Poetics* is far more diverse than most, it does leave out poets from Canada, South Africa, Australia, and New Zealand. Likewise Ramazani virtually passes over poets, other than Yeats, from Ireland, Scotland, and Wales. Such poets, some of whom both Patke and Bery consider, might complicate Ramazani's implicit equation of the postcolonial with the 'Third World'. Still, it is not hard to see how Ramazani's exciting model of what he terms 'an aesthetically attuned transnational literary criticism' could be extended to poets whom he doesn't mention. Harnessing fresh readings of individual poems to the wide-reaching claim that English-language poetry over the last century confounds national categories, *A Transnational Poetics* should send literary cartographers back to the drawing board.

Nathan Suhr-Sytsma, Yale University

Writing Singapore: An Historical Anthology of Singapore Literature
Edited by Angelia Poon, Philip Holden and Shirley Geok-lin Lim
Singapore: NUS Press 2009
ISBN: 978 9971 69 458 6 pb xxvi + 677pp S$48.00

Singapore Literature in English: An Annotated Bibliography
Compiled and edited by Koh Tai Ann
Singapore: National Library Board Singapore and Nanyang Technological University 2008
ISBN: 978 981 07 0060 7 pb 280pp Not retailed; Limited distribution

Writing Singapore: An Historical Anthology of Singapore Literature is the first comprehensive collection of English literature from Singapore. The anthology represents some of the key texts in the body of the national literature. Admittedly, the fact that it is a relatively young literature means that the scale of the collection is not overwhelming for the casual reader, but it is still hefty enough to be of value to those who approach it with scholarly intentions.

The selections stretch from the earliest recorded accounts of Singapore in the *Malay Annals*, to work published as late as 2007. These are arranged into three broad sections: writings up to 1965, when Singapore gained its independence; writings from 1965 to 1990, when the country's founding Prime Minister stepped down from office; and writings from 1990 to the present day. This is a sensible approach as it clearly delineates the major turning-points in Singaporean history, and their impact on the literary zeitgeist.

The first section contains items that range from Abdullah bin Abdul Kadir's autobiography, *The Hikayat Abdullah*, 1849, to Ee Tiang Hong's poems of 1960 and 1966. The opening pieces may feel slightly out of place, given their more pronounced historical quality. But their inclusion is to be understood, even necessary, considering the contextual contributions that these early texts make to the teleological considerations of an anthology such as this. Of more significance is the creative energy that emerges from works such as S. Rajaratnam's 'The Tiger' and James Puthucheary's poems. And if this first section is suggestive of the vitality of early Singaporean literature, the third and final section reflects the substantial developments within more recent decades. The range and depth of latter-day Singaporean writing has been breathtaking. And much of this collective achievement can be seen in the sophistication of ideas and execution in, for example, Wong May's poems and Stella Kon's play

Emily of Emerald Hill. To these ends, the texts included in the first and final sections are a good indication of the literary climate of their respective periods.

It is by these standards that the 1965-1990 period comes across as being slightly under-represented by *Writing Singapore.* To their credit, the editors are the first to acknowledge, in the sectional introduction, the limits of coverage that an anthology such as the present one must bear. And as they suggest, the dramatic changes that Singaporean writing underwent during those years would perhaps be better served by a larger, if autonomous, collection devoted specifically to those crucial nation-building decades. And on the evidence of the present anthology, it would certainly be fair to hope that Poon, Holden and Lim would helm such an undertaking, extending the scholarly care and devotion that they have demonstrated in the successful compilation of *Writing Singapore.*

A similar sense of dedication and commitment can be felt in *Singapore Literature in English: An Annotated Bibliography.* Given the publish-or-perish climate of academe in the present time, a bibliography certainly does not qualify as 'sexy' scholarship – and it would take an academic of courage and confidence to assume the responsibility of compiling one for a national literature. Koh Tai Ann approaches this project with acumen; and the entries in general exemplify her careful scrutiny and zealous energy. In this, *Singapore Literature in English* far surpasses previous bibliographical attempts in its accomplishments, and certainly dwarfs these earlier examples by the sheer scale of its ambitions. Koh's bibliography is not strictly selective, and is not burdened by the critic's evaluative proclivities. The result is a credible compilation that includes entries of varying literary merit that, nonetheless, are truly reflective. At the same time, the archival undertaking here is admirable, and includes material long thought lost – items held outside Singapore, and material in private possession. Similarly commendable is the quality of the annotations that the editor has elected to include alongside each entry. These are accurate descriptions and summaries of the works in question; each articulated with remarkable thoughtfulness. The reader would be forgiven for mistaking the bibliographer for curator.

And as a resource, *Singapore Literature in English* is the perfect companion to *Writing Singapore.* If the latter provides a progressive series of key items from Singaporean literature, then the bibliography must surely be an aggregated record of Singapore's writing and reading culture.

Lim Lee Ching, Nanyang Technological University

Notes on Contributors

David Birch holds the Chair of Literary and Communication Studies, Deakin University, Australia, which he will relinquish through early retirement in December 2010. He has written widely on Singapore, media, theatre and culture. He is writing a book on the language and style of Liturgical Latin and its underlying impact on 'the grammar of prayer'.

Kenneth Chan is Assistant Professor of Film Studies at the University of Northern Colorado. He is the author of *Remade in Hollywood: The Global Chinese Presence in Transnational Cinemas* (2009).

Terence Chong is a Fellow at the Institute of Southeast Asian Studies, Singapore, and co-ordinator of its Regional Social and Cultural Studies programme. He has published in *Modern Asian Studies, Asian Studies Review, Critical Asian Studies, Journal of Southeast Asian Studies*, and the *Journal of Contemporary Asia* on the sociology of culture, class and identity formations in Singapore, Southeast Asian studies and cultural globalization.

Avijit Gupta was educated at Presidency College, Kolkata, and the Johns Hopkins University, Baltimore. Currently he spends his time between the Department of Geography, University of Leeds, and the Centre for Remote Imaging, Sensing and Processing, National University of Singapore. He works on large rivers, environmental hazards, and application of satellite imagery.

Goh Poh Seng is the author of four novels, five volumes of poetry, and three plays. His novel *If We Dream Too Long* is widely regarded as the first Singaporean novel in English, while his play *When Smiles Are Done* was the first to use Singlish in drama. His first volume of short stories, *Tall Tales and Misadventures of a WOG*, was being prepared for publication when he passed away on 10 January 2010.

Heng Siok Tian has published three collections of poems, *Crossing the Chopsticks and Other Poems* (1993), *My City, My Canvas* (1999), and *Contouring* (2004). She has written short stories and plays, and attended the Iowa International Writing Programme in 2000. She is a teacher by profession.

Koh Tai Ann is Professor and Senior Associate at the Centre for Liberal Arts and Social Sciences, Nanyang Technological University, Singapore. She has published extensively on Singapore and Malaysian writing in English, Southeast Asian women's writing, and culture and the arts in Singapore. Her comprehensive *Singapore Literature in English: an Annotated Bibliography* appeared in 2009.

Kwok Kian-Woon is Associate Professor and Head of the Sociology Division at Nanyang Technological University, Singapore. His research areas include the sociology of art and the comparative study of cultural policy.

Lee Tzu Pheng has published four collections of poetry – *Prospect Of A Drowning* (1980), *Against The Next Wave* (1988), *The Brink Of An Amen* (1991), and *Lambada By Galilee & Other Surprises* (1997). Her interest in children's literature culminated in a guide for parents, *Growing Readers* (1987), still used today in a new edition. She has received many awards for her work both nationally and internationally.

Leong Liew Geok taught at the Department of English Language and Literature, National University of Singapore, from 1981-2002. The author of two collections of poetry, *Love is Not Enough* (1991) and *Women without Men* (2000), she is currently working on a third collection, *Passions*.

Suchen Christine Lim has published four novels, a short-story collection, a play, a non-fiction book and twelve children's books. A short story was adapted for television. The novel, *Fistful of Colours*, was awarded the inaugural Singapore Literature Prize and adopted as an A Level text. A Fulbright Fellow, she has held several writing residencies.

Neil Murphy is an Associate Professor of English at Nanyang Technological University, Singapore. He is the author of *Irish Fiction and Postmodern Doubt* (2004), and has edited three collections of essays, the most recent of which is *Aidan Higgins: Framing the Contemporary* (2010). He has published numerous articles and chapters on contemporary literature, postmodernism, and theories of reading.

A freelance writer of poetry, drama, fiction, journalism, criticism and songs, **Ng Yi-Sheng** won the Singapore Literature Prize in 2008 for his first poetry collection, *last boy*. His non-fictional work, *SQ21: Singapore Queers in the 21st Century*, was a national bestseller. He is currently 'Creative-In-Residence' at TheatreWorks.

Quah Sy Ren is an Associate Professor in the Chinese Division, Nanyang Technological University, Singapore. He is the author of *Gao Xingjian and Transcultural Chinese Theatre* and General Editor of the ten-volume *Complete Works of Kuo Pao Kun*.

Senior Lecturer in English at the National University of Singapore, **K.K. Seet** has published in *Theatre Research International, The Drama Review, Theatre Journal, World Literature Today, Camera Obscura*, and written critical introductions to collections of plays by Singapore playwrights. He has edited a volume of plays, *Five Under Twentyfive*.

Resident Playwright of The Necessary Stage, Singapore, **Haresh Sharma** has written more than sixty plays, many of which have been staged in Singapore and cities abroad. His publications include *Still Building, This Chord and Others*, and *Off Centre*, an O and N level Literature text. He has an MA in Playwriting from the University of Birmingham.

Wai-chew Sim is an Assistant Professor at the English Division, School of Humanities and Social Sciences, Nanyang Technological University, Singapore. His fiction has appeared in *The Straits Times* (Singapore), in *Silverfish New Writing* 5 (Kuala Lumpur), and in the e-zine *Julie Mango*.

Associate Professor of English at the National Institute of Education, Singapore, **C.J.W.-L. Wee** is the author of *Culture, Empire, and the Question of Being Modern* (2003) and *The Asian Modern: Culture, Capitalist Development, Singapore* (2007). His current research interest concerns questions of modernism, postmodernism, and contemporary art and culture in the East/Southeast Asian context.

Robert Yeo has published several volumes of poetry including *Coming Home Baby* (1971), *And Napalm Does Not Help* (1977), *A Part of Three Poems 1966-1988* (1989), and *Leaving Home, Mother* (1999). Three of his plays – *Are You there Singapore, One Year Back Home*, and *Changi* – have been republished as *The Singapore Trilogy* (2007). His memoir, *Routes*, is forthcoming.

Ovidia Yu writes plays, novels, and short stories. She is the recipient of the Junior Chamber of Commerce International (JCCI) Singapore Foundation Culture Award, the National Arts Council (NAC) Young Artist Award, and the Singapore Youth Award.

Forthcoming issues include

Michael Ondaatje

Volume 10 No 2 2010

and a special 10th anniversary
Creative Writing supplement

also
Locating the Caribbean; Postcolonial Europe;
(Con)figuring Sport

All titles subject to confirmation